THE BURDEN OF BUSING

THE BURDEN OF
BUSING

THE POLITICS OF DESEGREGATION
IN NASHVILLE, TENNESSEE

Richard A. Pride, 1942 –
J. David Woodard

THE UNIVERSITY OF TENNESSEE PRESS / KNOXVILLE

Publication of this book has been aided by a grant from the American Council of Learned Societies from funds provided by the Andrew W. Mellon Foundation.

The paper in this book meets the guidelines for permanence and durability of the Committee on Production Guidelines for Book Longevity of the Council on Library Resources. Binding materials have been chosen for durability.

Library of Congress Cataloging in Publication Data

Pride, Richard A. (Richard Alan), 1942–
    The burden of busing.

    Bibliography: p.
    Includes index.
    1. Busing for school integration—Tennessee—
Nashville—History.   2. School integration—Tennessee—
Nashville—History.   I. Woodard, J. David.   II. Title.
LC214.523.N37P75   1985   370.19'342   85–5302
ISBN 0–87049–474–0

ACKNOWLEDGMENTS

Many people helped us with the research summarized in this book. We made an effort to thank each one at the time of his or her contribution and we thank them again now. The list is too long to name each one individually but a few special acknowledgments are in order. Former Director Dr. Elbert Brooks and staff members Mr. Tom Caulkins and Dr. Ed Binkley of the Metropolitan Board of Education were very cooperative in our search for important data. At Vanderbilt, our friend and colleague Dr. Robert Birkby was a constructive critic throughout the project. To these men we give a special nod of appreciation. This book is dedicated to our children, but we want to thank Dana and Judy, our wives, and Mavis Bryant, our editor at the University of Tennessee Press, for their assistance, support and encouragement, especially during the difficult periods.

Our research was largely unfunded, but small grants from the Spencer Foundation and the Vanderbilt University Research Council were helpful at early stages. General resources of Vanderbilt University, especially the Institute for Public Policy Studies, also supported our efforts. We are grateful for these sources of aid.

We lived and worked in Nashville when many of the events described here took place, and indeed direct observation of events was one of our principal methods of inquiry. It is never easy to be objective about one's home town, but we have tried to the best of our ability to be fair and honest in our account. Richard Pride was responsible for research and the initial draft of Chapter 2, and Chapters 6 through 12; similarly David Woodard was responsible for Chapter 1 and Chapters 3 through 5. Beyond this, however, the book was fully collaborative. Many people helped to make this book possible, but we alone take responsibility for any errors which may have found their way into the final product.

CONTENTS

ILLUSTRATIONS

Photographs

Figures

Tables

for
Ethan, Sarah, and Katie
for
Jesse and Caleb
and for
all the children

THE BURDEN OF BUSING

Clearly, the Negroes cannot achieve their emancipation on their own. They are, quite literally, a minority in the society and they do not possess the political power to win the vast and comprehensive changes in public policy that are necessary if there is to be real equality.

Michael Harrington
The Other America, 1962

I have a dream that one day . . . little black boys and black girls will be able to join hands with little white boys and white girls and walk together as sisters and brothers.

Martin Luther King, Jr.
August 28, 1963

The word "integration" was invented by a Northern liberal. The word has no real meaning. . . . The black masses prefer the company of their own kind.

Malcolm X, 1965

Our nation is moving toward two societies, one black, and one white—separate and unequal.

National Advisory Commission on
Civil Disorders
February 29, 1968

I'm gonna shake up the Democratic Party. I'm gonna shake their eyeteeth out.

George Wallace, before the Florida
presidential preference primary
February 1972

Preferring members of any one group for no reason other than race or ethnic origin is discrimination for its own sake.

*Bakke v. The University of California
at Davis*
June 28, 1978

1

2

If the New Generation is to close the gap and catch up, they must do so b disciplining their appetites, engaging in ethical conduct and developing their minds.

Reverend Jesse Jackson
May 1978

In this case, we have a white majority of the school board, acting on the advice of a white desegregation expert, recommending to the court *more* busing to achieve *more* racial balance. . . . the black plaintiffs urge upon the court *less* busing.

Judge Thomas Wiseman
May 1980

CHAPTER ONE

Introduction

A round six o'clock every weekday evening, Gary Watson hooks a fifty-five foot trailer to his 1980 Kenworth tractor rig in a Nashville freight yard. He will spend the next eight hours on a regular run to Memphis and back. "If I'm lucky, I'll be home by three A.M.," says this husky forty-six-year-old father of five. Mr. Watson's night drive comes after he has worked a regular shift as the supervisor of a Tennessee State Highway Department crew. Gary Watson works two jobs so his children won't have to attend the public schools.

"We tried busing; we stayed in the Metro system two years after the 1971 order. But when I saw what was happening to my kids, I took this extra job so they could go to private schools." When asked about the experiences of his children, Mr. Watson's jaw tightens. "Well, in junior high my oldest had some money taken from him by the colored kids in the restroom." Discussions of fights and classroom disruptions follow this explanation, then Mr. Watson concludes, "I only got through high school, and the state job is the best I'll ever get, but I want more for my kids." We are interrupted by a squawking CB radio that repeatedly asks "Chickasaw Fats" about the traffic situation up I-40. This distraction cannot alter one conclusion: the busing plan in Nashville, Tennessee, means that Gary Watson works nineteen hours this day to keep four children in private school.

"For me, busing was a kind of culture shock." The speaker is Greg Bailey, today a respected journalist for the *Nashville Banner*, but in 1971 a diffident high school sophomore who experienced busing first-hand. "In the spring of that year, I saw a black guy hit a white kid with a school annual on the neck that killed him." The incident, widely reported both locally and nationally, occurred when a white and a black student quarreled over the ownership of a school yearbook. "It happened right outside the journalism office, the white guy hit his head on one of those heavy oak classroom doors as he fell and suffered a concussion." It was the most violent incident in a year of turbulence. For weeks after the fight uniformed police patroled the halls of Hillwood High School. "My parents tried to get me into BGA" (a local private high school), recalled Greg, "but they didn't have an opening."

When the original busing order was handed down Mr. and Mrs. Bronson Thompson bought a house in Bellevue, a community in Western Davidson County. Bellevue was exempted from the 1971 busing plan. "Both my husband and I worked so we could make the payments on our house." Each morning Mrs. Thompson leaves her driveway at 7:00 A.M. to begin a fifty-minute drive to her job at a dentist's office. Her trip may be longer after the latest busing order. "Now the judge wants to include Bellevue in the busing, and we're thinking of moving to Williamson County."

"This city," exclaims Mayor Tom Bain, "grew up on busing." The city is Brentwood, Tennessee, located just over the Davidson County line, eleven miles from downtown Nashville. In the 1970s Brentwood was the fastest-growing city in the state, with a population increase from 4,099 in 1970 to 9,605 in 1980. "They just resented being told what to do," exclaims one city official. "The federal government came in here and forced these parents into busing, so they just moved to the next county."

John and Kathy Copeland both work so they can pay the nearly $2,500 tuition costs for their two daughters' private schooling. "When they did away with prayers in the classroom we thought about leaving," says John. His wife echoes, "So we were thinking about Ezell–Harding Academy before busing. The desegregation plan just helped us make up our minds." Quality education concerns the Copelands, who want their children to be able to say prayers in the classroom and still have the benefits of good instruction.

Across the street, Lynn Johnson talks about busing as he waters the shrubs in his front yard. "I can't blame the Copelands," he says, "but I wish they would stay in the public schools. If everyone leaves the quality of education will go down." Mr. Johnson was born and raised in Nashville, and he wants his children to have the same good public school memories he had as a child.

In another part of the city, Shamana Roberts, a junior at Hillsboro High School, arises at 5:30 to catch the 6:10 bus to school. "I sometimes go to bed as early as 8:30," she says casually. Shamana has been bused from her home in the Edgehill housing project to seven different schools in eleven years of public education. "I don't have the same friends in class from year to year. I've known a few white kids, but it never lasts because we don't see each other after class." Because of the shortage of school buses and consequently staggered starting times, Shamana will be home from Hillsboro by 2:00 P.M. Her mother works as a cook in a restaurant and will not come in until 7:30 P.M. In the afternoon Shamana is supposed to study; instead, she often watches television with her friends.

Shamana's cousin Pam lives a few blocks from Edgehill and attends comprehensive Overton High School. Overton is "fully integrated," but almost all the classes Pam goes to are predominantly black. "Most of the white kids are on a different program," she explains with a shrug. "They're college prep, and we're vocational."

The names in these vignettes have been changed, but the experiences are real. Each incident was shared with one of the authors in the course of discussions about busing and school desegregation. The comments are an appropriate backdrop against which to ask questions about the consequences of civil rights policy in the United States. What effect has twenty-five years of school desegregation had on the lives of people and on the community?

This book responds to that question by examining school desegregation in Nashville, Tennessee. In one sense we want to tell a story of integration efforts in one southern city with a proud tradition of racial tolerance. In another way, however, we want to go beyond the chronicle of events and systematically examine some of the most important issues arising from the national policy of school desegregation.

Twenty years after more than 250,000 people heard Dr. Martin Luther King, Jr., make his "I have a dream" speech, political and social change has come to the South. In restaurants and hotels, in restrooms and at drinking fountains, in reception rooms and on television, blacks and whites are in close proximity. Business offices and department stores in downtown Nashville are desegregated; no "For White Only" signs are displayed. The city school system is "racially balanced" and "fully integrated."

But beneath all this change there is a lingering racial paradox. More blacks than ever are hired for jobs in the public and private sectors, but statistics show only a small incremental decrease in the gap between black and white incomes. In 1960 the annual median family income for blacks was 51 percent that of whites. By 1980 the gulf had narrowed some, but it was still only 59 percent of the white figure. In Nashville, churches have an "open door" policy where race is concerned, but on any given Sunday most white and black parishioners worship God separately. In fact, Martin Luther King's observation that "the most segregated hour in America is eleven o'clock on Sunday morning" is as appropriate today as it was when he made it in 1963.[1]

1. Martin Luther King, Jr., *Why We Can't Wait* (New York, 1963), 87–93. The income figures are calculated from information in: U.S. Department of Commerce, Bureau of the Census, *Statistical Abstract of the United States, 1960* and *1980* (Washington, D.C.).

It is not just the shallowness of black and white relations that is of concern, it is their unevenness as well. In any conversation about school desegregation the listener will hear expressions of outrage and satisfaction, disappointment and hope, determination and resignation. Few policies elicit such a wide range of heartfelt emotions.

Change certainly has come, but how significant are the transformations? Blacks and whites see progress on racial issues differently. Whites are apt to point out how far we have come; blacks, especially black leaders, emphasize how far we have yet to go before full racial justice is achieved. In 1980 the Gallup Poll found that 80 percent of whites believed the quality of life for blacks had improved during the previous ten years. Sixty-seven percent of them believed that treatment of blacks in their community was the same as that accorded whites. Whites consistently saw blacks as better off than blacks saw themselves, and far fewer whites than blacks viewed racial discrimination as an issue in the problems of blacks.[2] These different perspectives are critical when education issues are discussed.

The movement for racial equality began with the schools and, long after other issues of racial discrimination have been settled, the courts continue to act frequently and forcefully in education. Schools were touted as the vehicles to bridge the separation between the races. The original goal of school desegregation was to bring black and white together. The "table of brotherhood," to quote Dr. King, was to be found in public school classrooms, lunchrooms, and athletic fields throughout the land.

Busing for school desegregation was, and remains, the most visible and controversial issue of race in America. Yet few books have looked at the long-term results of school desegregation efforts. In the chapters of the three sections that follow, the reaction to busing is explained in terms of cultural conflict. Where social roles are impersonal, desegregation works; where intimacy begins, desegregation is problematical. Blacks have always been ambivalent about assimilation, and the initial "access" thrust of the civil rights movement has gradually given way to a separatist impulse. Many blacks have come to want cultural parity, not cultural assimilation.

Schools are the principal institutions bridging the worlds of society and community. For this reason they are the focus of intense subcultural conflict. We want to give the political and social roots of the policy of busing and to justify the conclusion that the conflict is and was about social status more than about educational services.

2. George H. Gallup, *The Gallup Poll: Public Opinion, 1980* (Wilmington, 1981), 154.

Our purpose is to provide a detailed examination of busing effects in one city, in the hope that such an analysis will provide insights into school desegregation nationally. All the drama of racial politics is captured in the history of Nashville. The city has a shameful past or a tolerant history, depending on whom you talk to. There is a legacy of civil rights marches, sit-ins, arrests, school bombings, the explosive rhetoric of an anti-busing rally, and the esoteric arguments of school desegregation briefs submitted to the U.S. Supreme Court.

Busing is an emotional topic. The *Economist* noted that it was hard to think of a printable word which stirred up more explosive feelings than "busing."[3] The word itself became, in Murray Edelman's terms, a "condensation symbol"—an emotional representation of all the oversimplifications and stereotypes associated with the complex and ambiguous situation of race relations in America.[4] To whites, who viewed the civil rights movement with mixed emotions anyway, busing was a threat to their lifestyle. Many of them had purchased homes in neighborhoods distinguished by good public school facilities. Suddenly the federal courts were telling them where they could enroll their children in school—hence the label "forced" to describe the policy. To other whites, desegregation (and ultimately desegregation through busing) was legitimate penitence. They did not like the burden it brought, but they accepted desegregation as a moral imperative, especially for the South.

Blacks, too, brought to school desegregation a range of intense emotions. For Malcolm X and others, "the word 'integration' was invented by Northern liberals . . . the word had no real meaning . . . the black masses prefer the company of their own kind."[5] Other blacks felt differently. For them, school desegregation was worth any price, because schools were the great nursery of racial separation. To integrate schools was to conquer the evil of racism in its cradle. These feelings and many more were present in Nashville as much as in the nation as a whole, and they provide an enduring backdrop for the analysis which follows.

The chapters in this book are grouped into three sections. After a brief conceptual chapter, Part I sketches the background of the struggle for racial equality in Nashville. Then, the characteristics of the 1971 busing plan are described, and the first-year effects analyzed. Chapters in Part II evaluate some of the longterm effects of busing during the decade of the seventies. White flight from the public

3. Harold Howe, "The Battle of the Buses," *The Economist* 221 (Oct. 1966), 60–64.
4. Murray Edelman, *The Symbolic Uses of Politics* (Urbana, Ill., 1964), 6.
5. Malcolm X, *The Autobiography of Malcolm X* (New York, 1964), 272–73.

schools, educational achievement, public opinion, and private school enrollment are covered here. Readers who do not care to follow the statistical basis of the argument may wish to skim these chapters. The narrative account resumes in Chapter 9. Part III focuses on the blacks' complaints about the effects of busing on their children and their community. Racial justice takes on a new meaning during the time period summarized by this section. These chapters tell the story of events which finally led a local district judge to order an end to busing in Nashville. His decision was subsequently appealed and reversed, but the case attracted national attention and took on national significance.

CHAPTER TWO

The Politics of Desegregation

Twenty years ago Dr. Martin Luther King, Jr., stood on the steps of the Lincoln Memorial in Washington, D.C., and spoke of his dream for racial harmony in America.

> In spite of the difficulties and frustrations of the moment, I still have a dream. I have a dream that one day this nation will rise up and live out the true meaning of its creed: "We hold these truths to be self-evident—that all men are created equal." I have a dream that one day . . . the sons of former slaves and the sons of former slave owners will be able to sit down together at the table of brotherhood . . . I have a dream that my four little children will one day live in a nation where they will not be judged by the color of their skin but by the content of their character. I have a dream that one day little black boys and black girls will be able to join hands with little white boys and white girls and walk together as sisters and brothers.

For those who remember Dr. King's booming voice and the magnificent simplicity of his hopes and demands for justice, the words ring out today as potently as they did on that summer midday in 1963.[1]

In this book we ask if King's words and the movement they inspired have brought much change in race relations. Specifically, we examine school integration efforts and results in one city, Nashville, Tennessee. Nashville was one of the first municipalities in the South to desegregate after the 1954 *Brown* decision. Seventeen years after *Brown*, the city again led the way with a comprehensive busing plan, the implementation of which resulted in an estimated 8,600 white students abandoning the public schools that first year. Each fall thereafter, public school enrollment has continued to decline. After ten years of busing for desegregation, a poll found that eight out of ten white parents and a majority of black respondents believed that the policy had hurt the educational development of both black and white students. By 1980 a federal judge could look across the bench at the civil rights lawyer who had handled the school case since 1956 and

---

1. *New York Times*, Aug. 28, 1983. The King speech was printed in its entirety to commemorate the twentieth anniversary of the civil rights march.

ask if desegregation "efforts have been less than fruitful, if not to some extent counterproductive."

Despite King's rhetoric, the crusade for racial equality has been a political as much as a moral movement. Politics is defined as who gets what, when, where and how, when the sanctions of governmental authority are ultimately involved.[2] Blacks have wanted "to get more of what there is to get," and they have sought different things, at different times, in different places, by different means. One thing has remained relatively constant, however; blacks have pursued redistributive policies *vis a vis* whites. Blacks have always sought to transfer benefits from advantaged whites to disadvantaged blacks.

School desegregation is only one facet of the political struggle for racial equality, yet the controversy surrounding this process may help to shed light on the whole fabric of racial politics in the United States. The politics of school desegregation in Nashville has, we think, a revealing history. In order to make better sense of this story, and of the people and events which comprise it, a general perspective must be established. We must look closely at the nature of politics itself and at specific facets of the black movement before the role of schools, as manifestations of racial politics, can be understood.

Wellsprings of the Black Movement

More than any other man, Martin Luther King, Jr., has embodied the black man's quest for racial equality. He not only spoke eloquently about the "promised land," but also led nonviolent protests to integrate the social and political life of the nation. Even in his ascendency, however, King did not speak for all blacks. Then, as throughout their whole history in America, black people have been divided concerning ultimate goals as well as the means of achieving those goals.

Differences among black leaders over the direction and nature of the struggle for equality certainly predate the confrontation of Booker T. Washington and W.E.B. DuBois at the turn of the century, but embedded in these two men's conflicting approaches lie the paradigmatic elements of subsequent black political action.

Washington came into national prominence at the Cotton States and International Exposition in Atlanta (1895), where he shared his vision of black progress for America: "It is at the bottom of life we must begin and not at the top." Blacks would enjoy social equality

2. Harold Lasswell, *Politics: Who Gets What, When and How?* (New York, 1956).

only as "the result of severe and constant struggle" and not from "artificial forcing." "The wisest among my race understand that agitation on questions of social equality is the extremest folly," he said. At the climax of his address Washington endorsed segregation, stating that blacks could be separate "as the fingers," yet one "as the hand" in society. Washington wanted blacks to focus their energies on economic gain and was prepared to accept subcultural separation, including explicit status inferiority. Through hard work in the marketplace, he felt, blacks could earn their piece of the American pie. Only after blacks achieved economic success could they deserve the respect of whites. "His way was not protest and agitation, but through hard work to win the respect and admiration of whites."[3]

In 1905 DuBois formally broke with Washington over the issue of the Negroes' place in American society. Five years later he assumed editorship of *The Crisis*, the official journal of the National Association for the Advancement of Colored Persons (NAACP). For the next twenty-four years DuBois led the crusade against white segregation practices. "We must complain," he wrote, "yes, plain, blunt complaint, ceaseless agitation, unfailing exposure of dishonesty and wrong."[4] His first interest was always "equality," which for him meant respect from white people.

Washington's and DuBois' ideas clashed at many points. They gave different answers to these questions: Is economic equality a precondition for social acceptance, or is equal respect necessary for economic advancement? Is equality earned, or is it demanded? Do blacks want to be a part of one American culture, or do they want two separate cultures within one economic system?

Washington and DuBois are not alone in giving different answers to these questions. The twists and turns of racial politics in America are revealed by the varied responses made by black leaders and organizations. Father Divine, Elijah Muhammad (Black Muslims), Roy Wilkins (NAACP), Vernon Jordan (Urban League), Jesse Jackson of the People United to Save Humanity (PUSH), Stokely Carmichael of the Student Nonviolent Coordinating Committee (SNCC), and Martin Luther King, Jr., of the Southern Christian Leadership Conference (SCLC), to name a few, have approached the issues in different ways.

3. Louis R. Harlan, *Booker T. Washington: The Making of a Black Leader* (New York, 1972), 207.

4. Julian Bond, "Emergence of the Black Right," *Tennessean*, Dec. 30, 1980. See also Julius Lester, ed., *The Seventh Son: The Thought and Writings of W.E.B. Dubois* (New York, 1971), 361; and W.E.B. DuBois, *Black Reconstruction in America* (New York, 1977), 219.

The Politics of Race: Who Gets What?

Politics is about who gets what, when, where, and how in the struggle over our collective destiny. It is the function of government to regulate the scramble over the distribution, or redistribution, of values and resources. The power and ultimate authority of government can be used to promote or hamper the interests of particular groups by dispensing or failing to dispense economic rewards or symbolic reassurances.

Human society involves inequalities, the two most important of which are economic class and social status. Groups within society occupy different rungs on these two ladders. Although there is a positive relationship between the two hierarchies, they are not identical. Among occupational groups, for example, doctors are high on both income and prestige, while migrant workers are low on both. But while long-haul truck drivers often make more money than teachers, they command less respect.

Individuals are conscious of the class and status dimensions of their lives and frequently want to improve their relative standing. When individuals organize themselves into collectivities which seek to use the power of government to protect or enhance their economic position or their claim to goods and services supplied by government, then they are engaged in *class* politics. When groups try to maintain or to increase the respect conferred on them by others, they are engaged in *status* politics. Class politics involves the clash over "bread and butter" interests; status politics involves confrontation over "lifestyles."

Class politics is about the struggle over economic interests or the instruments by which groups can pry out a bigger slice of the economic pie. This form of politics is familiar to observers of the American scene. Farmers regularly have employed political muscle to fashion governmental price supports for their crops. Labor unions fought for a minimum wage law. The American Trial Lawyers Association blocked passage of a no-fault auto insurance program. The conflict over economic interests is fought on many political battlefields—in courts, legislatures, and even the streets. Sometimes it involves few contestants, sometimes many; indeed, mass movements occasionally are formed around class-based issues, as, for example, the Labor and Grange movements were earlier in this century. The benefits to groups from engaging in the politics of economic interest are obvious; if they succeed, they get higher wages, increased profits, or improved services through governmental action.

The idea of status politics can be traced to the work of Richard

Hofstadter and Daniel Bell. Bell, writing the opening essay of *The New American Right* in 1955, contended that economic prosperity in the United States would lead to political conflict among groups striving to maintain or improve their status in society.[5] In the same book, Seymour Martin Lipset analyzed four movements (Know Nothing, 1856; the Anti-Catholic American Protective Association, 1880s; the Progressive movement, 1900–1912; and the Ku Klux Klan, 1920s) as status conflicts.[6] Joseph R. Gusfield used the status perspective to examine the American Temperance Movement, and later Louis Zurcher expanded the status approach by analyzing antipornography drives in the U.S.[7] Murray Edelman also cited status conflicts in his writings on symbols in politics.[8]

Status discontent occurs when the prestige accorded to groups is perceived as less than they expect. "The self esteem of the group member is belied by the failure of others to grant him respect, approval, admiration, and deference he feels he justly deserves."[9] Status politics results when groups try to do something about that difference. "When divergent styles of life claim equal or superior prestige, the bearers of these styles are involved in a clash to establish prestige dominance or subordination."[10]

Status politics is attitudinal rather than material. The conflict stems from an alteration in the amount of social respect conferred on one group by another. The temperance movement, an antipornography drive, and present- day campaigns for a "Moral Majority" (involving issues like the role of women, abortion, and school prayer) are status crusades. The crusaders are more interested in vague ideals such as "the sanctity of the family" or the "right to life" than in specific economic rewards. Their ostensible goals are often unclear (i.e. to right past wrongs, to rid society of sin). These movements seek symbolic benefits.

"As status groups vie with each other to change or defend their prestige allocation, they do so through symbolic rather than instru-

5. Daniel Bell, "The New American Right," in Daniel Bell, ed., *The New American Right* (New York, 1955). Also see Richard Hofstadter, "The Pseudo-Conservative Revolt," in Daniel Bell, ed., *The New American Right.*

6. Seymour M. Lipset, "The Sources of the Radical Right," in Bell, ed., *The New American Right.* Lipset, *Political Man* (New York, 1960).

7. Joseph R. Gusfield, *Symbolic Crusade* (Urbana, Ill., 1976). Louis R. Zurcher, *Citizens for Decency* (Austin, 1976).

8. Edelman, *Symbolic Uses of Politics.* Edelman, *Politics as Symbolic Action* (Chicago, 1972).

9. Gusfield, *Symbolic Crusade,* 17.

10. Ibid., 18.

mental goals."[11] The contemporary fight over school prayer is a case in point. When children in school prayed to God in the language of Christianity, the prestige of Christians was raised above that of secular non-believers and followers of other faiths. If school prayer is reestablished, even if not in a specifically Christian format, religious fundamentalists will have won a striking victory over "secular humanists." The same argument can be applied to other current political issues. Abortion, for instance, is a highly charged symbolic issue. The people who fight most strongly are not women of childbearing age whose lives are directly affected, but individuals who are concerned about the values involved. Abortion has become an important symbol of the struggle between traditional Christian fundamentalism and secular humanism. The respect accorded these contending groups and individuals will be greatly affected by the outcome of this struggle because both groups have accepted abortion as a symbol of their values, lifestyles, and relative standing in the broader community.

Booker T. Washington and W.E.B. DuBois both wanted black equality, but they differed profoundly on intermediate goals. Washington believed economic achievement should precede efforts to improve social status; DuBois placed status equality above all else. These twin tendencies can be observed in more contemporary black leaders. Vernon Jordan (Urban League) and Jesse Jackson (PUSH) have pursued "bread and butter" economic interests for blacks, but Martin Luther King, Jr., was most interested in status benefits.

Thomas Sowell has become a reluctant but controversial symbol of this tension within the black rights movement. Sowell, a black economist, published *Race and Economics* in 1975. Sowell's book rekindled the great debate between advocates of class and status politics. Sowell examined the history of ethnic groups in American life during and after the waves of immigration in the nineteenth and twentieth centuries.[12] He wanted to find out why blacks have remained at the bottom of the class and status hierarchies while other ethnic groups who also began life in the U.S. at the bottom have risen in education, occupation, wealth, and prestige.

Other ethnic groups, Sowell notes, lived in poverty, were illiterate in English, and suffered discrimination, yet they have "made it," while blacks have not. Skin color cannot be used as an excuse. Japanese and Chinese are racial minorities who have claimed their share of the good things in life. Sowell's central thesis is that blacks

11. Ibid., 21.

12. Thomas Sowell, *Race and Economics* (New York, 1975).

(and to a large extent the Irish) made the wrong choice between class and status. The racial and ethnic groups who have succeeded did so by going into business for themselves, accumulating skills and wealth that could be passed from father to son, and by pursuing education and the professions. On the other hand, blacks, like the Irish who remain the white ethnic group lowest on the class hierarchy, have made a public issue of their culture, fought battles over symbolic issues, and been dependent on government for jobs and social welfare. The clear implication of Sowell's work is that blacks should abandon status protest and focus their energies on individual and subcultural self-reliance and competitive achievement. "When social acceptance has come to ethnic minorities," he writes, "it has typically come *after* their [economic] rise and has not been a cause of that rise. Obvious as this may seem its implications are frequently overlooked by those wishing to make the fight against 'white racism' their number one priority."[13] In this, Sowell is the son of Booker T. Washington rather than W.E.B. DuBois.

The distinction between class and status is pertinent to school desegregation. During the period of dual school systems (*de jure* segregation) there can be no doubt that black schools received less than their fair share of resources allocated by local governments. Black teachers were less educated and received lower pay than their white counterparts. School textbooks, equipment, and facilities were dramatically poorer than those allocated to whites. There can also be no doubt that black schools and the children in those schools were looked down upon by the white community. Through school desegregation blacks hoped to get what the whites had in terms of services and facilities and at the same time to reduce the status differential.

In *Brown*, the seminal school desegregation case, the Supreme Court held that separate schools for blacks and whites were inherently unequal schools. The key issue in *Brown*, however, was not the inequality of educational services but the inequality of status. The court held segregation invalid because Negroes separated "from others of similar age and qualifications solely because of their race generates a feeling of *inferiority as to their status in the community* that may affect their hearts and minds in a way unlikely ever to be undone"[14] (emphasis added). It was racial isolation itself, more than the unequal distribution of class-based goods and services, that was the issue then and that has remained the major issue since. Indeed, when reluctant school boards in the South finally equalized resources

13. Ibid., 163.
14. Derrick A. Bell, Jr., ed., *Civil Rights: Leading Cases* (Boston, 1980), 112.

in desegregated schools, the courts found that action to be insufficient. Busing was ordered, not because of inferior textbooks, equipment, or facilities, but because racially identifiable schools continued to exist. Desegregation of schools by neighborhood during the 1960s did not alter the traditional status hierarchy between the races. If blacks' and whites' mutual stereotypes were to be broken down, children had to associate in equal-status situations. Busing for desegregation, it was believed, could achieve this end. An equal distribution of educational goods and services could have been achieved without busing, but only *busing* could redistribute status as well as class benefits within the society.

In the politics of race in Nashville both class and status issues have percolated to the top of the civic agenda over the decades, but status issues—both between and within the black and white populations—have dominated school desegregation in recent years.

The Politics of Race: Where?

Political efforts to pry loose social and economic benefits involve the question of where those benefits are to be distributed. The answer may be geographical—urban vs. rural, or North vs. South—but "where" may also mean the area of one's life that is affected by the outcome. In this case, "where" involves asking whether our *communal* or *societal* relationships are affected.

Ferdinand Tonnes is given credit for making this distinction.[15] Societal associations are those which are consciously willed. Most business associations, professional clubs, and governmental activities involve impersonal transactions between people. Such relationships are contractual, impersonal, routinized, and regulated by institutions of formal law. Societal associations are formed to meet specific ends; for example, business relationships are designed to transfer goods and services for money. By contrast, communal associations arise from mutual sympathy, habit, or common belief. Social clubs, churches, and family relationships are communal in nature. Such associations are characteristically ascriptive, permanent groupings controlled through traditions and group norms.

Each of us participates in both societal and communal relationships to a greater or lesser degree. We do not need to share personal values with a salesclerk when we buy something in a store, but we do

15. Werner J. Cahnman and Rudolf Heberle, eds., *Ferdinand Tonnes on Sociology* (Chicago, 1971).

assume shared values in other more intimate settings. Societal associations can be negotiated and renegotiated, but communal relationships establish the nature of man and God, the proper conduct of the two sexes, the manners and obligations of friendship, and more. These things are not easily changed.

The distinction between societal associations and communal relationships, and among the institutions which serve those interactions, is important to understand fully the politics of desegregation. As a general rule, the quest for racial equality has been more successful in desegregating societal institutions than communal ones.

Caste systems exist when the class and status hierarchies in a society are nearly identical, with sharp lines of demarcation and little or no movement from one group to another. Until the 1950s the American South could be described in those terms. As black people, allied with sympathetic whites, rebelled against this system, their first targets were societal institutions. On city buses and at lunch counters blacks demanded status equality in impersonal societal areas of life. The quality of goods and services was not at issue— coffee and hamburgers tasted just as good at black cafes as at white lunchcounters, and the bus moved just as quickly at the back as at the front. Black preachers are just as good as white preachers, too, but today buses and restaurants are fully desegregated while churches are not. The reasons for this difference are several, but one thing is clear: many whites resist black claims to status equality in communal relationships more strongly than they do claims to status equality in societal associations. And for blacks, desegregation of societal institutions did not put at risk their own communal base—their own churches, social clubs, and neighborhoods.

To be sure, blacks have sought access to white communal institutions, but these efforts have been for the most part symbolic gestures with token victories affecting few blacks. Similarly, few whites have chosen relationships with blacks in traditional black communal groups. To desegregate communal groups means the minority person has to adopt (or appear to adopt) the values found there. That is not easy to do.

For this reason, as if by mutual agreement, blacks and whites have chosen to associate with one another in specific ways. On any given Saturday black and white customers can be seen rubbing elbows at bargain tables in Nashville's numerous department stores, but on the following morning those same patrons prefer to attend churches which are all-white or all-black. Social relationships vary as to their intimacy, purpose, and reason for existence. Desegregation has been successful in places where social interactions are casual and short-lived (e.g., shopping centers) but intimate relationships—in churches, for instance—have been slow to change. The emotional price to be paid in desegregation of communal institutions is great indeed.

Schools are both societal and communal institutions. There are aspects of schools which are contractual, impersonal, routinized, and controlled by rules and regulations. As societal institutions, schools are places where teachers should teach and children should learn a set body of knowledge in a disciplined environment. But schools have always manifested a communal character. They taught, and continue to teach, values as well as grammar. The traditions, values, and symbols of a school reflect the lifestyle of its patrons. The "neighborhood school" traditionally was not a myth; it was a symbol as well as a building, a subcultural network as much as an intellectual factory.

Busing for desegregation in Nashville compromised the communal basis of schools in the eyes of many black and white parents. As black and white neighborhoods exchanged their children, subcultural values, traditions, and expectations were challenged. This was, of course, to be expected; busing was designed to alter racial stereotypes and by doing so to improve race relations. Efforts were made after busing began to build new traditions and a new community school. But this often meant that old traditions as well as old prejudices were to be set aside.

Busing threatened the communal base of schools, and Nashville parents reacted in different ways. Many whites fled busing and desegregated schools rather than have their children exposed to what they believed to be the values of the ghetto. Others remained in the public schools and sought to work with others, both black and white, to preserve the values they cherished. Over the years, however, many blacks came to resent the damage done to their own community by busing. Their schools, they said, had been taken over by whites or closed. Their children, they felt, suffered the indignity of perpetual minority status in schools dominated by white people and white values. In 1979–1980, after nine years of busing for desegregation, the frustrated communal spirit erupted on both sides, and busing was ultimately rejected by the district court.

This is the story we have to tell. Busing in Nashville was intended to reallocate prestige and respect between black and white people, and in many ways it succeeded in doing so. But this reallocation caused tension both between whites and blacks and within each race.

In one sense, the burden that busing shouldered is that it, almost alone among governmental policies, sought meaningfully to desegregate a communal institution. In a narrower sense, however, the burden of busing fell heavily on those families who submitted their children to the unknown enculturation of the desegregated school.

The Politics of Race: When?

The journey for black equality has been long and tortuous, and, as we have seen, there have been differences of opinion over *when* equality could come. Some black leaders have believed that equality had to be earned at the price of patience, compromise and hard work. Others have wanted equality *now* and sought through ceaseless confrontation and agitation to demand immediate benefits. Booker T. Washington took the first position and W.E.B. DuBois the second. During the civil rights movement of the 1950s and 1960s, status and later class benefits were demanded "NOW!" Thomas Sowell, who reopened this issue with his analysis of immigrant ethnic groups, found that it has taken other groups several generations, an achievement-oriented subcultural value system, and a strategy for intergenerational transfer of wealth and skills before relative parity was achieved.

It was thought that the benefits of school desegregation for blacks would occur in both the short and the long term. In the short term blacks would achieve another victory in their war against illegitimate status differentials. Through school desegregation, blacks would gain access to another white institution which had traditionally reinforced the subordination of blacks. There was, however, to be another short-term benefit. Scholarly research had shown that black children did better academically when they were in school with middle-class whites. Greater social respect and higher academic achievement for black children were good things in themselves. So when desegregation of neighborhood schools failed to secure these benefits for most black children, busing became necessary. Only when children were bused out of their neighborhoods could the redistribution of public respect and academic achievement be shared by all children. The long-term goals of desegregation were even more compelling. If black and white children associated with each other in equal-status situations today, in a generation or two racial prejudice would be significantly diminished.

School desegregation, then, and especially desegregation through busing, would pay dividends both now and in the future on both class and status dimensions of American life. The same, however, could be said of other public policies sought by blacks: immediate benefits would affect both the short- and longterm distribution of class and status. Affirmative action in employment, the 10 percent set aside for black contractors on federal construction projects, as well as the desegregation of schools, would work for black people now and in the future.

The Politics of Race: How?

How will blacks achieve greater respect and income *vis a vis* whites? The answer to this question is, of course, bound up in the blacks' and whites' response to the other questions concerning desegregation: "what," "where," and "when." Blacks can pursue class or status benefits. They can seek these benefits in communal or societal areas of life. They can demand immediate benefits or earn them over time. How these benefits are to be achieved, then, is a strategic decision: blacks can achieve them through *assimilation* or *separation.*

Assimilation is a process by which groups with different cultures, occupying the same geographical areas, come to have a common culture. "This means, of course, not merely such items of the culture as dress, knives and forks, language, food, sports and automobiles, which are relatively easy to appreciate and acquire, but also those less tangible items such as values, memories, sentiments, ideas, and attitudes."[16] *Separation is the process by which groups with different cultures preserve their distinctive cultures.*

America is a nation of immigrants, one where peoples of different cultures have regularly collided with each other. The pattern of these encounters and the dynamic quality of assimilation have been ably analyzed elsewhere, but a few key ideas are important here.[17] In *Assimilation in American Life,* Milton M. Gordon describes three approaches to assimilation—Anglo-conformity, melting pot, and cultural pluralism.

> In preliminary fashion, we may say that the "Anglo-conformity" theory demanded the complete renunciation of the immigrant's ancestral culture in favor of the behavior and values of the Anglo-Saxon core group; the "melting pot" idea envisaged a biological merger of the Anglo-Saxon peoples with other immigrant groups and a blending of their respective

16. Brewton Berry, *Race Relations* (Boston, 1951), 217.

17. Nathan Glazer and Daniel P. Moynihan, *Beyond the Melting Pot* (Cambridge, Mass., 1963). Michael Parenti, "Ethnic Politics and the Persistence of Ethnic Identification," *American Political Science Review,* 60 (1967), 717–26. Harry H. Bash, *Sociology, Race and Ethnicity* (New York, 1979). Joel Williamson, *The Crucible of Race* (New York, 1984).

cultures into a new indigenous American type; and "cultural pluralism" postulated the preservation of the communal life and significant portions of the culture of the later immigrant groups within the context of American citizenship and political and economic integration into American society.[18]

"Anglo-conformity" denotes the *absorption* of an ethnic minority into the prevailing culture. The "melting pot" metaphor indicates the *fusion* of separate cultures into a third new culture. "Cultural pluralism," however, accepts society and community as separate phenomena and denotes societal integration with subcultural separation.

As Gordon makes clear, the choice of assimilation or separation results from countless decisions by individuals, institutions, and governments. The ideology of assimilation prevalent throughout the nation's history has been Anglo-conformity.[19] English settlers arrived first and transplanted the society and culture of their homeland to the new colonies. Native American Indians were excluded or removed themselves, and the remnants of their separate cultures, remain alive on reservations today. As new waves of immigrants came to America, they were encouraged or compelled to assimilate into the prevailing white, Protestant, middle-class culture they found here.

The absorption of northern Europeans into the core culture went rather painlessly; the social and cultural distances were not great. As immigration of peoples from markedly dissimilar cultures increased dramatically in the latter part of the nineteenth century, the hegemonic aspects of Anglo-conformity became more widely noted. The melting pot metaphor, symbolizing the fusion of distinct cultures and peoples, emerged to depict another, perhaps better, approach to assimilation. The crucible of this new American race was to be the frontier experience and the settling of the vast new land. Out of this process would come a new, uniquely American lifestyle.

Whether by absorption or fusion, a single overriding culture was to emerge from the admixture of ethnic, religious, and racial groups. By World War I the popular name for assimilation was Americanization, and its realization was not left to chance. A prominent American educator of that time expressed the prevailing sentiment:

Everywhere these people tend to settle in groups or settlements, and to set up here their national manners, customs, and observances. Our task is to break up these groups or settlements, to assimilate and amalgamate these

18. Milton M. Gordon, *Assimilation in American Life* (New York, 1964), 85.
19. Ibid., 89.

people as a part of our American race, and to implant in their children, so far as can be done, the Anglo-Saxon conception of righteousness, law and order, and popular government, and to awaken in them a reverence for our democratic institutions and for those things in our national life which we as a people hold to be of abiding worth.[20]

The intensity of the Americanization movement, directed as it was toward southern and eastern Europeans, engendered an ideological counterattack—cultural pluralism.

The presumed goal of the cultural pluralists is to maintain enough sub-societal separation to guarantee the continuance of the ethnic cultural tradition and the existence of the group, without at the same time interfering with the carrying out of standard responsibilities to the general American civic life. In effect, this demands keeping primary group relations across ethnic lines sufficiently minimal to prevent a significant amount of intermarriage, while cooperating with other groups and individuals in the secondary relations areas of political action, economic life, and civic responsibility.[21]

Cultural pluralists resented the cultural dominance of the Anglo-Saxon core group and did not want to see the separate ethnic subcultures evaporate into some misty new assemblage. Indeed, for them, the strength of the nation lay in its cultural diversity. Cultural pluralism was rooted in an anti-assimilationist and separatist impulse.

The separatist impulse has not always originated exclusively with ethnic minorities themselves. In the South, the separation of races had come at the behest of whites. Under Jim Crow, separation and inequality had gone together. By the 1950s, the quest for racial equality seemed to require an end to racial and subcultural separation.

"Jim Crow" had been the code name for a separation by race, sanctioned by law. "Integration," that powerful, evocative slogan of the civil rights movement during the 1950s and 1960s, was an assimilationist's cry. King welcomed white people into his movement, just as he demanded blacks' access to white institutions. Black and white were to sit together at "the table of brotherhood." But the assimilationist stream was not the only one in the surge to equality. Another impulse found its most notable manifestation in the Black Muslims, but it was not limited to them alone. For these people, equality was not to be found in black access to white institutions, but in the power of a separate culture and even perhaps a separate economy.

One incident illustrates the tension between the assimilative and

20. Ellwood P. Cubberly, *Changing Conceptions of Education* (Boston, 1909), 15–16.
21. Gordon, 158.

separatist wellsprings within the black movement.[22] In June 1966, James Meredith was gunned down on Highway 51 south of Memphis. Shortly thereafter, civil rights activists organized a demonstration to finish his "march against fear" in Mississippi. The night before the march, Willie Ricks, a fiery SNCC orator, brought the black crowd to its feet by asking a rhetorical question, "What do you want?" The response was unanimous, "Black Power." The emotional reaction to the phrase prompted Martin Luther King to confront Stokely Carmichael and Floyd McKissack about the movement's mood and its new slogan. Their debate, which took place in a small Catholic parish house outside Yazoo City, Mississippi, lasted for five hours.

Why did these leaders spend so much time talking about a simple phrase? Because, although these activities of the black crusade were theatrical, a kind of play before a national audience, they identified, for supporters and opponents alike, the goals and ideals of the movement. Slogans ("Freedom Now"), songs ("Freedom," "We Shall Overcome"), and rhetoric ("I have a dream . . . ") of the early civil rights movement were pitched to a listener's emotions, but they reminded everyone of their common humanity. The early protests and slogans had been designed to appeal to sensitive whites for support. In June 1966, then, Martin Luther King was upset because he knew the phrase "Black Power" could alienate whites, who would interpret the slogan as a demand for separation and domination. Instead of equality through assimilation, the new black militants wanted equality through separation. A turning point had been reached, and just as King feared, sympathetic whites began to drop away or be cast aside by the newly separationist movement.

School desegregation is an assimilationist policy endorsed by blacks and mandated by the courts on the basis of public law and the Constitution. The Supreme Court has assumed that had it not been for slavery and governmentally imposed discrimination, blacks would have been assimilated into American life just as other groups had been. The central thrust of court decisions has been to make assimilation happen in schools. The *sine qua non* of equality was, for the Court, the assimilation of blacks. Busing for desegregation became the principal tool by which this was to be brought about, whether blacks or whites wanted it or not.

As the following story of busing in Nashville makes clear, many black people are ambivalent about assimilation if it means they have

22. Howell Raines, *My Soul Is Rested* (New York, 1978), 470. Stephen Oates, *Let the Trumpet Sound* (New York, 1982), 40. King, *Where Do We Go From Here* (New York, 1967).

to give up their communal base. Blacks, no less than whites, see schools as a communal as well as a societal institution. Under the "separate-but-equal" policy, schools in black neighborhoods reflected and reinforced the black culture. Under busing for desegregation, blacks surrendered this communal aspect of schools as the price of assimilation. And many of them did not like that.

The Politics of Race: Who?

Who benefits in the politics of redistribution? Clearly, as individuals and as a group blacks want to get a larger proportion of the good things of life. Not all public policies issuing from the surge toward equality in the past few decades, however, have taken from all whites and given to all blacks. Some have, to be sure, and these have generally produced status benefits. Nondiscriminatory access to white institutions was one such status benefit in which all blacks could share. All blacks benefited when a national holiday was declared to celebrate Martin Luther King, Jr.'s birthday. All blacks shared in this public display of deference, and most white southerners were shamed at the same time. The rest of the nation's respect and admiration for southern whites, never very high, dipped lower still during the struggle over civil rights.

Policies which affect all blacks equally and all whites equally are rare, and they usually reallocate status benefits. More often redistributive public policies reward some blacks more than others and cost some whites more than they cost others. Inevitably, perhaps, such policies have created tensions within each racial group as much as between them. For example, when white universities adopted affirmative action programs in admissions and employment, they were able to attract the best, brightest black students and professors. As a result, traditional black colleges lost class and status benefits. In Nashville, Fisk University and Meharry Medical College nearly foundered in the wake of assimilation. Supporters of these two schools were not happy about that.

Among whites, too, the assimilationist thrust of school desegregation had its differential consequences. In "separate-but-equal" schools and even in "desegregated-but-neighborhood" schools, the class and status differences among the community's schools were apparent. Busing, however, reduced these differences not only between the races, but also within the white race itself. For example, for generations before busing, residents of Belle Meade, a wealthy white suburb of Nashville, used Parmer, the local public elementary school.

But when busing was introduced, they removed their children from the school, not because the educational quality was worse (its excellent faculty remained), but because Parmer was no longer the "in" place to be. The "better schools" were the ones the "better people" went to. Busing destroyed much of this status distinction among white parents. Those who wanted to retain the status benefits once attached to their local public school soon found that they had to pay private school tuition. Some could and did; others couldn't and resented their loss of face. Other white parents, who could pay private school tuition but kept their children in the public schools out of conviction, felt morally superior to but were separated from the private school patrons. Busing split the white middle class into distressed new factions.

Conclusion

The chapters which follow elaborate on the definition of politics which serves as an analytic framework for this book. As the story unfolds the reader should remember that we are focusing on the nature of and reasons for conflict in society. Thus it is important to keep asking which issues caused divisions of opinion within each racial group and between blacks and whites as two separate groups. The patterns of conflict which emerge answer questions about who benefits and who pays in the struggle over racial policies. The answers to these questions are not trivial. The differential impact of costs and benefits is always the source of the seemingly inevitable next round in the battle over the role of race in American life.

September, 1957, parents and students watch as black children arrive at a formerly all-white school. Courtesy: *Nashville Banner*

Hattie Cotton School the morning after a dynamite blast destroyed one wing of the recently desegregated school, September 10, 1957. Courtesy: *The Tennessean.*

Pickets protest segregated lunch counters in downtown Nashville in April, 1960. Courtesy: *Nashville Banner.* Photo by Vic Cooley.

Anti-busing leader Casey Jenkins addresses protesting parents outside Judge
L. Clure Morton's courthouse, March, 1971. Courtesy: *Nashville Banner.*
Photo by Bill Goodman.

Parents gather in War Memorial Auditorium in March, 1971, to register their
opposition to the idea of busing for desegregation. Courtesy: *The Tennessean.*

Busing for racial balance begins, September, 1971. Courtesy: *Nashville Banner.* Photo by Charles Warren.

Police assist parents who brought their children to school cross a picket line,
September, 1971. Courtesy: *The Tennessean.*

A child ignores the boycott called by protestors, September, 1971. Courtesy:
The Tennessean.

A protest march against busing, September, 1971. Courtesy: *The Tennessean.*
Photo by Jimmy Ellis.

Avon N. Williams, counsel for the plaintiffs in *Kelley, et al.* v. *Metro* Board of Education, makes his point forcefully. Courtesy: *Nashville Banner*. Photo by Dean Dixon.

U.S. District Court Judge Thomas A. Wiseman, Jr. Courtesy: *Nashville Banner.*

Board of Education members with an assimilationist impulse, Fall, 1979: George H. Cate, Jr. (above left), Isaiah T. Creswell (above right), Barbara E. Mann (bottom right) and Cynthia Morin (bottom left). Courtesy: *Nashville Banner*. Photos by Bill Goodman.

Board of Education members with a separatist impulse, Fall, 1979: Ruby Major (above left), Troy Lynn (above center), Delois J. Wilkinson (above right), John Bottom (bottom right), and Ted Ridings (bottom left). Courtesy: *Nashville Banner.* Photos by Bill Goodman and Donnie Beauchamp.

Consultant Donald Waldrip presents a high school desegregation plan to the Board, February, 1980. Courtesy: *The Tennessean.* Photo by Gerald Holly.

Marian Harrison and William R. Willis, attorneys for the school board, encounter a reporter outside the board's conference room. Courtesy: *The Tennessean*. Photo by Robert Johnson.

Kent Weeks, chairman of the elected board, appears pensive moments before announcing secret negotiations with plaintiff, March, 1982. Courtesy: *The Tennessean*. Photo by Dan Loftin.

Part I

After the Civil War many black people came to Nashville, a regional center and the state capital, in search of better lives. During Reconstruction the newly freed slaves entered the sometimes benevolent, sometimes exploitative, but always paternalistic embrace of the Freedman's Bureau, the Union Army, and northern liberals. Whites started schools for blacks—schools which later became Fisk University and Meharry Medical College—and whites continued to govern the black schools and to supervise the conduct of their students well into the twentieth century. During Reconstruction, too, blacks were politically organized, and important posts in state and local government went to black citizens, then one-quarter of Nashville's population.

The paternalism of Reconstruction receded as waves of newly reenfranchised whites came to power in the 1870s and 1880s. Legal separation of the races in public places in Nashville preceded the separate-but-equal doctrine issued by the Supreme Court in *Plessey vs. Ferguson* (1897). With the ascendency of the Democratic party and its "white primary" and poll tax, blacks soon lost their political power. Blacks, regardless of their individual attributes, were returned to the bottom of Nashville's class and status hierarchies by an exercise of social, economic, and political power by the whites.

At the turn of the century, leaders of the black community in Nashville supported many of the ideas of Booker T. Washington, especially communal separation, patience, cooperation, and self-help. These leaders organized businesses, including a bank and a newspaper, and sought to build a cohesive if separate community while fighting a rear-guard action against the extremes of "Jim Crow" separatism in public facilities. The pattern of this period persisted through the Great Depression, when many black businesses failed, and through World War II. The physical and psychological mobilization for the war set the stage for the black assault on inequality in Nashville.

By the mid-1950s blacks were no longer prepared to accept second-class citizenship. They demanded equal status in societal institutions. They wanted nondiscriminatory access to public facilities. A confluence of forces made change possible, if not inevitable. A magnificent coalition emerged, consisting of courageous black community leaders, determined black citizens, sympathetic white supporters, skillful and persistent civil rights attorneys, activist courts, and later the aggressive force of the federal government.

The white South had violated the American culture's most elementary norms of fairness, and it was forced to change. Schools, hotels, restaurants, buses, and waiting rooms were desegregated. Discrimination against blacks in the sale or rental of property was outlawed. Voting rights were guaranteed.

In the late 1960s the magnificent coalition began to come apart. Richard M. Nixon was elected President, and he wanted to restrain the federal government from actively pursuing any further efforts to redistribute class and status benefits. The morally inclusive integrationist rhetoric of Martin Luther King, Jr., was displaced by the confrontational and separatist chants of "Black Power." Racial justice was no longer defined as equal access; it came to mean compensation—a payment to be extracted from whites for their past sins. Affirmative action was required.

Busing for desegregation was one form of affirmative action sanctioned by the courts. Though southern misdeeds attracted special attention, the logic of the policy did not stop at the Mason-Dixon Line. In 1973 busing went north and west, and resistance to busing in Boston was as great as it had been in warmer climates. Every geographical area, it seemed, was guilty of racial isolation. The redistribution of prestige and educational benefits through busing became a national policy, and white resistance became widespread.

In 1971, as one important facet of the complex nexus of racial politics in the United States, desegregation of public schools through the use of busing came to Nashville. To understand the meaning of this event and the politics of desegregation after busing, a historical context is necessary. In Part II we look at the past in order to better understand the present consequences of busing in the city.

CHAPTER THREE

Integration Efforts in Nashville

// "This is the city," wrote Nashvillian David Halberstam in 1960, "whose integration plan has been called a model for other southern cities; where white mobs were quickly and cleanly handled during school openings, where Negroes have voted and enjoyed justice in the courts, where bus segregation was ended by quiet agreement between city and Negro leaders, where the racist demogogue John Kasper is now meditating in the county jail . . . It is a good city . . . Yet early this month, in the words of a photographer who had just watched white hoodlums stuff cigarette butts down the collars of Negro college students, it was 'a good city gone ugly.' "[1]

On any resident the city of Nashville can bestow a history rich in all that is noble or profane in southern culture. The city's designation, "Athens of the South," suggests an openness and a tradition of a civic excellence. The city is home to a variety of religious denominations; music, banking, business, and printing interests; and more than a dozen colleges and universities. Nashville is the capital of the State of Tennessee. Its two newspapers boast a tradition of award-winning journalistic excellence. Yet this Athens can become a Sparta on occasion. Nashville was the scene of the first school bombing after the 1954 *Brown* decision. Post–Civil War Nashville served as a nesting ground for the Ku Klux Klan, founded by Tennessean and former Confederate Gen. Nathan Bedford Forrest. An upsurge in Klan sympathy in the 1920s resulted in beatings, mob protests, a student strike, and a lynching.

In this chapter we highlight the early awakenings of racial protest in Nashville's history and white responses to each confrontation. The objective of black protest activity was admission to white societal institutions. Schools were the embodiment of social and economic differences, so school desegregation lay at the heart of the racial conflict. All the paradoxes and emotions of community life were revealed in the process of school desegregation. The depth of white feelings about race was reflected in decisions about whether to

---

1. David Halberstam, *The Reporter,* Mar. 31, 1960, 17–19.

put a child in private school, abide by court–ordered busing, or move to another neighborhood or county. Some schools experienced the special rewards reaped when parents and teachers of both races worked together to educate children. In other neighborhoods and schools, racial tension was the order of each school day.

The character of the black community was forged in adversity. Even before school desegregation began, Negroes had a tradition of civic pride unique in the South. Early struggles for racial equality had had the practical effect of making black neighborhoods independent, autonomous, and proud.

A Segregated City

"Whites make their own history," said local black activist lawyer Avon N. Williams, Jr., in a 1970 newspaper interview. "[They] write it the way they want it, and write the Negro out of American history."[2] There is a ring of truth to Williams' statement, especially when the subject of study is blacks before the Civil War. History is written from the viewpoint of the articulate—those who had the ability and fore-sight to put their thoughts on paper. The Negro was not articulate, at least in the literary sense. Hence not much material is left to tell about Afro-Americans in Nashville. Early records show only that non-whites were roughly one-fourth of the population in Davidson County. Slavery was the rule in the area, although a few free blacks pursued skilled occupations such as blacksmithing and carpentry.

The end of the Civil War brought Mr. Lincoln's Freedman's Bureau to Tennessee. Ex-slaves flocked to Nashville for the rations and medical care offered by the Bureau, as well as for better job opportunities and the excitement of city life. By 1865 there were 10,744 freedmen in the Davidson County, compared to fewer than 4,000 before the war. Black Bottom, the area of town south of Broad Street, became a land of promise. During Reconstruction, Negroes served on the City Council, voted, and bought land. Northern "carpetbaggers" and local "scalawags" organized the blacks into potent political blocks. The Nashville *Union and American* newspaper declared in 1870 that blacks were "lured to the cities by the wily Radicals who

2. *Tennessean*, Feb. 9–15, 1969. J. Merton England, "The Free Negro in Ante-Bellum Tennessee," *Journal of Southern History*, 21 (1955), 54–56. Paul D. Phillips, "White Reaction to the Freedman's Bureau in Tennessee," *Tennessee Historical Quarterly*, 25 (1966), 30–62.

held out to the views of the darkies the glittering boon of the franchise, with hopes of office and position in the future."[3]

More likely blacks came to the city for services rather than for political favors. In Nashville, a black could learn to read and write at the Freedman's Bureau school, get the lingering ailments of slavery treated at hospitals, and best of all, buy things previously reserved only for "massuh." Freedom meant that blacks could imitate whites by addressing each other as "Miss" and "Madam," attend dressy social functions, and travel as they pleased. Many adopted new last names, such as Jefferson, Washington, or Hamilton. Couples with children and grandchildren were legally married; later they bought homes in some of Nashville's new "colored" neighborhoods.

The black community flourished around the cultural amenities of local churches and fledgling educational institutions. But free Negroes soon realized that dressing in master's clothes did not gain them admission to his world. The best means of advancement in the white culture was a formal education. After the war, abolitionists and representatives of various northern aid societies sought to build a normal school for blacks. They succeeded in 1866, when Fisk University was founded. Central Tennessee College (1866) and Meharry Medical School (1876) were also opened. These schools were the living embodiment of white hopes for Reconstruction—church-affiliated and benevolent in purpose, but white in administration. Fisk University was named for the white general, Clinton Fisk, who helped establish the Freedman's Bureau in Nashville after the war. This paternalism was in keeping with the Reconstruction ideal that whites should assist blacks to reach their proper station in life. Later this assistance would become a barrier to integration, as whites contended that blacks already had "a place" in society and should stay "in their place." Very few whites, early or late, believed in absolute status equality between the races.

Black aspirations were stymied by the return of Bourbon rule. Congressman Horace H. Harrison, elected in 1873, became the last Republican Nashville sent to Washington. Black politicians campaigned for the party of Lincoln until 1887, when their activities were curbed by a poll tax law. Disenfranchisement became complete when whites pledged themselves to the Democratic Party. In Nashville, it was understood that white people would vote only for the Democratic nominee in the general election, thus dooming the Republican

3. Howard N. Rabinowitz, *Race Relations in the Urban South, 1865–1890* (New York, 1978), 22–23. James Summerville, "The City and the Slums: Black Bottom in the Development of South Nashville," *Tennessee Historical Quarterly,* 40 (1981), 182–92.

choice. The Democratic primary, a nongovernmental institution, became a white man's political club in which "family" disputes were settled. The one-party tactic worked to perfection. A newspaper article of the period described what happened when a black attempted to speak at a Democratic political rally. "The speaker was pelted with eggs, potatoes and heavier missiles. . . . the box upon which he stood was knocked from under him five or six times."[4] Blacks would one day form a crucial part of the Democratic coalition in Tennessee, but in the 1870s prudence dictated that they avoid party assemblies altogether.

By intimidation whites forced blacks to adopt a policy of appeasement. One day in 1868, M.M. Hiland opened his mail to discover a note demanding that he close his school for Negroes immediately. "If this notice fails to effect its purpose, you may expect to find yourself suspended by a rope with your feet about six feet from terra firma (signed) Grand Cyclops." Threats by the Ku Klux Klan were commonplace in post-war Tennessee. The Klan was originated and nurtured in Middle Tennessee; its first secret meeting convened at the Maxwell House Hotel in Nashville in April 1867. National black leaders realized that their dreams of equality would not soon be realized in such an atmosphere. The white racist attitude helps to explain the importance of Booker T. Washington's "Atlanta Compromise" speech in 1895. The speech served as a harbinger of *Plessy v. Ferguson*, a 1896 court case which institutionalized "separate-but-equal" public facilities.[6] The ruling served to legitimize established policy in Tennessee, where statutes on the books prohibited interracial marriage and schooling. Later Jim Crow legislation banned association in factories, restaurants, theatres, hotels, and other public places.

Segregation, intended to separate the races, really consigned blacks to an inferior caste. In the white community, allegiance to the color line was absolute. When Teddy Roosevelt invited Booker T. Washington to the White House for dinner, Tennessee's U.S. Senator Edward W. Carmack wondered if the President was trying to turn the White House into "a nigger restaurant." The Memphis *Commercial Appeal* editorialized about the visit by inquiring if the executive mansion had subsequently been "disinfected, or even the chair, knife,

4. Mingo Scott, Jr., *The Negro in Tennessee Politics* (Knoxville, 1966), 74. Herbert L. Clark, "The Public Career of James Carroll Napier: Businessman, Politician, and Crusader for Racial Justice, 1845–1940" (D.A. diss., Middle Tennessee State Univ., 1980).

6. August Meier, *Negro Thought in America* (Ann Arbor, 1969) 100–101.

fork, plate and napkin deodorized."[7] In Nashville, blacks indeed had their place—at the back door, in the rear of the streetcar, in shanties along Jefferson Street, and at menial jobs throughout the city.

Yet there were exceptions to the inferior position assigned blacks. The Nashville Negro community had an unusually large number of preachers, teachers, lawyers, and businessmen who were immune to the economic threats of whites. The 1890 census showed that the city had more professional "colored" men than the comparable municipalities of Atlanta and Richmond.[8] Men like James C. Napier and Dr. R. H. Boyd provided community leadership. Napier was born free. Between 1878 and 1889 he served three terms on the Nashville City Council and was the first black to preside over that body. He helped establish Pearl and Meigs High Schools and was a founder of the One Cent (now Citizens) Savings Bank. Dr. R. H. Boyd was a preacher, missionary, entrepreneur, publisher, banker, educator, and writer. Boyd believed in the ideals of Negro initiative and self-help and was a life-long supporter of Booker T. Washington. In 1909 Boyd, Napier and others sponsored a state-wide tour for Washington. J. H. Keeble, a North Nashville politician, had such faith in the financial abilities of the black citizenry that he took out an advertisement in city newspapers, both black and white, urging "every colored man in Nashville . . . to buy a home. There is no use in saying you can't, for no man is too poor to buy one or two lots at sale next Tuesday."[9] At the turn of the century Nashville had more businessmen, black lawyers (nine as compared to Atlanta's two), physicians (with Meharry Medical School), and politicians than any comparable city in the South.

The independent character of the black community was forged on the anvil of segregation. When the state legislature passed a Jim Crow streetcar law, blacks in Nashville responded with a transportation boycott. Negroes could get to work just as quickly at the back of the streetcar as at the front, but their self-respect and their social status were at stake. So, in August 1905, Napier, Boyd, and other black leaders established the Union Transportation Company. Twenty-five thousand dollars in capital stock were issued, and enough was bought to enable R. H. Boyd to purchase five "auto-buses." The boycott was immediately successful, and hopes of forcing repeal of the Jim Crow law were high until winter set in. Then problems developed—the steam-driven autos were too slow; the engines broke down often; and

7. Stanley J. Folmsbee, Robert E. Corlew, and Enoch L. Mitchell, *Tennessee, A Short History* (Knoxville, 1969), 574.

8. Rabinowitz, *Race Relations in the Urban South*, 66.

9. Ibid., 103.

the line had a hard time staying on schedule in December snow.
Whites harassed blacks as they waited for the cars. Finally the finan-
cial burdens became too great, and the company folded in mid-1906.
The boycott tactic, which would prove successful fifty years later in
Montgomery, was symbolic even if it failed—it showed that the
Negro community could organize and resist white denigration.

The Reverend James A. Jones of the St. Paul A.M.E. Church said
before the boycott, "self-respecting, intelligent colored citizens of
Nashville will not stand for Jim-Crowism on the street car line in this
city."[10] He was right. Even in failure, the black community was
united, dignified, and purposeful. Evidence of new self-respect is
nowhere more apparent than in the early editions of the black-owned
newspaper, the Nashville *Globe*. The *Globe* was founded in 1906 by
R.H. Boyd and his son, Henry Allen Boyd. Early editorials berated
segregation as a practice resulting in pervasive and inequitable treatment of blacks by whites. In the early 1900s, Negroes were hired only
for menial tasks such as road building, brick making, sewer digging,
street cleaning, and, for the women, domestic chores. Whites believed these jobs were suited to the lazy and unreliable nature of the
black race. Words in a new weekly newspaper about self-respect did
not compensate for the daily indignities blacks suffered on the job.

World War I changed the self-images and occupations of blacks.
About one-tenth of the American Expeditionary Force in Europe was
Negro. These men did traditional jobs such as unloading ships and
building roads, but they drew the same pay as their white counterparts. Negroes in Europe were treated with courtesy and kindness by
French civilians. After the war, some of these veterans came to
Nashville to attend Fisk University. Men who had faced the Germans
in trenches across Europe were called "boy" in Nashville and told to
address the white administrators at Fisk as "suh." This treatment did
not sit well with them. Veterans led student efforts to establish a
student newspaper, change the dress code, and bring a branch of the
newly organized NAACP to campus. Fisk President Fayette
McKenzie vetoed the latter idea and expelled responsible male student leaders for their "Bolsheviki spirit."[11]

Nevertheless, after 1920 student complaints became more numerous. Racial tension reached the boiling point in 1924. Fisk was the
scene of a student strike which forced McKenzie to resign as presi-

10. Lester C. Lamon, *Black Tennesseans, 1908–1950* (Knoxville, 1977), 23–24.
11. Lamon, "The Black Community in Nashville and the Fisk University Strike of
1924–1925," *Journal of Southern History,* 40 (1974), 225–44. Alrutheus A. Taylor, "Fisk
University and the Nashville Community, 1866–1900," *Journal of Negro History,* 39
(1954), 111–26.

dent and changed the course of black and white relations. The scene had been set a year before when Ku Klux Klan activity and the trial of a black veteran for the rape of a white woman had split the community. "During the year a local Negro minister was killed by a police officer, a black businessman was shot down in his store by a white saloonkeeper (who went completely unpunished), and during November two Negro women, one of them a student at the Tennessee Agricultural and Industrial Normal School, were beaten on streetcars by unchallenged white men."[12] Late in 1923, a Negro youth was taken from the county hospital by a gang of white men and lynched.

Fisk University president Fayette McKenzie responded to the community tension by clamping down on the students under his charge. Rules had been a part of the school since it was founded; card playing, betting and tobacco usage had always been grounds for dismissal. Social relationships were tightly controlled. Between 1917 and 1923 six men were expelled for fornication, "at least a dozen for gambling, one for possession of a deadly weapon, and one for threatening a fellow student with a pistol."[13] In the Roaring Twenties, Fisk remained (to quote one of its graduates) "a Victorian nunnery."

Across town, at prestigious Vanderbilt University, the rules of student conduct were no less strict; but there the rules were made by white men to control white men. At Fisk whites made and enforced the rules for blacks. McKenzie's strict discipline, in conflict with student demands for a newspaper, athletic association, and self government, culminated in a schoolwide boycott in February 1924. The president called the city police to break up the student demonstration and appealed to the white community for support to keep the blacks in their proper place. Almost without exception, the whites— at civic clubs, in daily newspapers, and on the Fisk Board of Trustees—backed McKenzie. Despite this pressure, the students stayed away from their classes for two months and finally forced McKenzie's resignation. The Fisk student strike, like the earlier streetcar boycott, unified and strengthened the black community. The neighborhood around Fisk became a kind of fortress where blacks rallied to resist white injustice.

The impulse for racial reform in mid-century came from forces outside Nashville—from the federal government and Negro leaders and liberals in the North. Their initiatives created a local environment conducive to change. Beginning in 1947, the President's Committee on Civil Rights recommended that segregation be outlawed in

12. John Egerton, *Nashville: The Faces of Two Centuries, 1780–1980* (Nashville, 1980), 193. Egerton, *A Mind to Stay Here* (New York, 1970).
13. Joe M. Richardson, *A History of Fisk University* (University, Ala., 1980), 86.

federal government hiring practices, the public schools, and places of public accommodation. Southern Democrats lost a fight to remove reformist civil rights proposals from the party platform at the 1948 national convention. In Tennessee, the poll tax law was repealed in 1943. The first black patrolman walked Nashville streets five years later. The first black president of Fisk University, Dr. Charles Spurgeon Johnson, took the helm in 1946. The first black city councilman since Reconstruction was elected in the early 1950s. But the real catalyst for racial reform in Nashville, as throughout the nation, was the *Brown* decision of 1954.

National Efforts at School Integration

In no area of the nation is the legacy of local control of education more pronounced than in the South. The southern custom contained "an intense distrust of, and indeed downright aversion to, any actual exercise of (governmental) authority beyond the barest minimum essential to the existence of the social organism."[14] Yet it was in Dixie that the federal government mounted its offensive against segregation in the 1950s and 1960s. The first salvo in this battle to change established social customs was the *Brown v. Board of Education of Topeka* ruling in May 1954.

In a unanimous opinion authored by new Chief Justice Earl Warren, the Supreme Court ruled that "In the field of public education the doctrine of 'separate but equal' has no place." The opinion emphasized the importance of education, and affirmed that "segregation of children in public schools solely on the basis of race . . . deprive[s] the children of the minority group of equal education opportunities."

The Court did not issue an enforcement order with the ruling but instead cited "the great variety of local conditions" which must be taken into account in formulating desegregation plans.[15] A year later, more arguments were heard on guidelines for implementing the decision. The May 1955 decision, usually called *Brown II*, assigned supervision of desegregation policies to the federal district courts. The ultimate objective of the policy was clear: admission to public schools on "a racially nondiscriminatory basis." But there was little guidance as to how the goal should be achieved.[16]

14. W.J. Cash, *The Mind of the South* (New York, 1969), 32–43.
15. Derrick Bell, *Civil Rights*, 114–16. Also see Reed Saratt, *The Ordeal of Desegregation: The First Decade* (New York, 1966).
16. *Brown v. Board of Education*, 349 U.S. 294 (1955), in Derrick Bell, *Civil Rights*, 114–16.

Most local educators resisted integration. Some school districts, to slow the rate of desegregation, simply refused to comply until they were faced with federal court injunctions. By 1960, however, with the adoption of grade-a-year plans, a compromise was reached on the degree of segregation in the South.[17]

The grade-a-year plan had its genesis in Nashville and was used to acclimate whites to the realities of integration. Local school boards set on resistance to integration adopted other less benign procedures to frustrate judicial intent: state payment of private school tuition for students in lieu of providing public school funding; amending compulsory attendance laws to provide that no child be forced to attend an integrated school; artificial concerns over the "public welfare"; and the requirement that schools faced with desegregation schedules simply close down.[18] Between 1954 and 1958, the eleven southern states enacted 145 statutes designed to thwart the *Brown* ruling.[19]

These procedures had the desired effect, for southern schools remained segregated. White parents in Alabama, Mississippi, and Georgia formally complied with the federal desegregation order but then asked for reassignment under relevant state statutes. The state law provided "freedom of choice" for each child in the selection of a school. Southerners knew that blacks as well as whites would prefer to go to school with their friends. The intrepid black youngster who ventured into the hallways of a white school was intimidated by indifference, threats, or abuse. By 1964 barely 12 percent of the schools in the eleven-state southern region were integrated; in the Deep South (Georgia, Alabama and Mississippi), the figure was closer to 2 percent.[20]

Early desegregation efforts were stimulated by the John F. Kennedy administration, which, in response to civil rights demonstrations, pressured the Justice Department to increase the pace of desegregation in the South. Lunchcounters endured numerous sit-ins and

17. *Kelley v. Board of Education of the City of Nashville,* 270 F. 2d 209 (6th Circuit, 1959). *Calhoun v. Members of the Board of Education, City of Atlanta,* Civil No. 6298, N.D. Ga., Dec. 30 1959. The grade-a-year plans were not consistently approved; see *Cooper v. Aaron,* 358 U.S. 1 (1958). *Northcross v. Board of Education of the City of Memphis,* 333 F. 2d 47 (5th Circuit 1964). *Armstrong v. Board of Education of the City of Birmingham,* 333 F. 2d 47 (5th Circuit, 1964).

18. Southern Regional Council, "School Desegregation 1966: The Slow Undoing," (Dec. 1966), 47. Benjamin Muse, *Virginia's Massive Resistance* (Bloomington, Ind., 1961).

19. Henry A. Bullock, *A History of Negro Education in the South From 1619 to the Present* (Cambridge, Mass., 1967), 260.

20. U.S. Commission on Civil Rights, "Survey of School Desegregation in the Southern and Border States, 1965–1966" (Feb. 1966).

boycotts in 1961. State institutions of higher learning witnessed white opposition to federally enforced integration; a gun battle accompanied James Meredith's enrollment at the University of Mississippi in 1962. The next summer Governor George Wallace stood in the University of Alabama's front door to prohibit even token integration there.

The movement for civil rights reached its climax in Spring 1963 in Birmingham, Alabama. Nonviolent protests saw 3,000 Negroes jailed while thousands more knelt in prayer before lunging German Shepherd dogs and fire hoses spouting jets of water. Television news brought the scene into millions of American living rooms; the macabre sight crystalized public opinion in favor of the protesters and stimulated similar outbursts in other cities.

Early Desegregation Efforts in Nashville

"This had to be done. It was time. And the only question was who would do it." That is how Robert W. Kelley remembered his involvement in the Nashville desegregation case twenty-five years afterwards. "All I wanted is for people to be able to do what they want to do as long as their choice is good."[21] On September 23, 1955, Kelley, along with twenty-one other plaintiffs, filed suit to end segregation practices in the Nashville public schools. Just three weeks earlier he had tried to enroll one of his children at East High School. Principal William H. Oliver politely but firmly refused the request. *Kelley v. Board of Education* was the result.

In 1955 Nashville was a community where blacks and whites lived in racial separation. The city itself, 40 percent black, was surrounded by a number of predominantly white independent suburbs. The desegregation issue centered on the sacrosanct housing patterns which characterized the community. "Colored town" was in the northern part of the city around Fisk, Meharry and Tennessee State Universities. Black neighborhoods also flourished south of the downtown area along major transportation arteries. Middle-class white people lived in the green-grass suburbs of West and South Nashville. Across the Cumberland River lay the working-class areas of East Nashville, Donelson, and Goodlettsville.

The Davidson County school board responded to the 1954 *Brown* decision by saying that the Supreme Court decisions "do not require immediate action, but rather suggest careful study as related to local

21. *Tennessean*, May 13, 1979.

conditions."[22] "Careful study" lasted until March 1956, when Judge William E. Miller ordered the city (as distinct from the county) schools to desegregate. At that time there were two black school systems, consisting of twelve black schools in the city and thirteen in the county. These included two high schools, Haynes and Pearl, which served the black community. By contrast, the two white systems were composed of nearly eighty schools (including a dozen high schools) with a combined enrollment of over 60,000.[23]

Robert Kelley's court suit resulted in the "Nashville Plan," a stair-step, grade-a-year program for desegregation starting in the first grade. To the city school board's way of thinking, the plan had two virtues. First, it complied with the *Brown* decision, and second, it had "due regard" for existing racial patterns in the community.

This latter point troubled NAACP attorneys Z. Alexander Looby and Avon Williams. They contended that the plan relied too much on neighborhood schools and geographical zoning. The program simply reinforced existing residential housing patterns. Avon Williams later said of the Nashville Plan, "The purpose of the gradual plan was not in good faith, but rather for a regrouping of forces and achieving de facto segregation."[24] Nevertheless, the grade-a-year plan became a model for school systems in the South.

Nashville was officially integrated September 9, 1957, when thirteen black children registered in formerly all-white first-grade classes. About two o'clock the next morning, a dynamite bomb blew a gaping hole in one wing of Hattie Cotton School. One Negro girl had attended classes at the facility the day before. In the wake of the blast, Police Chief Douglas E. Hosse addressed his morning police detail with resolve, "This has gone beyond a matter of integration. These people have ignored the laws and they have shown no regard for you or any other citizen."[25] This bombing, the first violence since the *Brown* decision, shook white Nashvillians from their apathy. Many in the community made amends by supporting the school board's plan.

Even with black children at the school door, some parents refused to accept the inevitable. On September 9, white protesters picketed five formerly all-white schools. They were led by John Kasper, an avowed segregationist from New Jersey who travelled throughout the

22. Ibid.
23. U.S. Office of Education, Federal Security Agency, *Directory of Secondary Schools in the United States* (Washington, D.C., 1949), 360. U.S. Office of Education, *Public Secondary Day Schools: 1958–1959* (Washington, D.C., 1959).
24. *Tennessean*, Feb. 9–15, 1969.
25. *Tennessean*, Feb. 10, 1969.

South to organize resistance to integration. Kasper had just served a six-month jail term for interfering with desegregation in Clinton, Tennessee, where a crowd of one thousand had finally been dispersed by National Guardsmen with fixed bayonets supported by seven tanks and three armored personnel carriers. In Nashville, Kasper held rallies where his rhetoric and the distribution of anti-black and anti-Jewish literature made the tense situation even worse. One flyer featured a photograph of a black man kissing a white woman with the inscription, "When they put the niggers in school with your kids in September, load your shotguns to defend your wife and home."

Finally, Kasper was arrested and charged with inciting to riot. His flamboyant behavior at a six-day trial attracted national attention. Two hundred twenty-five character witnesses were subpoenaed in Kasper's behalf; fifty-five gave testimony. His attorney was the staunch segregationist Raulston Schoolfield, an impeached criminal court judge from Chattanooga. In the end, Kasper was found guilty and sentenced to six months in the workhouse with a $500 fine.

The emotional quality of this trial was poignantly illustrated in an incident which occurred at the close of proceedings one day. As Nashville City Attorney Robert H. Jennings was leaving the courtroom, he overheard Kasper make a wisecrack, a threat which ended with the challenge, "What are you going to do about it?" Jennings turned in anger, put his finger under Kasper's chin, and said, "Prosecute you to the fullest extent of the law, that's what." Reporters snapped a picture of the confrontation and circulated it with the story to newspapers throughout the South. Such publicity helped the city's image; Nashville was a good city—one which would not slip into racebaiting.[26]

Support of integration was made palatable to whites by a plan which did not call for compulsory integration. Both black and white children were allowed "freedom of choice" to refuse to attend schools previously all white or all black. The 1957 plan was based on pre-*Brown* geographical attendance zones; the plan assigned only 115 black first graders to enter previously white schools and 55 white students to enroll in black schools. But even this modest start toward full societal integration was doomed to failure. The school's transfer policy offered a way out, and 102 black children and all 55 white children opted to transfer to other schools. In 1957, the first year of desegregation in Nashville's first grade, only ten of the original thirteen black youngsters completed a full year in a desegregated classroom.[27]

26. Interview with Robert H. Jennings, Feb. 1982.
27. Connie Pat Mauney, *Evolving Equality: The Courts and Desegregation in Tennessee* (Knoxville, 1979), 110.

The school board's policy was derived from the Tennessee School Preference Act, one of a host of segregation laws passed in 1957 by the state legislature. The Preference Act, as the name implies, allowed parents to choose where their children would go to school. In early September 1957, Judge Miller declared this act unconstitutional; in July 1958, he made the grade-a-school-year plan compulsory for city schools. By fall 1958, desegregation was the law in Nashville. But the law was not popular. Another bomb damaged the Jewish Community Center, named by an anonymous caller "the center of integrationists in Nashville."

The grade-a-year plan was widely imitated; it provided a gradual approach to an explosive situation. The Nashville proposal, which cleared a judicial test in 1960, scheduled integration through 1968, when the school system would be fully in compliance with the *Brown* mandate. In November 1960, the Davidson County school system was ordered to follow the grade-a-year plan already operating in the city school system. When the two systems merged in 1963, the new Metropolitan Board of Education adopted the city plan for the entire county. In 1965 the Metropolitan Board mandated that the 1966–1967 school year would mark desegregation for all twelve grades in the public schools.

But the school administrators were accelerating a plan that wasn't working. The 1960s began with forty-four black students in white schools. All these pupils were in the city school system; no county facilities were desegregated. Children attended schools in their neighborhoods, and school zones reflected the housing patterns of the community. The grade-a-year plan changed the pattern of segregation some, for the percentage of black students attending school with whites rose from 9.7 percent in school year 1964–1965 to 12.3 percent in school year 1965–1966. But overall gains were insignificant. A 1969 study showed that 83.3 percent of the white students in Davidson County attended classes which were 90 to 100 percent white. Nashville was desegregated in name only. Segregated housing patterns led to continuing racial isolation in neighborhood schools.[28]

Despite these inequalities, Nashville's integration record was a source of pride among whites. The city's approach was moderate; it met the letter if not the spirit of the *Brown* ruling. A standard of educational quality was being maintained while all this "progress" took place. But behind the smiling mask of racial harmony lay the frowns of racial tension. Frustration was evident in 1965 when Martin Luther King, Jr., spoke to packed black Nashville churches. His

28. Leo C. Rigsby and John Boston, "Patterns of School Desegregation in Nashville, 1960–1969," *The Urban Observatory* (Nashville, Jan. 1971; mimeographed).

words brought new hope to Negroes in the city, and many began to organize and discuss the changes which were overdue for their race. School integration had shown that adjustments were possible, but more rapid changes were needed. In Nashville, the index of black expectations was on the rise.

The Civil Rights Act of 1964

After the murder of John Kennedy, the new president, Lyndon Johnson, told a joint session of Congress, "We have talked long enough in this country about equal rights. We have talked for one hundred years or more. It is now time to write the next chapter, and to write it in the books of law."[29] Southern resentment of the new laws was immediate and furious. It boiled to the surface in 1964 when George Wallace ran for the presidency, trying to capitalize on a "white backlash" to the federal mandates. Black leaders responded to the challenge by registering Negroes to vote.

In March 1965, Dr. Martin Luther King, Jr., called for a "march on the ballot boxes throughout Alabama." On "Bloody Sunday" (March 7, 1965) state troopers reinforced by a sheriff's posse met the marchers on the Edmund Pettus Bridge outside Selma, Alabama. The ensuing melee resulted in over fifty injuries to the demonstrators, seventeen of whom required hospitalization.[30] A week after the incident, President Johnson compared the events in Selma to the historic battles at Lexington, Concord, and Appomattox. The issues were important because something more substantial than a dough-nut at a lunchcounter was at stake. Nondiscriminatory access to the ballot box was a lever of power in the politics of race.

The first school years after passage of the civil rights laws were marked by confusion. Educators remained obdurate in the face of the new law. Office of Education officials responded by handling each school district individually. No universal desegregation standards were set. Funds were released for school districts on a case-by-case basis.

In the decade following passage of the Civil Rights Act, the Justice Department initiated five hundred school desegregation suits, and the Department of Health, Education and Welfare (HEW) brought six hundred more actions.[31] Strict guidelines governing desegregation

29. Lyndon B. Johnson, *The Vantage Point* (New York, 1971), 38.
30. Francis P. Simpkins and Charles P. Roland, *A History of the South* (New York, 1972), 609.
31. Richard Kluger, *Simple Justice: The History of Brown v. Board of Education and Black America's Struggle for Equality* (New York, 1975), 958.

were issued in March 1966. These measures addressed faculty hiring practices and unequal facilities, programs, and activities for black students. Many parents reacted by pulling their children out of the public schools. Forty thousand students in Virginia, South Carolina, Alabama, Mississippi, and Louisiana were in private academies by fall 1966.[32] The Alabama legislature enacted a law to nullify all HEW measures and lost $30 million in federal aid as a result. But these insurrections only served to strengthen federal resolve. Late in the school year 1966–1967, the Atlanta Office of Education ruled that school districts must achieve higher integration ratios by fall 1967.

Supreme Court decisions continued to dismantle desegregation barriers erected by recalcitrant school boards and state legislatures. In *Bradley v. Richmond School Board* (1965), the Court held that further delays in desegregation were "no longer tolerable." Grade-a-year desegregation plans were outlawed. In 1968 "freedom of choice" plans were struck down in *Green v. County School Board of New Kent County.* A passive program was no longer acceptable to federal officials.

The last two years of the Johnson presidency witnessed a full-scale assault on *de jure* segregation in the South. Congress continued to supply HEW officials with fat federal education grants to entice reluctant local school districts into compliance. The Civil Rights Division of the Justice Department updated standards for integration. Assaults on *de facto* segregation in the North and West were rare; such cases required extensive research and tedious litigation to prove the existence of official conduct which reinforced racial isolation.

By the end of the 1960s, domestic racial concerns were submerged by protests against the Vietnam War. Racial issues were only one item on the public's troubled agenda. In retrospect the Civil Rights Act of 1964, the Great Society programs, and the events of the decade seem more important for the principles they espoused than for the changes they effected. The legislation guaranteed blacks access to places once denied them to be sure. Legal mandates gave blacks equal status but not the economic means to better themselves. Economic assistance in the form of welfare payments to Negroes rewarded dependence on government and were often ineffective in transfering benefits. The Great Society programs were so embroiled in turmoil that their political insufficiencies outweighed the good intentions that gave rise to them. Daniel Moynihan examined the Community Action

32. U.S. Commission on Civil Rights, "Survey of School Desegregation, 1966–1967" (Washington, D.C., 1967), 11. U.S. Commission on Civil Rights, "Survey of School Desegregation, 1965–1966," 19–23.

Programs (CAPS) and concluded that the legislative intent of "maximum feasible participation" by the poor resulted in a "maximum feasible misunderstanding."[33] Misunderstanding was in fact the norm for those times.

Civil Rights in Nashville

"Gentlemen," said NAACP President Dr. Edwin Mitchell in a speech before the city's Chamber of Commerce, "Nashville is indeed fashioning a new face . . . but tall buildings which allow you to gaze outward upon the green grass of suburbia cannot long shelter you from the despair, frustration and bitterness that continue to build around you." In Mitchell's mind the despair was rooted in continuing racial injustice. "In a city that unites its governments but leaves its people divided a cruel mockery is made."[34]

The first racial incidents of the sixties in Nashville were typical of those in communities across the South. Initially blacks desegregated lunchcounters. The Reverend John Copeland of Zion Baptist Church remembers marching from First Baptist Church Capitol Hill downtown, to places like Woolworth's where "the rabblerousers would stand around and throw things at you." The climax came when an early morning dynamite blast wrecked the Meharry Boulevard home of Nashville lawyer, black activist, and City Council member, Z. Alexander Looby. The next day hundreds of people packed Fisk University Gymnasium to hear pleas for nonviolence. Finally, a series of meetings between black and white community leaders ended segregation at lunchcounters, in bus terminals, and on transportation lines. This sensible arrangement enhanced Nashville's reputation as a city where cool heads controlled the South's hottest problem.

By the middle 1960s it appeared that Nashville was worthy of the "Athens" title. But the worst incidents of the decade lay ahead. In 1966 the Student Nonviolent Coordinating Committee (SNCC) met in annual conference in Nashville. The atmosphere was ugly with frustration. Malcolm X had been assassinated, Julian Bond had been denied his rightful seat in the Georgia State Legislature, and the killers of civil rights workers Goodman, Chaney and Schwerner, murdered in 1964, were still free. In such an environment the gentle, religious John Lewis was elected chairman, but later he was unexpectedly opposed and ousted. In his place the twenty-five-year-old black

33. Daniel P. Moynihan, *Maximum Feasible Misunderstanding* (New York, 1970).
34. Egerton, *Nashville*, 258.

power advocate Stokely Carmichael was installed. SNCC's position changed from nonviolence to violence, from cooperation to separatism. "Freedom Now" gave way to "Black Power."

In April 1967 Stokely Carmichael returned to Nashville and spoke at Vanderbilt University. His advocacy of black separatism and black power fell on sympathetic ears in the mostly Negro audience. When Martin Luther King was killed a year later, this militancy surfaced. The King assassination triggered sporadic violence requiring mobilization of the Tennessee National Guard to enforce a city curfew. There were no massive eruptions of hatred or burned-out buildings, but the peace between black and white was uneasy.

This distance between the races was not lost on attorney Avon Williams. In November 1969 the original black plaintiffs in the *Kelley* suit filed a brief with the U.S. District Court. This time the complaint had to do with the construction of new facilities to house an expanding public school student population. During the 1960s, quality education meant innovation. The metropolitan public schools were among the first in the South to experiment with new curricula, develop open classrooms, and use individualized instruction. Middle-class parents wanted their children to take advantage of these latest educational innovations. So it was no surprise that when the system expanded late in the decade to accommodate the post-war boom babies, the location of schools became a critical issue. Not surprisingly, new schools were scheduled to be built in the suburbs. Construction reflected housing patterns in the county and the growth of the suburbs, so blacks were to be left with the older downtown facilities.

Williams believed that the geographical school zones actually hindered integration; most of the attendance zones were still pre-*Brown* configurations. He pointed out that black pupils attended older downtown schools while white children were educated in modern suburban facilities. Plaintiffs contended that the pace of desegregation, one grade a year, had allowed whites to move to the suburbs, thus triggering a type of resegregation. To build new schools in the outlying white areas would simply reward those escaping desegregation. Given that city and county boundaries were now the same, black citizens asked that all schools in the system be integrated with approximately an 80 percent/20 percent white-to-black ratio.

Late in 1969 District Court Judge Miller enjoined the board from constructing new schools or purchasing new sites until officials presented a new plan that would end the effects of the dual school systems. After examining the issue from the standpoint of legal precedent, he came to the conclusion that "there appears to be fairly

general agreement that unavoidable segregation resulting from bona
fide racial residential patterns is constitutionally permissible." Nevertheless, the judge said that the board could and must alter zone
lines and plan construction in order to maximize integration. Moreover, Judge Miller ruled that placement of black teachers in white
schools must be increased. At that time an average of two black
teachers taught in each predominantly white school, while fourteen
taught in each black school. Miller gave the board thirty days to come
up with a comprehensive plan addressing the issues. Before the court
was reconvened, however, Miller stayed the proceedings. He wanted
to wait and see what the Supreme Court would say in a pending case
dealing with schools in Charlotte-Mecklenburg County, North Carolina. But Avon Williams didn't want to wait; he asked the Sixth U.S.
Circuit Court of Appeals to lift the stay and order more rapid desegregation in Nashville. The appeals court agreed with Williams, and
Miller was ordered to press ahead.

Both the school board and the community were unprepared for the
court order which was handed down on July 16, 1970. A new school
superintendent, Dr. Elbert Brooks, had been at his post only sixteen
days, having assumed his job after the untimely death of Dr. John
Harris. Many parents believed it was too late in the summer to
organize a fullscale desegregation effort by the fall. In a surprising
move, Judge William Miller instructed the school board to submit a
plan in thirty days which would: (1) desegregate the staff, (2) desegregate the student population, and (3) identify the construction of
facilities which would enhance desegregation. If the board succeeded,
busing of students would almost certainly be required.

On August 19 the board submitted its limited, hastily drawn plans
and requested time for more thorough study to guide future planning.
Judge Miller accepted the board's plan to desegregate the teaching
staff and ordered it implemented when schools opened that fall. The
plan for desegregation of teachers and principals required staff assignments in the 80 percent white to 20 percent black range in each
school. The judge then vacated his order for student desegregation in
order to permit a more orderly implementation of the pupil assignment plan. This delay disturbed plaintiff's attorney Williams, who
again appealed to the Sixth Circuit Court in Cincinnati.

Halfway through the regular school board meeting of August 25,
1970, a note was passed to Dr. Brooks. The superintendent interrupted the proceedings to tell all present that he had an unusual
announcement. The floor was then turned over to board attorney
Robert Kendrick, who read as follows: "In the absence of further and
more specific guidelines from the Supreme Court, no lower federal

court is in a position to make a definite ruling on these important issues." Applause and cheering erupted from the 250 black and white parents in the hearing room. Busing in Nashville was delayed. The U.S. Circuit Court in Cincinnati felt that immediate implementation of the policy "might result in harm to those whose interests must be deemed paramount, the students."[35]

Some in the audience that summer night believed there would be no "forced busing" ever. The reasons for their confidence included Richard Nixon's presidential rhetoric, the belief that Nashville was already integrated, and the assurances of local politicians that busing would never happen here. But their belief was misguided; in fact, Nashville had been targeted for full integration since 1967. In that year the Justice Department had begun an investigation of "artificial zone boundaries" in the Nashville school system. Even with the grade-a-year plan and community support for the goals of integration, Nashville remained segregated. Davidson County had a population 20 percent black in the 1970 census, yet only 19 out of 125 schools were 15–35 percent black. School zones reflected housing patterns, and segregated housing meant racial separation. Racial separation resulted from past unconstitutional state action. For this reason some type of busing plan was inevitable if the illegal racial separation was to end. The only real question was, "How much busing is enough?"

Many Nashville parents realized that the 1970 delay was but an Indian summer; soon the winter winds of the busing conflict would sweep the community. Scores of these concerned people sought to find an integration compromise before it was too late; after four months of school, a group of them worked out a new plan with the twin goals of racial balance and quality education. The parents, who called themselves Concerned Citizens for Improved Schools (CCIS), sought to stimulate dialogue between black and white factions in the dispute by redefining the term "neighborhood." The CCIS plan took a more expanded view of what neighborhood schools should be. The first section of their plan called for a massive reorganization of the school system, resulting in four to six administrative areas, each with a student population of 75 percent white and 25 percent black. Racial ratios would vary from school to school, but each area would reflect the Davidson county ratio. The CCIS proposal was a compromise, a modest attempt by citizens to solve the integration conundrum.

Meanwhile the school board itself initiated other action. During the 1970–1971 school year, a citizen's committee, consultants, and

35. *Banner*, Sept..15, 1971.

district staff undertook a Building and School Improvement Study (BASIS). They surveyed public opinion, interviewed community leaders, and carefully examined the existing educational program. The BASIS report contained four plans, none of which involved busing for desegregation in the lower grades. Elementary desegregation would depend on newly drawn neighborhood attendance zones, but desegregation would occur most notably in the larger attendance zones of several "great schools," which soon became known as "comprehensive high schools."

Comprehensive high schools were attractive for two main reasons: greater educational opportunities for students and natural desegregation. In comprehensive high schools students would have many more programs and courses from which to choose. Each such school would contain as many as twenty vocational programs ranging from construction trades and auto repair to data processing and commercial art. These programs were intended for students who wished to enter the work force upon graduation. New opportunities would exist also for students interested in college. In the older traditional high schools eight or ten students—too few to justify a class—might want Latin or calculus. But when students from two or three traditional high schools were put together in a single comprehensive facility, there would be enough students to create these special courses. Just as important as student opportunities was the natural desegregation which such a facility, with its large attendance zones, would entail. Such schools contrasted happily with the smaller traditional high schools, which were often disproportionately one-race institutions· and which would require "cross-town busing" to be brought into an acceptable ratio.

When the BASIS report was being developed, McGavock Comprehensive High School was under construction. When it opened in fall 1971 it would bring together students from three high schools— Two Rivers, Cameron and Donelson—as well as other students who sought its special programs. McGavock was to be the prototype for desegregated secondary education in Nashville.

The school board debated the recommendations of the BASIS report and in the end developed two desegregation plans for submission to the court. Both plans were very limited. They did not incorporate cross-town busing, but they did endorse the concept of a large comprehensive high school. Even though these plans failed to satisfy the court, the development of inclusive secondary education facilities and programs continued to be the central thrust of the board's planning during the next decade.

Nashville's commitment to comprehensive high schools was based on rational calculations. Comprehensive programs in large facilities would provide the maximum choice for students, and the schools would be desegregated through the use of large attendance zones. The board also anticipated the use of state funds for the construction of the vocational education wings of the comprehensive schools. Indeed, in 1973, when the Vocational Education Act became law, substantial funds were made available to local school districts. Metro schools ultimately obtained grants to finance 95 percent of the cost of its vocational education facilities.

Swann v. Charlotte–Mecklenburg Co., 1971

Until the 1968 election campaign of Richard Nixon, the federal government supported civil rights reform efforts in the South but said little about racial segregation in the North. The Republican strategy that year was designed to pry the southern states out of the traditional Democratic (New Deal) coalition. Thus, Nixon showed his sympathy for southerners by pointing to school segregation in northern cities, most of which voted Democratic on election day.[36] A popular campaign speech cited the fact that only twelve HEW field investigators were assigned to northern cities, while over fifty examined southern school systems.

Nixon's "Southern Strategy" forged an alliance between Republican voters in the mountains and Piedmont areas and the conservative, white, middle-class urban and suburban communities of the South. Republican strategists conceded the extremist white vote to George Wallace, while they cast Nixon as a moderate. On racial issues, Nixon said he would "uphold the laws of the land," but he left little doubt that desegregation would not be forced.

When Nixon assumed office, southern politicians brought enormous pressure to bear on the president to make good his promises and ease federal guidelines demanding full school desegregation in September 1969. Powerful Republicans such as Strom Thurmond and John Tower consistently emerged from the White House saying that the president believed "the government had gone too far" in pushing busing. An intra-administration debate on desegregation guidelines soon broke out. Attorney General John Mitchell favored giving southern districts more time, while HEW Secretary Robert Finch advocated immediate implementation of firm standards. Finch had prom-

36. Kevin Phillips, *The Emerging Republican Majority* (Garden City, 1970), 25–42, 187–289.

ised civil rights leaders there would be "no erosion of the guidelines."[37] In April, HEW followed through on a cutoff of funds to recalcitrant southern school districts, but the issue of how fast desegregation should proceed remained open.

By 1970 busing was political dynamite. The controversy surrounding the policy was multi-faceted, but it stemmed from white concern that blacks were "pushing too fast." Parents seemed to resent the moralizing attitude of the court order as much as the ideals embodied in the policy. Busing was labeled "forced busing." It was controversial because the court order moved children around at will and distributed black children in suburban facilities originally designed for the neighborhood white youngsters. Similarly, whites were obliged to send their own children into black neighborhoods. This latter provision was especially odious to whites, who often responded to a busing proposal by withdrawing their children from the public schools. Equality of educational service was a laudable goal as long as whites were not required to sacrifice their children to the ghetto environment.

Black leaders countered by saying the federal government was not doing enough to bring justice to the land. They consistently charged that desegregation statistics failed to show how shallow integration was. Schools were considered integrated if they accepted any black students, even though they might remain overwhelmingly white. Moreover, the federal figures did not report all-white private academy enrollments. If most black and white children remained in racially separated schools, then the lessons of racial tolerance and mutual respect could not be learned. The unwarranted status differential would remain even though schools formally were open to children of any race.

Civil rights groups returned to the courts to go beyond token integration of the schools. They were rewarded with a significant victory in the Supreme Court decision, *Swann v. Charlotte-Mecklenburg Co.* This landmark ruling in May 1971 established the pattern for busing in school districts across the nation. The Supreme Court, in yet another unanimous opinion, upheld the plan of a local district court which used mathematical ratios as part of a scheme to end racial separation in the school district. The court outlined the elements of an "acceptable" busing plan as: (1) busing outside the neighborhood could be required in order to achieve "effective desegregation," (2) "pairing" and "gerrymandering" were introduced as alternatives to neighborhood schools, (3) the racial ratio of each school should reflect the racial composition of the entire school

37. "Schools Make News," *Newsweek*, Feb. 17, 1969, 260–73.

district, (4) a small number of all-black schools could remain, provided they were not the result of discrimination, and (5) state anti-busing laws which obstructed desegregation efforts were unconstitutional. Pairing and grouping of schools in distant noncontiguous parts of the district was an acceptable desegregation practice. "Our objective in dealing with the issues presented by these cases is to see that school authorities exclude no pupil of a racial minority from any school, directly or indirectly, on account of race." The Supreme Court standard became clear: the removal of racial isolation in local school systems.[38]

In *Swann* the Supreme Court revealed most clearly the assumption on which it built its school desegregation policy. Had it not been for illegitimate governmental action the Court implied, blacks would have been fully assimilated into majority American culture. Busing for racial balance would end racial isolation in schools and juxtapose blacks and whites as they would have been naturally, had unlawful discrimination not occurred. *Swann* sanctioned belated assimilation.

The court decisions, coupled with the liquid administration position on the subject, made busing the hottest issue of the 1972 presidential campaign. George Wallace's victory in the Florida primary shocked political experts; it showed that beneath the South's new racial integration lay its old racial animosity. Few aspirants to the presidency in 1972 endorsed busing for purposes of desegregation. A groundswell of public opinion rose against the policy, and soon this antipathy began to show up in various court cases. On June 6, 1972, the Fourth Circuit Court of Appeals limited busing in Richmond, Virginia, to the city schools; no merger of city and county systems was required. Various bills were introduced in Congress restricting federal authority over busing plans. Busing, never a popular issue, came in for criticism by judges and politicians as well as the Nixon administration. This reaction came at a time when appeals were pending regarding many *de facto* segregation cases. Judicial mandates were less clear in these latter cases than in *de jure* instances. Implementation of busing programs in southern school districts was doubly difficult given the campaign rhetoric. How could school officials and politicians in Charlotte or Nashville urge parents to accept busing when nightly television news programs showed a parade of presidential contenders denouncing the policy?

---

38. Derrick A. Bell (ed) *Civil Rights: Leading Cases* (Boston, 1980), 260–73.

Conclusion

On a brisk April morning in 1960 a Negro picket kept vigil outside the downtown Woolworth's store, bearing a sign which read, "Make Nashville Great—Desegregate." The sign was a compliment, in a way; it signified the hope for racial justice in the city. Integration, especially school desegregation, touched the entire community in an intimate way. Emotions ran high because parents, both black and white, were worried about changes which affected their children. In such an atmosphere it was a credit to Nashville that no angry outbursts led to rioting, looting, and violence. Instead, cool heads prevailed in the streets, and the issue was debated and resolved in community discussions, school board meetings, and court proceedings.

Many things changed in Nashville between 1954 and 1972. The civil rights movement and the power of federal law altered the social landscape. Separation of the races, by law and custom, all but disappeared in places of public accomodation. There were no longer separate drinking fountains, waiting rooms, or hotels. Still, the actual mixing of races continued to be limited largely to impersonal transactions. Interactions between the races in such situations were often awkwardly formal, excessively polite, and especially brief.

In the schools racial separation continued to exist for the vast majority of students. As long as school attendance zones reflected local neighborhood segregation patterns, the situation was not likely to change. Leaders in the black community, recognizing that confrontation usually produced results, pressed for racial balance in the schools. But that meant busing. Whites responded that "enough was enough."

These were the lines of confrontation in a familiar lawsuit. Throughout the school year 1970–1971, all parties to the dispute and the community at large waited for the Supreme Court to set a pattern for busing. The *Swan* decision fixed the standard to the racial ratio of the school district. Now the question before the courts in the Nashville case was whether a minimum busing plan met the *Swann* integration standard.

CHAPTER FOUR

The Nashville Busing Plan

U.S. District Judge L. Clure Morton assumed responsibility for the integration plan when Judge William E. Miller was elevated to the Sixth Circuit Court of Appeals. Morton had begun his career in law enforcement, serving as an FBI agent during World War II. When he took his oath as judge in October 1970, he brought to the federal bench thirty-three years of experience as a trial lawyer. In a newspaper interview, he described his judicial philosophy simply: "to be a fair arbiter in the courtroom." As a Republican, Morton was recommended for his post by Senator Howard Baker and appointed by President Nixon. Three months after assuming his new position, Judge Morton ruled on the *Kelley* case. He was destined to become known as Nashville's "busing judge."[1]

Morton was charged by the circuit court with making "a judgment as to whether the plan proposed [by the school board] was a good faith compliance . . . or whether it was designed to evade and frustrate the Constitutional purposes." Judge Morton carefully exercised his responsibilities, considering the plans developed by CCIS, the school board, and the plaintiffs. For a variety of reasons, he rejected each one and impatiently called for a team of outside experts from the Department of Health, Education and Welfare (HEW) to come in and draw up an appropriate plan.

On April 20, 1971, three weeks after the HEW team began its work, the Supreme Court announced its decision in *Swann*. In this case, involving Charlotte-Mecklenburg County, North Carolina, the Supreme Court affirmed busing for racial balance as the principal instrument for school desegregation in the South. With this decision the fate of Nashville's schools was sealed.

In 1971 the Charlotte-Mecklenburg County school system was the nation's forty-third largest district. The racial ratio was typical for a southern county, 71 percent white and 29 percent black. Prior to the court order nearly all black children in that system attended all-black schools. The desegregation plan grouped nine black inner-city ele-

1. *Tennessean*, Mar. 14, 1971.

mentary schools with twenty-four white suburban schools. Blacks were to be transported to the suburbs in Grades 1–4, and whites traveled to the downtown schools in Grades 5 and 6. Attendance zones for the junior high and high schools were altered to produce schools which reflected the overall racial makeup of the system.

In *Swann*, the Supreme Court affirmed the use of mathematical ratios in the plan. "School authorities . . . might well conclude . . . that in order to prepare students to live in a pluralistic society each school should have a prescribed ratio of Negro to white students reflecting the proportion for the district as a whole." The Court went on to say that not every school had to meet the prescribed ratio, but "awareness of the racial composition of the whole system is likely to be a useful starting point in shaping a remedy to correct past constitutional violations."[2]

The HEW team had been handicapped by the confusion over what standards were appropriate for the Nashville desegregation plan, but once the *Swann* decision came down, they were able to work with certainty and speed. Even though Judge Morton never told the team to use busing for racial balance, such a remedy was implicit in the Supreme Court opinion. The local officials obtained a map of Davidson County and spread it over a school gymnasium floor. Metro school personnel placed data on each city block of the map giving the race and age of each child on that block. With this data in place, the HEW team outlined new school zone boundaries and established pairing relationships between white and black neighborhoods.

All the elements of the *Swann* decision (mathematical ratios, pairing and grouping of schools, and the use of busing) were used in the Nashville plan. The first HEW plan did leave a few all-black schools in North Nashville, but Judge Morton insisted that they be desegregated. In the final HEW plan, none of Metro's 131 schools were to have a majority of blacks; however, several of them would be over 90 percent white. Before the plan was submitted to the court, it was personally inspected by Attorney General John Mitchell, HEW Secretary Elliott Richardson, Senators Howard Baker and William Brock, and Tennessee Governor Winfield Dunn. We don't know what opinion these officials had of the plan, but the reaction of the community was clear.

2. *Swann v. Charlotte-Mecklenburg Board of Education* 402, U.S. 1 (1971), in Derrick Bell, *Civil Rights*, 260–73.

Community Reaction

A hallmark of school integration policy in the South is that most changes have been precipitated by federal court order. So it was not surprising that on March 12, 1971, a Metro Council member named Casey Jenkins led five hundred irate white parents to the building where Judge L. Clure Morton convened hearings on the HEW desegregation plan. The courtroom could accommodate only a hundred visitors, so the remainder of the crowd stood in the hallways. Soon their noise became disruptive, and Judge Morton adjourned the hearings until the next week. Before television cameras, on the sidewalk in front of the courthouse, Casey Jenkins pledged to have fifteen hundred protesters at the next session of the hearings.[3]

In March 1971, Nashville came as close to violence over the race issue as at any time in its history. Fifteen hundred parents jammed War Memorial Auditorium in downtown Nashville to hear Jenkins proclaim, "Busing to create racial balance is an ugly creature, busing is unconstitutional . . . busing deprives us of our freedom of expression, of our freedom of choice, of our property rights and our civil rights." All over town parents congregated in homes, churches, and schools to discuss the latest busing rumor and to speculate on the court decision.

The Metro Council became a stage for antibusing rhetoric. Councilman Jenkins helped sponsor a resolution asking the courts not to "deprive any student in the public schools . . . of his constitutional right *not* to be transported" (emphasis added). The Nashville *Banner*, in an unusual front-page editorial, expressed its outrage under the headline, "Busing to Achieve Racial Balance in Public Schools Is Not Required by Law, And Is Opposed by the Congress, By the President, And by the People." On March 15, 1971, hundreds of school children were kept away from the public schools by parents sympathetic to the antibusing movement.[4]

All this activity was directed at one man, Judge L. Clure Morton. The desegregation hearings resumed amid tight security. Federal marshals patroled the halls and admitted only persons with "legitimate business." Doors at all but one entrance to the courthouse building were locked. Such security made rumors about the proceedings all the more salacious; each press report added kindling to the community tinderbox. In early June the HEW plan was made public.

3. *Tennessean,* Mar. 12–14, 1971.
4. *Banner,* Mar. 11, 1971; *Banner,* Mar. 17, 1971.

It called for busing an additional 15,000 children.[5] On June 28, 1971, Judge Morton accepted the HEW plan with minor modifications.

The next morning Assistant Metro Attorney Thomas S. Nelms was dressing for work when he received an unusual phone call from Mayor Beverly Briley. "Get downtown," he said, "I've called a press conference to discuss this busing decision." Briley was on record as opposing busing. "The courts should stay out of education, and education should stay out of the courts."

By summer Briley had a new reason for opposing the policy—the additional $2,122,800 needed to buy 127 new buses for the fall term. "We don't have the money . . . I don't know where such an additional amount of money can come from . . . there is no money in the budget for this purpose." Twelve years later attorney Nelms would remember that the newspapers couldn't print the expletives the mayor used to describe busing. "Bev was mad, and he wasn't about to increase taxes to buy school buses." The estimates for school buses varied. E. Carlisle Beasley, director of transportation for the Metro Schools, had earlier testified in Judge Morton's court that busing twenty thousand additional students would require another 240 school buses, more than doubling the existing fleet of 193 vehicles. Beasley placed the cost of the buses and bus driver salaries in the neighborhood of $4.3 million.[6]

The mayor was not alone in his opposition to busing. An overwhelming majority of the Metropolitan Council was also against any additional appropriation to pay for the massive busing program. Councilman Kenneth Miller of the 22nd District summed up a common sentiment: "If the federal government is not going to provide monies to implement the program . . . then I think the board of education would have the right to revert to its previous (desegregation) program."[7]

The topics of money and compliance with the court order became prime issues in a summer political campaign for Metro mayor and council positions. Councilman Casey Jenkins, capitalizing on the anti-busing sentiment, forced incumbent Mayor Briley into a run-off election in which the principal issue was who could remain more obdurate in the face of the federal court order.

In the middle of the summer political strife, the school board voted, by a majority of one, to appeal Judge Morton's decision. Attorneys for the school board pushed the appeal all the way to the Supreme Court.

5. *Banner*, Mar. 17, 1971; *Tennessean*, June 2, 1971.
6. *Tennessean*, Dec. 19, 1970; *Banner*, June 30, 1971. *Banner*, Apr. 10, 1971. Interview with Thomas S. Nelms, July 1982.
7. *Banner*, Oct. 13, 1971.

When, in August 1971, the Court refused to hear the petition, school administrators were forced to implement the busing order.

With appellate litigation ended, community leaders resolved to face the inevitable. Sentiment was growing in Nashville that no matter how odious the ruling, it was still the law and as such ought to be obeyed. There was consensus on one point, that no violence should accompany the opening of school. Beverly Briley's mayoral victory over Casey Jenkins quieted the antibusing rhetoric. In the wake of his election triumph, Briley pledged to implement the judge's order. Later the mayor used his considerable influence to lobby the Metro Council for supplementary funds so the school buses could roll on a staggered fall schedule.[8] The *Banner*, which had earlier characterized busing as "an outrageous, arbitrary, disruptive imposition on the whole community," joined in the spirit of resolution and dubbed Casey Jenkins the "Pied Piper of Pickets."[9] The paper subsequently called for obedience to the court order. In July, forty Southern Baptist pastors called for calm and issued a statement asking local "elected officials to refrain from inflaming emotions . . . at this time of crisis and decision." One month later Mayor Briley joined prominent ministers and two defeated mayoral candidates (but not Casey Jenkins) in a televised plea for calm and restraint. The Sunday before school busing began was a time when ministers of all denominations sermonized on suffering and obedience.[10]

The first children bused in Nashville's new desegregation plan were picked up at 6:15 A.M. on September 15, 1971. Forty-one schools in the city were being picketed by white parents. Casey Jenkins, leader of the picketing Concerned Parents Association (CPA), said there were "beatings and attacks in the halls" of various schools. "Mrs. Trudy Toberlin of Old Mt. View Road told police that children threw rocks at her head, missing by inches," while she picketed a Nashville junior high.[11] The awful vision of a desegregation "incident" haunted school officials.

Would it take federal marshals to keep the peace in this southern city? The picture of a small black child being escorted through a sea of white protesters chanting "keep our white schools white" was in the mind's eye of every city and school official that fall. U.S. Attorney Charles H. Anderson recalled years afterward that "the local police

8. *Tennessean*, Sept. 4–10, 1971.
9. *Banner*, Sept. 15, 1971.
10. *Tennessean*, June 28, July 21, Aug. 18, Aug. 23, Aug. 24, Aug. 25, Sept. 6, 1971.
11. *Banner*, Sept. 15, 1971. *Tennessean*, Sept. 16, 1971.

(did) an excellent job and there (was) no evidence of any need for additional help."[12]

An uneasy truce settled over the school system after the first few fall days. The pickets went home and the antibusing rallies faded into history; but protest against busing for purposes of school desegregation simply took on another face. The visible protest subsided, but many white parents did not send their children to the new schools.

The Busing Plan

Throughout the Nashville desegregation effort, Metro officials clashed with HEW team members over which schools would be involved in what pairing arrangements. HEW guidelines held that the pairing concept (predominantly white zones and predominantly black zones exchanging children) met the letter of the court ruling. Metro officials objected to pairing because they felt that the integration plan should accommodate a child's development from first grade through high school. They emphasized the need to have continuous friendship patterns and classroom associations throughout the public school experience.

School board officials pled for some flexibility and deviation from the rigid racial ratios used in the Charlotte case. They liked to quote from Section V of the *Swann* decision, "Conditions in different localities will vary so widely that no rigid rules can be laid down to govern all situations."[13] Still, there was a conscious attempt to keep the community reaction, already hostile, to a minimum. Grades 1–4 were generally assigned to suburban schools, while Grades 5 and 6 were placed in older black community schools. The plan projected that each school would be a microcosm of the larger community; black children would make up 25 (± 10) percent of each school in the court-ordered area.

An example of the "pairing" concept is provided by the zones illustrated in Figure 1. The pairing plan divided the neighborhood into geographical zones suitable for busing exchanges. Wharton Elementary School was predominantly black before busing. The 1971 busing order carved the Wharton Elementary School district into three zones, represented by the letters A, B, and C. For the first four years of their formal schooling black students from these areas were transported to the suburban schools associated with each letter. In

12. *Banner,* Sept. 15, 1971.
13. *Swann v. Charlotte-Mecklenburg,* in Derrick Bell, *Civil Rights,* 272.

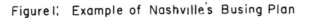

Figure I: Example of Nashville's Busing Plan

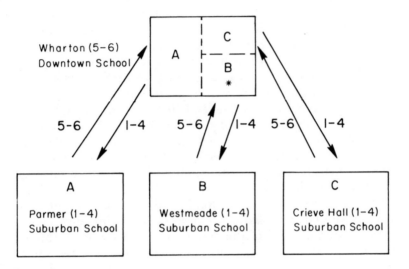

Wharton (5-6)
Downtown School

5-6   I-4   5-6   I-4   5-6   I-4

A
Parmer (1-4)
Suburban School

B
Westmeade (1-4)
Suburban School

C
Crieve Hall (1-4)
Suburban School

NOTE: Wharton school district was subdivided into three zones (A , B , C here). Students from these zones were transported to the suburbs for the first four years of their schooling. White students were bused downtown to Wharton (represented by the * here) for the fifth and sixth grade.

the fifth and sixth grades white students were bused into Wharton
School from three elementary school zones in suburban Davidson
County. The criteria for assignment of students were their grade level
and where they lived.

The broad outlines of the busing plan were affirmed by the court
without consulting school officials. The original HEW/Metro proposal was limited at the elementary level; it had envisioned only a
moderate amount of busing between paired contiguous neighborhoods that ringed the downtown area. Under this plan there were
some all-black schools and some all-white schools. The HEW plan
required neighboring school zones to exchange children; busing was a
trade between school zones which were contiguous but different in
their racial makeup. But the judge found this HEW proposal too
limited and paired downtown schools with outlying white areas—
while still allowing the original pairing between contiguous neighborhoods to stand. As a result, children from outlying white areas
were bused to a downtown school through a ring of school zones
involved in contiguous exchanges of children (Figure 2). Thus, a child
from West Meade (Zone A) would travel all the way downtown (to
Zone C) to complete his elementary school education, while a child
from the Sylvan Park area (Zone B) would only travel several blocks to
a contiguous school zone also in Zone B.

No single pairing concept dominated the Nashville plan; some
schools were Grades 1 through 3, some Grades 1 through 4, and some,
in the outlying areas of the county, retained Grades 1 through 6.
School officials had to work out a plan which involved the transfer of
22,000 elementary school children in seventy-one schools. Because
of the logistical complexity of busing, each school was practically a
unique case involving some type of alteration in the general plan.
However, to the extent that overarching principles guided the planners, the concepts outlined in Figures 1 and 2 held.

Some neighborhoods were content with the Metro plan. White
parents in the suburbs had their children in their local school until
the fourth grade, after which time the child was transported to a
downtown school for two years. Metro Schools officials hoped this
plan would reduce community hostility by allowing white parents to
keep their children in the suburbs until they were about ten years old.

The one hundred court-ordered school zones contained 67 percent
of the white children and 95 percent of the black children in the
school system. Thirty-three schools containing the remaining students were exempt from the court order. These schools (Zone D in
Figure 2) were so far from the urban core that it was judged impractical to bus children from them in any pairing relationship. These

Figure 2: Nashville-Davidson County Busing Plan

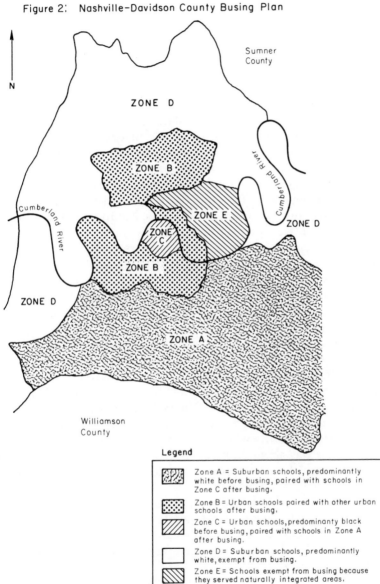

Legend

Zone A = Suburban schools, predominantly white before busing, paired with schools in Zone C after busing.

Zone B = Urban schools paired with other urban schools after busing.

Zone C = Urban schools, predominanty black before busing, paired with schools in Zone A after busing.

Zone D = Suburban schools, predominantly white, exempt from busing.

Zone E = Schools exempt from busing because they served naturally integrated areas.

outlying schools became havens for white parents trying to avoid busing. The court order had anticipated this white flight and sought to limit it by prohibiting new construction or the use of portables at such facilities. Nevertheless, their classrooms were soon choked with students.

The White Flight Response

Perhaps the first question to ask about Nashville busing is this: how valid was the plan? In other words, if every student in the metropolitan school system had followed the new assignment policy, would racial isolation have been eliminated?

To answer this question it is necessary to describe each school zone used in the busing plan. HEW officials used the existing Metro zones (i.e., the neighborhood around the school facility) in the pairing schemes. Schools were paired to achieve racial mixes roughly proportional to the Davidson County black-white ratio. For example, schools that were all white were matched with schools and neighborhoods that were nearly all black. If all the students attended their assigned schools, the resulting mixture at each school should reflect the 75–25 percent racial ratio (white to black) in the school-age population of the county.

Table 1 examines the pairing relationships between the various elementary schools. Was the busing plan based on the ideal of having the most racially isolated schools exchange students with one another? Or were compromises made and the all-black schools paired with already integrated facilities? The HEW desegregation architects had the option, for example, of pairing suburban Glendale School with a downtown facility which was almost all black, or with a closer facility which was about 50 percent black. The student population ratios were such that either match would have met the racial ratio test.

Table 1 compares the racial characteristics of each school zone. The statistics show that predominantly white school zones (those with a neighborhood characteristic of 0-5 percent black) were matched with predominantly black zones (those greater than 50 percent black). At the same time, over half (56 percent) of the black school zones were paired with white (0-5 percent black) schools. The basic goal of the busing plan was to mix whites and blacks in equal proportions throughout Davidson County. Table 1 shows that this goal was met, at least in theory.

The busing exchanges in Table 1, showing pairing arrangements in

Table 1: *Racial Characteristics of Matched Schools in the Nashville Busing Exchange, 1971 (Percent of Schools)*

RACIAL CHARACTERISTICS OF THE SCHOOL'S MATCHED BUSING PAIR (PERCENT BLACK)	RACIAL CHARACTERISTICS OF A SCHOOL ZONE (PERCENT BLACK)			
	0–5	5–25	25–50	MORE THAN 50
0–5	0%	18%	9%	56%
5–25	9	18	18	32
25–50	15	46	9	6
Greater than 50	76	18	64	6
Total	100%	100%	100%	100%
N	(33)	(11)	(11)	(16)

Number of Schools: 71 elementary schools in the court-ordered area. Chi Square: 42.78 significant at .001 level
Gamma: .682

the Metro system, were appropriate only if white students attended the public school to which they were zoned. But in September 1971 many white pupils did not show up. Enrollment patterns varied from school to school throughout the city.

The next question, then, is: what were the patterns of white flight in the school system? In other words, given the pairings of the busing plan, did some schools experience more white flight than others when the plan was implemented in fall 1971? Since school officials were required to gather extensive data on the racial composition and age of children in the school zones, the difference between the projected enrollment and the actual enrollment is a good indicator of the amount of protest by parents against the busing order. This difference is defined as "white flight," and is measured this way:

$$\text{White flight} = 1 - \frac{\text{Actual number of white students enrolled}}{\text{Number of white students projected to enroll}}$$

As an example of this method of white flight calculation, compare the following figures for a predominantly black Nashville school (Wharton) and similar figures for a school in a white neighborhood (Eakin).

$$\text{Wharton white flight} = 1 - \frac{147}{724} = .797 \text{ or } 79.7\%$$

$$\text{Eakin white flight} = 1 - \frac{224}{253} = .035 \text{ or } 3.5\%$$

In this measure, as white flight increases the number gets larger. In some non–court ordered schools white enrollment exceeded projections. In such cases the white flight figure had a minus sign, which means the school actually gained white students. Schools exempt from busing, in Zone D of Figure 2, frequently experienced this growth. The white flight for one such school, Harpeth Valley, is given below:

$$\text{Harpeth Valley white flight} = 1 - \frac{357}{330} = -.081 \text{ or } -8.1\%$$

When one looks at system-wide aggregate enrollment data for court-ordered schools the year before busing and the first year of busing, it appears that Nashville lost between 15 and 20 percent of its white students. This figure includes some students who were planning on attending private school regardless of the busing situation. The true character of white flight, however, cannot be judged from gross system-wide estimates. Within-system patterns reveal much more about the problem. Table 2 shows these patterns.[14]

Table 2 shows that the pattern of white migration was not uniform throughout Nashville. Whites left schools in the court-ordered area in disproportionate numbers. Schools exempt from busing experienced almost no white flight. In fact, junior highs and senior highs excused from the order actually gained white students. Court-ordered schools uniformly experienced white student losses, ranging from a low of 14.4 percent in Grade 1–4 schools to a high of 25.9 percent at the 5–6 level. Half of the student exodus came from two sources—the Grade 5–6 schools and the high schools impacted by the court order. The pattern of white flight within the Metropolitan-Davidson County school system is the most striking finding in Table 2.

In September 1971 unsuccessful mayoral candidate Casey Jenkins called an "antibusing" rally at the State Fairgrounds. In a speech to thousands of angry white parents, Jenkins said that boycotting the public schools was a legitimate protest to busing. Two weeks later many white parents, knowingly or unknowingly, followed Jenkins'advice. The 1971–72 school year would be remembered for its public demonstrations and racial rhetoric, but as the year ended the loudest statements were being made by those white parents who had quietly left the public school system.[15]

14. The HEW projections were accurate reflections of the school age population, but they did not try to estimate private school enrollments. The projections were based on school system data and 1970 census profiles. What about "black flight"? The incidence of black students leaving the public schools was rare, so the projected black enrollment figures were very accurate (2 to 3 percent error) in 1971.

15. *Tennessean*, Sept. 4, 1971.

Table 2: *Patterns of White Flight in Nashville, Tennessee, 1971*

GRADE LEVEL	WHITE FLIGHT IN COURT-ORDERED SCHOOLS	WHITE FLIGHT IN NON-COURT-ORDERED SCHOOLS
Elementary (Grades 1–6)	White Flight: 17.6% Students Missing: 4,344 No. of Schools: 71	White Flight: 6.8% Students Missing: 767 No. of Schools: 22
Elementary (Grades 1–4)	White Flight: 14.4% Students Missing: 2,509 No. of Schools: 51	
Elementary (Grades 5–6)	White Flight 25.9% Students Missing: 1,835 No. of Schools: 20	
Junior High (Grades 7–9)	White Flight: 16.3% Students Missing: 1,646 No. of Schools: 16	White Flight: −2.9% * Students Gained: 84 No. of Schools: 4
High School (Grades 10–12)	White Flight: 20.3% Students Missing: 2,533 No. of Schools: 13	White Flight: −13.1% * Students Gained: 545 No. of Schools: 31
Whole System:	White Flight: 17.7% Students Missing: 8,661 No. of Schools: 131	

* Negative white flight percentages indicate that these schools gained students as a result of the busing plan.

Source: *Ten Year Analysis of Enrollment Patterns*, Nashville-Davidson County Metropolitan School Board, 1981.

Note: These white flight figures are based on the HEW enrollment figures, which did not take into account normal white losses from the system. Hence these data slightly overestimate the amount of white flight.

Conclusions

The dual school systems which existed in Nashville and Davidson County prior to 1955 had reinforced the inequality of blacks along both class and status dimensions of community life. Black leaders sought school desegregation in order to reduce these inequalities. But desegregation of neighborhood schools, especially on a grade-a-year basis, did little to alter the pattern of inequality. By 1967, when the grade-a-year program was completed, because neighborhoods were themselves racially segregated, the great majority of children of both races still attended identifiably one-race schools in their communities. Moreover, newer and presumably better school facilities were being constructed in the suburbs as whites migrated to outlying areas. Nondiscriminatory access to schools had not achieved the desired result; blacks remained unequal.

Blacks wanted equality in terms of educational services and social status, not just access to the schools on an individual basis. The Supreme Court agreed with this demand for equality. In *Swann* the Court turned from a "means" solution to the problem of race (equal access) to an "effects" solution (busing for racial balance). Behind the Court's decision lay a powerful assumption. Had it not been for unconstitutional action by the state, the logic ran, blacks would not have been socially and geographically isolated in society. In the absence of discrimination by government, assimilation would have been achieved; so assimilation was required now in order to bring blacks to the position they would have occupied naturally. Busing for racial balance, the principal tool for desegregation after *Swann*, would create in each school a social *microcosm* of the larger community. Identifiably one-race schools would be abandoned, and blacks and whites would no longer be isolated from each other. Busing would remove the status and class inequalities between black and white children now, and over the long term within the entire society.

In Nashville, blacks supported busing because it redistributed class and status benefits between blacks and whites. Even in 1971, however, many black leaders were aware of the intractable nature of the inequalities; for them busing was not the end of the struggle, only a new phase. Nor was the redistributive nature of busing lost on Nashville whites. Most white parents accepted the plan, albeit reluctantly, and sent their children to the "new" schools. A significant minority of whites, however, left the public schools, saying in effect that assimilation could be left to others.

Part II

Desegregation of neighborhood schools in the 1960s did not change things in Nashville very much. By the end of the decade most black and white children were still schooled in predominantly one-race institutions. The incremental grade-a-year desegregation plan allowed white families to escape neighborhood schools with ease, and since neighborhoods were largely segregated anyway, desegregation affected few families. The prevailing patterns of inequality both between and within the two races remained. Equal educational opportunity meant that blacks had the right to attend schools with whites, but it was a largely symbolic victory that had been achieved by blacks and their white supporters.

Desegregation of schools by neighborhoods did not immediately threaten the educational services and social values of most whites. But busing for racial balance did. Busing was clearly intended to reallocate class and status benefits between blacks and whites. Most whites said they accepted the abstract ideal of equal educational opportunity, but at the same time they rejected busing, the policy designed to implement this ideal. It seemed to them that the rules of the game of life had been changed. Desegregation of neighborhood schools meant that individual black families could choose to live in white areas, to share in that community and its values, and to reap the benefits of this association in terms of educational achievement and social acceptance. That might be acceptable. Busing, however, was not voluntary and not selective; it affected everyone.

Now a new language of protest developed. Whites complained that busing wasted children's time, destroyed the nexus of school and community, placed children in schools too far from parents, broke up family and friendship groups, exposed well-behaved children to undisciplined or even violent school milieus, and undermined educational achievement. Fearful whites who felt trapped in the Metro public schools took to pickets and boycotts to protest the coming of busing. Those who were afraid and financially able moved or put their children in private schools. Although many anxious whites stayed in the schools and fought to make sure their values were upheld there, a large segment of the white community turned its back on the public system; these were no longer "their" schools.

There can be no doubt that many whites were afraid for their children as busing for racial balance became a fact of life in Nashville's schools after 1971. In Part II we examine the levels and patterns of white flight, achievement test scores, and public opinion in order to understand better the hopes and fears of those who protested busing and its consequences. As we shall see, white flight from the public schools was associated with the *blackness* of those schools and not their quality. Busing had no significant effect on the achievement of white children.

CHAPTER FIVE

First-Year White Flight

Pickets and rallies were the most visible ways whites used to protest against busing, but the silent withdrawal of white children from the public schools was the most significant form of rejection of the policy. About 18 percent of the white Metro school students fled from the public schools when busing was implemented in 1971. As will be shown in Chapter 6, many of these children would have gone to private schools or moved from the county as part of normal out-migration, but most left because of busing. Busing was seen for what it was—a redistributive policy—and many white families did not want to pay the price. They sought to preserve their share of the good things schools had to offer by leaving the public schools of Davidson County, even at the cost of private school tuition or family relocation.

What were the good things they sought elsewhere? Were they class or status benefits? Schools provide both. If parents withdrew children from the public schools because they feared their children would learn their academic lessons less thoroughly, then they were worried about the loss of class-based educational services. If they fled the schools because they feared the social values their children would acquire there, then they were responding to status concerns. In this chapter we seek to discover which of these two dimensions of social life underlay the protest against busing that we call white flight.

Grounds for Busing

Racial prejudice, and the racial segregation that is its behavioral manifestation, is a status issue. Racial prejudice is rooted in in-group and out-group loyalties, and it establishes a clear hierarchy of superior and inferior character traits between groups. One race is described in terms of virtues and the other in terms of vices. Racial prejudice found fertile soil in the American South. In 1944 Gunnar Myrdal described segregation as "an American dilemma"[1] that disfigured a

1. Gunnar Myrdal, *An American Dilemma* (New York, 1944).

region and its people. His research was cited in the now famous Footnote 11 of the Supreme Court's *Brown* decision. In its opinion, the Court also cited a "modern authority" whose research showed that racial segregation had a profoundly damaging effect on black children. The authority was Dr. Kenneth B. Clark, who had conducted a series of doll experiments.[2] Clark had given black and white dolls to children in segregated settings. He found that white children preferred the white doll, but so did black children. The white doll was described as the "nice" one. Clark concluded that the "fundamental effect of segregation [was] basic confusion in individuals in their concepts about themselves." Segregation damaged the self-esteem of black children, just as it reinforced the prejudice of white children.

Kenneth Clark's conclusions were later challenged, but their legal importance cannot be overstated.[3] In *Brown*, the NAACP legal brief was accompanied by a statement supporting Clark signed by thirty-two prominent anthropologists, psychologists, and sociologists; the statement testified to the damage done to black children by segregation. The *Brown* decision opened the door for social science research to be introduced as evidence in subsequent desegregation litigation. Although desegregation research now has become mired in academic and political controversy, in the early days its themes were clear and consistent. School desegregation would enhance black children's self-concepts and academic achievement. Both black and white children would find their racial prejudices blunted by personal experience with children of the other race. White children's academic performance would not be hurt. Everyone, in short, would gain something, and ultimately race would dissolve as a contentious issue in American life.

The case for integration was made by psychologist Gordon Allport in his book, *The Nature of Prejudice*. In one of its most important passages Allport stated:

> Prejudice (unless deeply rooted in the character structure of the individual) *may be reduced by equal status contact between majority and minority groups* in the pursuit of common goals. The effect is greatly enhanced if this contact is sanctioned by institutional supports (i.e., by law, custom, or

2. Kenneth Clark and Mamie Clark, "Emotional Factors in Racial Identification and Preference in Negro Children," in Martin Grossack, ed., *Mental Health and Segregation* (New York, 1963), 53-63.

3. Edmond Cahn, "Jurisprudence," *New York University Law Review,* 30 (1955), 150. Monroe Berger, "Desegregation, Law and Social Science," *Commentary,* 23 (1957), 471–75. Herbert Garfinkel, "Social Science Evidence and the School Desegregation Cases," *Journal of Politics,* 21 (1959), 37. Ernest Van den Haag, "Social Science Testimony in the Desegregation Cases," *Villanova Law Review,* 6 (1960), 69.

local atmosphere), and if it is of a sort that leads to the perception of common interests and common humanity between members of the two groups[4] [emphasis added].

Allport's "contact theory" became the social science benchmark around which the forces of integration could rally. If blacks and whites could meet in "equal status" situations with "institutional supports" to pursue "common goals," racial prejudice might be reduced. Schools were the natural arenas within which to pursue these aims.

The academic genesis of busing as a logical policy of desegregation was a piece of sociological research by James S. Coleman entitled *Equality of Educational Opportunity* and commonly known as the Coleman Report. It included data on 600,000 children, as well as information on teachers and schools. The report undermined much of the conventional wisdom regarding education in the United States. Instead of finding that curriculum, pupil expenditures, and class size influenced educational achievement, Professor Coleman found that individual learning was affected more by a student's family background and the family backgrounds of his classmates.[5] This result implied that lower-class black students needed to be assigned to middle-class white schools in order to improve their educational performance.

Because of segregated residential housing patterns, busing was the vehicle employed to mix students. The first experimental busing programs were tried in Boston, Massachusetts, in 1967. Upon the advice of the Boston School Committee, that city undertook a program to transport 200 Roxbury blacks to four suburban school systems. The program was called METCO, an acronym for Metropolitan Council for Equal Opportunity, and was the forerunner of similar experiements in Hartford, Connecticut, and Berkeley, California. As the Johnson presidency ended, however, these programs were only part of larger desegregation effort spearheaded by the Office of Education in HEW. In later years educational officials at all levels would remember 1968 not as the time when busing began but as a year when government officials and social science researchers were in harmony regarding the approach needed to end the devastating effects of segregation on both black and white children.

Almost without exception, government programs of the late 1960s relied on social science research findings to buttress the case for

4. Gordon Allport, *The Nature of Prejudice* (Garden City, 1958), 267.
5. James S. Coleman, *Equality of Educational Opportunity* (Washington, D.C., 1966).

integration. The social sciences enjoyed a period of high visibility where race relations were concerned. The *Brown* decision, the Coleman Report, and the entire debate on busing used social science data. Prominent researchers such as Kenneth Clark, Christopher Jencks, and James Coleman became as familiar to judges, parents, educators, and politicians as they were to their academic colleagues.[6] Still, their prestige proved fickle when the abstract ideal of racial harmony hit the wall of school desegregation reality. Even whites who accepted the ideals of integration opposed busing. Social science research, once so clear about how integration would work, became by the mid-1970s an amalgam of confusing jargon, contradictory findings, and political rhetoric. The consensus concerning the costs and benefits of busing had broken down.

White Flight Research

"White flight," the withdrawal of white children from the public schools by their parents in response to the implementation of a busing plan, became an important topic of research in 1975. In that year James Coleman showed that large city school systems were becoming resegregated.[7] Busing policies, aimed at increasing the overall contact between the races, were actually having the opposite effect. When schools in large cities were forceably desegregated, white parents moved to areas exempt from the busing plan or enrolled their children in private schools. These findings led some commentators to conclude that courts and federal agencies should be less active in school integration. Among scholars, Coleman's analysis produced considerable controversy.

The withdrawal of white children from the public schools in systems experiencing court-ordered busing became a focus of much social science research, and the field was characterized by disagree-

6. Christopher Jencks, *Inequality* (New York, 1972), 3–16. Gregg Jackson, "Reanalysis of Coleman's Recent Trends in Social Integration," 5 *Educational Researcher* (Feb. 1976), 3–4. Reynolds Farley, "Racial Integration in the Public Schools, 1967–1972," *Sociological Focus* 8 (Jan. 1975), 3–26. Farley, "Is Coleman Right?", *Social Policy* 6 (Jan.-Feb. 1976), 14–23. Michael W. Giles, Everett P. Cataldo, and Douglas S. Gatlin, "Is Coleman Right?", 6 *Social Policy* (Jan.-Feb. 1976), 46–48.

7. James S. Coleman, Sara D. Kelley and John Moore, *Trends in School Segregation, 1968–1973* (Washington, D.C., 1975). Coleman, "Racial Segregation in the Schools: New Research With New Policy Implications," *Phi Delta Kappan* 57 (Oct., 1975), 75–78.

ments over research methods and findings.[8] Early studies emphasized the toll of post–World War II suburbanization on white public school enrollments within cities. Several of these studies, unlike Coleman's found no evidence of declining white enrollments as a consequence of desegregation.[9] Criticism of Coleman's 1975 findings centered on his selection of school systems and his neglect of long-range outmigration trends associated with the general exodus of whites from urban areas.[10] Robert Green and Thomas Pettigrew, using a different analytic method on Coleman's data, concluded that busing was not correlated with white flight.[11]

Other scholars entered the fray. Christine Rossell collected data from eighty-six school districts and concluded that the loss of whites from public school systems was minimal to nonexistent, depending on how carefully officials prepared the public for the changes required by busing. Her study examined longitudinal patterns of white enrollent to see if the busing effects mentioned by Coleman were unexpected and permanent. Rossell's analysis constituted a serious challenge to Coleman's position that white flight was accelerated by desegregation policies.[12] However, Rossell's research itself was challenged by Diane Ravitch, who criticized the method used to calculate the rate of white flight. Ravitch contended that measuring flight by

8. Jencks et al., 3–16. After evaluating 120 studies, Nancy St. John concluded that "research has produced little evidence of dramatic gains for children and some evidence of genuine stress for them." St. John, *School Desegregation: Outcomes for Children* (New York, 1975), 136. Farley, "Racial Integration in the Public Schools," 1967–1972, *Sociological Forces* 8 (1975), 3–26. Willis Hawley, "The New Mythology of School Desegregation," *Law and Contemporary Problems* 42:3–4(1978), 214–33.

9. Christine Rossell, "Assessing the Unintended Impacts of Public Policy: School Desegregation and Resegregation" (Washington, D.C., 1978), mimeographed.

10. Jackson, "Reanalysis of Coleman's Recent Trends in Social Integration," 3–4. Farley, "Racial Integration in the Public Schools," 3–26. Farley, "Is Coleman Right?" Giles, Cataldo, and Gatlin, "Is Coleman Right?"

11. Robert L. Green and Thomas F. Pettigrew, "Urban Desegregation and White Flight: A Response to Coleman," *Phi Delta Kappan* 57 (Feb. 1976), 399–402. *Harvard Educational Review* 46 (Feb. 1976), 1–53. Coleman, "A Reply to Green and Pettigrew," *Phi Delta Kappan* 57 (Mar. 1976), 454–55. Green and Pettigrew, "Conflicting Views of Research and Social Justice," *Phi Delta Kappan* 57 (Apr. 1976), 555–56. Coleman, "Response to Professors Pettigrew and Green," *Harvard Educational Review* 46 (May 1976), 217–24. Meyer Weinberg, "A Critique of Coleman," *Integrated Education* 13–14 (Sept.-Oct. 1975–76), 3–7. Stanley S. Robin and James J. Bosco, "Coleman's Desegregation Research and Policy Recommendations," *School Review* (May 1976), 352–63. Charles T. Clotfelter, "The Detroit Decision and 'White Flight,' " *Journal of Legal Studies* 5 (Jan. 1976), 99–112.

12. Rossell, "School Desegregation and White Flight," *Political Science Quarterly* 90 (1975–76), 675–95.

percentage change in white pupil enrollment reduced the real effects of white withdrawal. By using absolute numbers to measure the decline in white student enrollments, Ravitch concluded that "In view of the rate of white exodus form the public schools of Boston, Denver and San Francisco, as well as the projected declines in Los Angeles after the implemenation of busing *it is impossible to contend that court-ordered racial assignment does not accelerate 'white flight' in large cities.*"[13]

David Armor examined the issue of busing and white flight and concluded that "(1) there is a substantial anticipatory effect the year before the start of desegregation . . . (2) the first-year effect is truly massive, with a loss rate four times higher than it would have been without desegregation, and (3) long term effects are also substantial with actual losses still nearly twice the natural losses. . . ."[14]

The controversy surrounding the issue was no mere academic tempest in a teapot. Because methodology affected the research findings and their interpretations, and these in turn had implications for national policy, much of the scholarly debate concerned issues of research methodology.[15] If white flight did not exist, then there was no reason to alter the policy course. If it did exist, however, then courts and other decision makers would have to take probable losses into account in assessing the costs and benefits of the policy of busing for desegregation. White rejection of busing would be weighed in the balance as a cost, just as enhanced black achievement and self-esteem would be as benefits.

Private Schools

During the period 1959–1975 national non-public school enrollment declined from 14 percent to 9 percent. The reasons cited for the

13. Diane Ravitch, "The 'White Flight' Controversy," *Public Interest* 51 (Spring 1978), 135–49. This controversy has been extensively debated in Rossell and Ravitch, "A Response to 'The White Flight Controversy,' " *Public Interest* 51 (Fall 1978), 109–13. Both Farley and Rossell have changed their stands on white flight effects since these articles appeared. The original Rossell sample was northern and went through fall 1972; hence, it included little mandatory reassignment of whites. Mandatory reassignment of whites is the key variable. When the study was updated to include southern school districts and data through fall 1975, her analysis did show significant white flight.

14. David J. Armor, "A Response to 'The White Flight Controversy,' " *Public Interest* 51 (Oct. 1978), 113–115. Armor, *White Flight, Demographic Transition, and the Future of School Segregation* (Rand Corporation, Aug. 1978), 5931.

15. Gary Orfield noted that massive losses of whites in school systems such as Atlanta and Memphis skewed Coleman's findings. Orfield, "Is Coleman Right?" *Social Policy* 6 (Jan.-Feb. 1976), 24–29. Ravitch noted that Rossell concluded that only two districts (Pasadena and Pontiac) experienced any significant white flight.

decline varied, but they included tuition costs, outward expansion of urban housing, the decreasing influence of religion, and the declining birth rate. The decline in private school enrollment during the 1960s was not uniform, however; there were many cities where it increased substantially. In the North and West, even in the absence of court-ordered desegregation, cities with large black populations and declining white school-age populations experienced substantial gains in private school enrollments. Private school growth was directly linked to racial factors in the cities' demographic trends.[16]

The movement of white children to private schools was examined by David Armor. He found that private school enrollments increased sharply when busing plans were implemented. During the early 1970s in Boston roughly 34 percent of the white children attended private schools; by 1980 over 50 percent did so. Los Angeles moved from 22 percent to 43 percent between 1974 and 1980. Similar sharp increases were found in other cities which implemented busing plans. But once again, researchers did not agree. Armor pointed out that three other studies evaluated countywide desegregation plans and concluded there was little growth in private school enrollments in suburban areas as a result of busing, while two more studies of central-city school districts found a substantial amount of white flight to the suburbs and to private schools.[17]

Tipping Points

Almost all of the research about the existence and magnitude of white flight used system-wide data for comparisons across a range of school systems, very few looked at within-system patterns of white flight. One stream of research which did look at white enrollments within school systems searched for a "tipping point," a point in the ratio of black-to-white students beyond which white withdrawal accelerates dramatically, leaving the schools all, or nearly all, black.[18] Research by Stinchcombe et al. (Baltimore), Molotch (Chicago) and Bosco and Robin (Kalamazoo and Pontiac) examined the results of

16. Henry J. Becker, "The Impact of Racial Composition and Public School Desegregation on Changes in Non-Public School Enrollment by White Pupils," (Center for Social Organization of Schools, Johns Hopkins Univ., 1978, mimeographed).

17. Armor, "On School Busing and the 14th Amendment," Hearings Before the Constitution Subcommittee of the U.S. Senate Judiciary Committee, 1981 (mimeographed).

18. Nilo E. Kopanen, "The Myth of the 'Tipping Point,' " *Integrated Education* 4 (Aug.-Sept. 1966), 42–57.

school desegregation within a city or individual school system.[19] Lord and Catau's examination of intra-district migration patterns focused on the Charlotte-Mecklenburg (North Carolina) system in the wake of the important *Swann* decision of 1971.[20] Giles, Cataldo, and Gatlin surveyed parents in seven desegregated school districts in Florida. In other research, Giles focused on the patterns of white withdrawal within the Jacksonville-Duval school system.[21] The results of these studies were mixed. Some found tipping points, others did not.

Why White Flight?

By the end of the 1970s there was general agreement on the existence and magnitude of white flight, but not on its causes. Rossell, who had earlier denied the existence of white flight, reviewed the white flight literature most thoroughly and found an emerging consensus on several points: white flight was greater (1) when whites were assigned to formerly black schools, (2) when the proportion black in the school or school district was above 35 percent, (3) when white elementary grades were involved, and (4) among whites with higher incomes. Rossell also found that the educational service-related factors—test scores, busing distance, etc.—were not uniformly associated with white flight. Her results clearly supported a racial motivation underlying white flight, but because the studies surveyed relied mainly on aggregate data, they could not reveal fully the calculus of parental decisionmaking.[22]

To monitor the dynamics of family choice more closely, survey research was required; yet few opinion surveys of communities undergoing desegregation examined why parents moved their children from public to private schools. Three deserve mention here:

19. Arthur L. Stinchcombe, Mary McDill, and Dollie Walker, "Is There a Racial Tipping Point in Changing Schools?", *Journal of Social Issues* 25:4 (1969), 127–36.

20. Dennis Lord and John Catau, "School Desegregation Policy and Intra–School District Migration," *Social Science Quarterly* 57 (1977), 784–96.

21. Giles, Cataldo, and Gatlin, "White Flight and Percent Black: The Tipping-Point Re-examined," *Social Science Quarterly* 56 (June 1976), 85–92. Gatlin, Giles, and Cataldo, "Policy Support Within a Target Group: The Case of School Desegregation," *American Political Science Review* 72 (1978), 985–95. Giles, "Racial Stability and Urban School Desegregation," *Urban Affairs Quarterly* 12 (1977), 499–510.

22. Rossell, "Busing and 'White Flight,'" *Public Interest* 53 (Fall 1978), 109–11. Rossell, "Is It the Distance or the Blacks?" (Boston, Boston Univ., 1979). Rossell, "Assessing the Unintended Impacts of Public Policy: School Desegregation and Resegregation."

Louisville, Los Angeles, and Boston. In these studies opposition to busing and white flight were explained in different ways. While there is now agreement on the existence and magnitude of white flight, there is still none on its causes.

Using a panel design, McConahay and Hawley investigated opposition to busing in Louisville. They sought to determine if opposition was grounded in individual self-interest or something else. They concluded that opposition was caused by a new form of racism, "symbolic racism."

> The low relationship of antibusing attitudes to self-interest and its much higher relationship to racial and other symbolic issues is strong evidence that "busing" is a symbolic issue similar to the prohibition debates . . . [People] argue as if they were concerned with harm to children or the family or the community or the nation, but they shout past one another because *the debate is really over whose values will dominate public life* . . .[23] [emphasis added].

David Armor criticized the McConahay-Hawley study and reported the results of his own Los Angeles survey. Armor said the results of his survey showed that "White flight originates not from a commitment to neighborhood schools alone, but from the *combined* result of believing in neighborhood schools and *not* believing desegregation is beneficial for minority children or their own children."[24]

Where McConahay and Hawley found antibusing attitudes grounding in "symbolic racism," Armor found it based on the desire for community and on calculations of educational costs and benefits to children.

In a report based on sociologist Michael Ross's surveys of Boston parents, Leigh Estabrook concluded that parents appeared to become dissatisfied with their children's schools when those schools were desegregated and that parents' evaluations were more negative for issues of behavior and discipline than for those related to academic performance.[25]

The results of these three studies are not as divergent as they might seem. A general theme ties them together. Whites oppose busing whether or not they have children of school age because busing unfairly redistributes social status. It breaks up the nexus of school

---

23. J.B. McConahay and W.D. Hawley, "Is It the Buses or the Blacks?" (Center for Policy Analysis, Duke Univ., 1977, mimeographed).

24. Armor, "White Flight and the Future of School Desegregation," in Stephan and Faegin, *Desegregation*, 220.

25. Leigh S. Estabrook, "The Effects of Desegregation on Parents' Selection of Schools" (Ph.D. diss., Boston Univ., 1980).

and community—the communal basis of schools. Parents are more concerned about behavior and discipline and the social values which underlie these in newly desegregated schools than about academic issues. Desegregation of impersonal societal institutions is acceptable, but many white parents are unwilling to place their children in a communal institution (the school) which may permit or encourage values the parents disapprove of. The black children issue from a separate, and for many whites, inferior culture. Whites are afraid that their children will acquire the bad habits and values of the ghetto. That is the underlying message of these studies.

First-Year White Flight in Nashville

In 1971-72, the year busing was implemented, there was a substantial amount of white flight in Nashville; 8,600 white children left the school system. Some of these students would have left under normal outmigration, but it is clear that most left because of busing. The magnitudes and configurations of white flight were closely associated with aspects of the desegregation plan: (1) when black children were bused into white neighborhood schools (Grades 1–4), over 14 percent of the white children were withdrawn; (2) when white children were bused into black neighborhood schools, 26 percent of them fled; (3) in the court-ordered area, junior high schools lost 16 percent and high schools 20 percent of their white students, while white enrollments in the non-court-ordered areas increased by 3 percent and 13 percent respectively.

White parents offered many reasons for removing their children from the Metro public schools. Many argued that busing diminished educational services; others said busing destroyed the community nexus of schools. Very few said publicly that they were pulling their children out of schools because they did not want them to associate with black children. If they said that, they might seem to be racists.

The authors of this book sought to find out why white parents withdrew their children from the public schools the first year busing was implemented by looking for factors associated with varying levels and patterns of white flight from schools of different types. We grouped the reasons given for white flight into three broad categories—educational services, racial status, and social homogeneity—and searched for empirical indicators of each theme *for each school or neighborhood*. These empirical indicators were then compared to the level of white flight using a sophisticated analytical technique, multiple regression analysis. In this chapter we summarize this process;

readers who wish to examine our methodology more closely are referred to our other work.[26]

The Educational Services Theme   The first rationale is that the principal objections to busing were educational in nature. The reasons for white flight, in this view, are that busing diminished the quality of education, undermined discipline, and wasted children's time. Citizens were not antiblack as much as they were antiplan.

Our measure of white flight during the first year of busing was based on the HEW team's projections of white enrollment in each school if all whites attended the schools to which they were assigned in fall 1971. The actual white attendance in June 1972 was subtracted from this figure to find out how many whites remained after a year of busing. Enrollment reports for the schools during the year indicated that some white flight occurred before school opened, but a larger proportion occurred during the year as white families relocated.

Achievement tests were administered to all students in selected grades in fall 1970 and 1971. The test score averages in these two years reflect some white flight, but since most white flight occurred after they were administered, they can be used as a measure of the "quality" of the individual schools and therefore as a predictor of white flight. The greater the decrease in a school's average achievement test scores, we hypothesized, the more white flight occurred.

Student achievement, school discipline, time on the bus, and school starting times are educational services. If these factors correlate with the levels and patterns of white flight, then we can conclude that parents relocated children in order to obtain better educational services from the schools.

The Racial Status Theme   If racial characteristics of schools or of neighborhoods around schools are more clearly associated with the levels and patterns of white flight than are other factors, then we place a racial interpretation on our findings. Old-fashioned racial prejudice is the easiest explanation to make; after all, the South has a tradition of trying to keep the black man in his place. Such an interpretation suggests that white attitudes and values have not

26. J. David Woodard, "Busing Plans, Media Agendas and Patterns of White Flight: Nashville, Tennessee and Louisville, Kentucky" (Ph.D. diss., Vanderbilt Univ., 1978). Richard A. Pride and J. David Woodard, "Busing Plans and White Flight: Nashville and Louisville," paper presented at meeting of the Southwestern Political Science Association, Houston, Apr. 1978. Pride and Woodard, "Busing and White Flight: Implementation Plans in Three Southern Cities," paper presented at meeting of the Southern Political Science Association, Gatlinburg, Tenn., Nov. 1979.

changed since the Jim Crow era, and that the civil rights successes of the past twenty years are regarded as illegitimate (perhaps temporary) alterations in the natural order.

In Matthews and Prothro's 1966 study of Negroes and political participation in the south, it was found that 64 percent of the whites surveyed wanted strict segregation. The attitudes, fears, and hatreds reflected in the survey, despite the fact it was taken before busing began, lend support to the racial prejudice explanation for opposition to busing.

> At the time of our interviews, the desegregation of the public schools was uppermost in their minds . . . eighty-five percent of those mentioning the matter were opposed to even token desegregation. "What puzzles me, is that they are so dirty . . ." a housewife in Texas said. "I wish they could change and be more like we are. Of course, I wouldn't want a child like that, all dirty and filthy, in school with my children."[27]

The Texas housewife was certainly prejudiced. She makes the classic comparison: in-group virtue versus out-group vice. But she also betrays the possibility of acceptance if "they could change and be more like we are." If blacks shared similar values and prejudices, she suggests, then she would not be upset by desegregation. Racial prejudice centers on skin-color; communal prejudice looks beneath skin color to the lifestyle of the group.

In order to test for the effects of race on white flight, we collected data on the percentage black *projected* to be in each school by the desegregation plan, since white parents who fled the schools the first year would have known only this aspect of the school. We also collected data on the racial makeup of the neighborhood around each school, since that too would have been known by white parents before busing began.

The Neighborhood Homogeneity Theme Unlike the previous model, the "neighborhood homogeneity" explanation is not so much anti-black as it is pro-community. This justification is cultural, holding that each locality has its own norms and social patterns which are reflected in local activities. The neighborhood schools model is critical of busing because it alienates students from their familiar environs. The reasoning here is that middle-class parents are proud of their suburban social standing and are reluctant to share it with others from a "substandard" area. The model asserts the importance to middle class parents of pride in home, property values, and climb-

27. Donald R. Matthews and James W. Prothro, *Negroes and the New Southern Politics* (New York, 1966), 332.

ing the social ladder by escaping from a lower-class residential area. Such values are measured here by census data on length of residence within a community and education/income levels of the neighborhood. William V. Shannon, writing in the *New York Times* on September 8, 1976, suggested how these precepts applied to teenagers. "Their [parental] concern is not academic instruction but the values and opinions, the tastes and expectations that older children in the sixth through twelfth grades acquire from one another. These values are quite different from those loving parents try to inculcate."

Shannon aptly summarized the fears that many parents have concerning the "paired" school. They are unsure what kind of environment their children will be exposed to. Most parents know teachers, principals, and other school personnel in their neighborhood school. But usually they do not know any of the people who operate the school to which their child is bused. The neighborhood schools explanation does not impute racism to concerned parents, but rather parochial loyalty. The model asserts that community facilities such as churches, YMCA, Little League, and shopping areas combine with local schools to provide a congenial community atmosphere specific to a certain section of the city. The Nashville busing protest was not so much black verus white as it was Edgehill and West End versus Donelson, Crieve Hall, and Hermitage.

The neighborhood schools explanation focuses attention on community stability and social class. We hypothesize that the higher a white neighborhood's residential stability, educational level, and home ownership indicators, the more that white area has a clearly defined communal orientation and the more it would resist busing. We also hypothesize that the character of the "paired" neighborhood would affect white flight; the higher the social class of the "paired" neighborhood, the less white flight we would expect.

Analysis

The first year of busing resulted in uneven patterns and levels of white flight. Schools exempt from the busing mandate gained white students, while schools involved in busing for racial balance lost white population. This analysis presents variables associated with each of the three explanations for busing protest, and correlates them with the white flight figures for each school zone.

Suburban Grade 1–4 Schools Table 3 gives the characteristics of variables associated with Grade 1–4 elementary schools. Data con-

Table 3: *Characteristics of Nashville Court-Ordered Schools,*
Grades 1–4   *(N = 51)*

VARIABLE	AVERAGE
Dependent Variable: White flight from Grade 1–4 schools	14.4 percent
Independent Variables: Educational Services Model:	
1. Change in school starting time	42 minutes
2. Change in reading test scores	+.80 stanines
3. Number of suspensions in the school	1.45 suspensions
Racial Status Model:	
1. Percent black population in the neighborhood (1–4) school zones	9.42 percent
2. Percent black population in the paired (5–6) school zone	66.10 percent
3. Projected black enrollment percentage in the neighborhood (1–4) school zone	31.41 percent
Neighborhood Homogeneity Model:	
1. Income level of the neighborhood (1–4) school zone	$10,426.52
2. Percentage of individuals owning homes in the neighborhood (1–4) school zone	66.30 percent
3. Stability of the neighborhood (1–4) school zone, the percentage of residents currently residing in the school zone who lived there five years before the 1970 census	49.83 percent
4. Income level of the paired (5–6) school zone	$6,869.00
5. Percentage of individuals owning homes in the paired (5–6) school zone	44.41 percent
6. Stability of the paired (5–6) school zone, the percentage of residents currently residing in the school zone who lived there five years before the 1970 census	47.75 percent

tained in the 1970 census tract surveys and information provided by
school administrative personnel were used to calculate the variables
in the table. The 1970 census data are especially appropriate for
Nashville because busing was initiated in fall 1971. A wealth of
information is contained here. For example, one can tell at a glance
that the average black population in the suburban school zones was
only 9.42 percent, and that the projected black enrollment for these
schools was 31.4 percent. The busing plan clearly embodied the
assimilation ethic of the courts.

To answer the question of what caused white flight from the
suburban Grade 1–4 schools we used the following procedures. Each

variable was individually correlated with the dependent variable. Next, variables which were significantly correlated were entered into a stepwise multiple regression model. When these results were obtained, the explanatory potential of each protest theme was evaluated. The final step in the research process was to discover how much variance in the dependent variable was due to the effects of the respective themes of protest. With the effects of multicolinearity removed, the significant independent variables were hierarchically entered into a multiple regression equation.

Grade 1–4 elementary schools in Nashville's busing plan were generally in white neighborhoods, and they averaged about 14 percent white flight the first year. Table 4 summarizes the three potential explanations for this white flight. After the two-stage regression procedure, only two variables, the change in school starting times and home ownership, emerged as statistically significant independent variables. Together, these variables explained only 27 percent of the variance in white flight from these schools.

Because Metro did not have enough buses to transport all students simultaneously under the new busing plan, starting times for schools were staggered. In this way buses could make two circuits each morning. Under the plan, elementary schools generally began their day later than they had done the year before; 19 percent of the variance in white flight was associated with the change in school opening times. The more the change, the greater the white flight. The change in starting times—an educational service variable—had a modest association with white flight from Grade 1–4 schools.

The principal finding issuing from the analysis of these schools is the failure of the three sets of factors to explain more of the white flight variable. The number of student suspensions and achievement test scores—important indicators of educational services—did not stand up under the statistical examination. The racial factors of the neighborhoods and the schools did not appear to be significant, nor did the homogeneity of the neighborhoods. The relative social class of incoming black children made no difference. Something else must have accounted for the level and pattern of white flight from the Grade 1–4 elementary schools.

Urban Grade 5–6 Schools   We turn next to the schools with the highest level of white flight in Nashville, the Grade 5–6 schools involved in the court ordered desegregation plan. Table 5 summarizes the school zone characteristics of these twenty schools. In the 1971 desegregation plan, children from inner suburbs were transported to downtown schools for the fifth and sixth grades. The highest levels of

Table 4: *Explanations For Nashville Court-Ordered Schools,*
Grades 1–4   *(N = 51)*

VARIABLE	BETA (STANDARDIZED)	EXPLAINED VARIANCE
Educational Services Model:		
1. Change in school starting time		
2. Change in reading test stanine scores	.3524	.1878
3. Number of suspensions in the school		
Racial Status Model:		
1. Percent black population in the neighborhood (1–4) school zone		
2. Percent black population in the paired (5–6) school zone		
3. Projected black enrollment percentage in the neighborhood (1–4) school zone		
Neighborhood Homogeneity Model:		
1. Income level of the neighborhood (1–4) school zone		
2. Percentage of individuals owning homes in the neighborhood (1–4) school zone	.3007	.0839
3. Stability of the neighborhood (1–4) school zone, percentage of residents residing in the school zone 5 years before the 1970 census		
4. Income level of the paired (5–6) school zone		
5. Percentage of individuals owning homes in the paired (5–6) school zone		
6. Stability of the paired (5–6) school zone, percentage of residents residing in the school zone 5 years before the 1970 census		
Total Explained Variance		.2717
F = 8.9566 Significant .001 level		

white flight were in these Grade 5–6 schools; about 26 percent of the whites assigned to these schools did not stay.

The desegregation plan paired these downtown schools in black neighborhoods with two or three suburban facilities. So it is not surprising to see lower income, home ownership and stability figures for these school zones than their Grade 1–4 suburban counterparts. Two variables presented in Table 5 were associated with white flight from these schools after the two-step regression analysis. As Table 6 shows, the income level of the suburban school and its racial composition were statistical "explainers" of white flight variance. In

Table 5: *Characteristics of Nashville Court-Ordered Schools,*
Grades 5–6 (N = 20)

VARIABLE	AVERAGE
Dependent Variable: White flight from Grade 5–6 schools	25.9 percent
Independent Variables:	
Educational Services Model:	
1. Time suburban students (Grades 1–4) spent in transit to downtown schools	31.9 minutes
2. Change in school starting time	56.6 minutes
3. Change in reading test scores	−.53 stanines
4. Number of suspensions in the school	4.50 suspensions
Racial Status Model:	
1. Percent black population in the neighborhood (5–6) school zone	61.66 percent
2. Percent black population in the paired (1–4) school zone	9.31 percent
3. Projected black enrollment percentage in the downtown (5–6) school zone	31.86 percent
Neighborhood Homogeneity Model:	
1. Income level of the neighborhood (5–6) school zone	$7,092.75
2. Percentage of individuals owning homes in the neighborhood (5–6) school zone	42.14 percent
3. Stability of the neighborhood (5–6) school zone, the percentage of residents currently residing in the school zone who lived there five years before the 1970 census	47.51 percent
4. Income level of the suburban (1–4) school zone	$9,833.70
5. Percentage of individuals owning homes in the suburban (1–4) school zone	64.91 percent
6. Stability of the suburban (1–4) school zone, the percentage of residents currently residing in the school zone who lived there five years before the 1970 census	48.79 percent

other words, parents in high-income suburban school zones with few
black residents tended to avoid busing at the Grade 5–6 level. These
two variables explained fully 68 percent of the variance in the dependent variable, most of it by income alone.

Junior and Senior High Schools The white exodus from the secondary schools was almost as high as it was from the Grade 5–6 centers.
That first year of busing over 3,500 students left the junior and senior

Table 6: *Explanations for Nashville Court-Ordered Schools,*
Grades 5–6   (N = 20)

VARIABLE	BETA (STANDARDIZED)	EXPLAINED VARIANCE
Educational Services Model:		
1. Time suburban students (Grades 1–4) spent in transit to downtown schools	_____	_____
2. Change in school starting time	_____	_____
3. Change in reading test stanine scores	_____	_____
4. Number of suspensions in the school	_____	_____
Racial Status Model:		
1. Percent black population in the neighborhood (5–6) school zone	_____	_____
2. Percent black population in the paired (1–4) school zone	−.3718	.0996
3. Projected black enrollment percentage in the downtown (5–6) school zone	_____	_____
Neighborhood Homogeneity Model:		
1. Income level of the neighborhood (5–6) school	_____	_____
2. Percentage of individuals owning homes in the neighborhood (5–6) school	_____	_____
3. Stability of the neighborhood (5–6) school zone, percentage of residents residing in the school zone 5 years before the 1970 census	_____	_____
4. Income level of the suburban (1–4) school	.5684	.5850
5. Percentage of individuals owning homes in the suburban (1–4) school zone	_____	_____
6. Stability of the suburban (1–4) school zone, percentage of residents residing in the school zone 5 years before the 1970 census		
Total Variance Explained		.6847
F = 18.4625 Significant .001 level		

high schools in Davidson County. However, the factors associated with their leaving were different from those for the earlier grades. We had far fewer variables to use in this analysis, for the school zone demographic characteristics were blurred by gerrymandering the districts. In the Grade 1–4 schools white flight was only modestly associated with the change in school starting times. In the Grade 5–6 schools suburban income levels explained the withdrawal from the public schools with greater accuracy. At the junior high and senior high level, as Tables 7 and 8 show, racial factors stand out. One

Table 7: *Characteristics of Nashville Court-Ordered Schools,*
Junior and Senior High Schools   (N = 29)

VARIABLE	MEAN
Dependent Variable: White flight from junior high and senior high schools	20.2 percent
Independent Variables: Educational Services Model:	
1. Number of suspensions in the school	127.31 suspensions
Racial Status Model:	
1. Percent black population around the senior or junior high school	31.09 percent
2. Projected black enrollment percentage in the senior or junior high school	28.59 percent
Neighborhood Homogeneity Model:	
1. Income level of the senior or junior high school zone	$9,463.76
2. Percentage of individuals owning homes in the school zone	58.53 percent
3. Stability of the senior or junior high school zone, the percentage of residents currently residing in the school zone who live there 5 years before the 1970 census	49.83 percent

variable, the projected black enrollment percentage of the school,
explained nearly 60 percent of the variance in white flight. Median
family income in the white area explained 18 percent.

Conclusion

What can we conclude from these results? One answer is that race
and income are important factors in white flight. Higher-income
whites had more to lose from the redistributive effects of busing, and
many sought to protect their children by pulling them out of the
public schools.

Table 9 summarizes the statistical findings. Grade 1–4 elementary
schools had been predominantly white before busing and were located in white neighborhoods. These schools had the lowest level of
white flight (14 percent in school year 1971–72) precisely because
they were in white neighborhoods. No other factor seems to explain
the lack of flight. There was some variation in the level of white flight
from school to school, and though we sought to discover what factors
explained this variation, we were largely unsuccessful. Variation in

Table 8: *Explanations for Nashville Court-Ordered Schools, Junior and Senior High Schools* (N = 29)

Variable	Beta (Standardized)	Explained Variance
Educational Services Model:		
1. Number of suspensions in the school	_____	_____
Racial Status Model:		
1. Percent black population around the senior or junior high facility	_____	_____
2. Projected black enrollment percentage in the senior or junior high school	.5735	.5875
Neighborhood Homogeneity Model:		
1. Income level of the senior or junior high school zone	−.4668	.1807
2. Percentage of individuals owning homes in the school zone	_____	_____
3. Stability of the senior or junior high school zone, the percentage of residents currently residing in the school zone who lived there 5 years before the 1970 census	_____	_____
Total Explained Variance		.7682
F = 16.5760 Significant .001 level		

Table 9: *Factors Affecting First-Year White Flight From Metro Schools, 1971–72*

Grade Level	Average White Flight	Significant Independent Variables	Total Explained Variance
1–4	14%	Change in school starting Times (19%) neighborhood home ownership (8%)	27%
5–6	26%	Median family income (58%) Percent black in suburban school zone (10%)	68%
7–12	20%	Projected percent black in the school (59%) Median family income (18%)	77%

the level of white flight from Grade 1–4 schools was not associated with differences in test scores, pupil suspensions, or demographic differences within the black or white neighborhoods. Only the change in school starting times was meaningfully related to the level of white flight from school to school, and it had only a modest impact. White flight was an undifferentiated response to the busing of black children into previously white schools.

The level of white flight from Grade 5–6 elementary schools in 1971– 72 was substantial; almost one in every four assigned white children fled them. These Grade 5–6 schools had been predominantly black before busing began and most were located in black neighborhoods. These two factors explain the higher rate of white flight from these schools. There were, however, variations in the level of white flight across these Grade 5–6 schools, and again we tried to discover what characteristics of these schools or of the students assigned to these schools might explain the differences. Two of our indicators together explained 68 percent of white flight variance. Whites felt more threatened when their children were to be sent to black neighborhoods, and those who withdrew their children came from higher-income white areas. Income facilitated white flight from Grade 5–6 schools, but it did not explain the overall level or the reasons behind white flight.

At the junior high and senior high level, an average of 20 percent of white students did not finish the school year in the schools to which they were assigned. Most of these schools were not in black areas of the community. There was a substantial amount of white flight from some schools and far lower amounts in others. These differences were largely associated with the percentage of black students who were assigned to the school in the busing plan; fully half of the variance in the level of white flight from these schools was accounted for by this factor alone. The median family income of the white areas assigned to the school was a second important factor.

The aggregate data clearly link race and class with white flight, but the data do not tell us why whites fled. What was it about blacks (and about the whites themselves) which caused them to flee the public schools? The history of Nashville and the South gives important clues. Racial separation reflects racial prejudice, whether it springs from Jim Crow laws or personal choices—that is the obvious answer. But is it accurate? Parents who left the schools gave other answers: busing destroyed good educational progams, wasted children's time, and subjected white children to undisciplined environments. In short, black children "dragged down" white children. However, those parents who withdrew their children the year busing began hardly gave the policy, the schools, or the children a fair test.

White parents who withdrew their children from the public schools were often defensive; they did not want to be considered racists. They wanted it known that they were protecting their children's futures. As one parent wrote in a letter to the authors:

If you have seen, as I have, the public schools intentionlly weakened to serve a predetermined social "received truth," it is depressing to see the natural reactions of caring parents to that damage called a problem with "white attitudes." The future, to many of us, lies in the skills, hopes and attitudes of our kids. For many people, to damage their own kids' future so that no-one has to publicly pronounce unpleasant words, is almost an evil. In fact, it is true that poor, underpriviledged people of any color draw down a school—any school—of which they are a large part. It's sad, but true.

Middle-class white parents wanted a good education for their children. A good education meant that children learned their lessons and the habits and values of self-discipline, ambition, respect for authority, and hard work. Parents had bought homes in areas where schools were favorably regarded for these virtues. When busing came to Nashville these parents felt threatened; busing, it seemed, would undermine their values and their way of life. Many white parents removed their children from the public schools rather than face this prospect; others remained in the public schools and fought to make sure their children got a good education there. There was, however, one big difference between the two groups: one pursued their aims in racially balanced schools, while the other did not.

CHAPTER SIX

Busing and Academic Achievement

"One clear answer has already emerged from the research literature on desegregation: virtually every writer on the subject has agreed that the test performance of white students is unaffected by school desegregation. It is safe to assume the issue is settled. . . ."

That's the way the national experts put it.[1] But the issue was far from settled in the minds of Nashville parents. Whether in pairs over coffee or in dozens at school meetings, white parents worried about the quality of the schools. Many, perhaps most, agreed that busing undermined the educational achievement of children. They had only to look at the newspaper to find fuel for their anxiety. Average achievement test scores and other educational rankings were printed each year.

Statistics showed that the Metro schools were among the best in the state, but that achievement only reinforced the general perception of educational mediocrity. In 1970 Tennessee ranked forty-sixth in the nation in per pupil public school expenditures. The likelihood of academic improvement was hindered by a state populace which ranked behind all but two states in median school years completed. The average salary of a classroom teacher in the state was $2,000 below—and only 80 percent of—the national average. Five school systems in the state outstripped the Nashville–Davidson County rankings on important indicators like per pupil expenditures, teacher salaries, and capital funds outlay. By every measure, the Metro educational system was below the national average.[2]

Black parents were just as concerned about educational quality as white parents. Before busing, black children performed more poorly than white children and, as the gap between black and white test scores remained great after five years of busing, many came to see

1. Robert L. Crain and Rita E. Mahard, "Desegregation and Black Achievement: A Review of the Research," *Law and Contemporary Problems* 42 (Summer 1978), 18.

2. U.S. Office of Health, Education and Welfare, *Digest of Educational Statistics, 1972, 1973* (Washington, D.C.), 15, 50, 65. Center for Business and Economic Research, Univ. of Tennessee, *Tennessee Statistical Abstract, 1980*, (Knoxville, 1980), 603–06.

busing itself as the problem. Busing, blacks said, disrupted the lives of black children and continued the historically racist policies of neglect.

If black parents had read the scholarly research reports accumulating on library shelves, they would have been reassured. After a systematic review of the literature on desegregation and black achievement, Crain and Mahard concluded: "Twenty-four of these evaluations report achievement gains, and five show losses—a four-to-one ratio favoring positive outcomes. The average gain in achievement (on the few studies where we have been able to code quantitative data) is around one-half of a grade-equivalent change in the first one or two years."[3]

There can be no doubt that many black and white parents were genuinely worried about the effects of busing on children's academic achievement. But for others, the issue of academic achievement was a mask for racist attitudes. These people opposed busing on other grounds and simply used the issue of academic achievement to cover their real feelings of racial antipathy.

Parents and others in the community linked busing and educational quality. Scholarly studies done elsewhere might carry no weight in public or private discourse, but Dr. Elbert Brooks, the Director of Schools, believed that research done in Nashville might inform the debate. The results of the study he commissioned, prepared by Dr. Richard A. Pride, are summarized in this chapter.[4]

Achievement Tests and Busing

Before 1975, Metro did not do systemwide achievement testing at all grade levels. In the early 1970s achievement tests were given in selected grade levels or only when requested by teachers, parents, and principals for diagnostic purposes. Teachers used the test results to identify children's strengths and weaknesses so they could select appropriate instructional tools and programs. But after 1975, systemwide achievement tests were given in the fall each year to all elementary grades. Teachers continued to use the tests for diagnostic purposes, but increasingly the scores were viewed as the measure of school quality. Newspapers published the Metro average test scores

3. Crain and Mahard, "Desegregation and Black Achievement," 48.
4. The sample was drawn and achievement test scores were merged by Metro schools' data processing section. The data were analyzed at Vanderbilt University by Richard A. Pride, whose report, "Desegregation and Achievement Test Scores in Nashville, 1975–1979," was submitted to the school board in June 1980.

by grade level each year. Such reports stimulated periodic waves of critical comment. The overall scores revealed modest increases toward the national average and, for those who inquired more deeply, a continuing gap between white and black average scores.

Parents received reports on their own children. A neat little printout showed how the child was doing on math, reading, and language tests, including the embedded sub-tests. Parents were shown the national distribution of scores and told where their child placed relative to the national norm. A parent could know, for example, that Johnny was in the 79th percentile in reading, but only in the 48th percentile in math. Parents did not often share their child's scores with others, but they could follow the "progress" of their child from year to year. If their child's scores fell, they often concluded that it was because of busing.

Critical Questions

The incremental rise in average achievement test scores over the decade of the 1970s was heartening, but it did not fully address some of the issues raised by parents in connection with court-ordered desegregation. Our study addressed four such questions which elaborated the relationship between the desegregation plan and academic achievement more fully than the systemwide averages reported in the newspapers did.

Question 1: Did moving from school to school affect achievement test scores?

Question 2: Did children in the county's outlying schools perform better on achievement tests than those in the court-ordered schools?

Question 3: Did white children who were in schools with a higher percentage black enrollment do relatively less well than those in schools with a lower percentage black? And did blacks in schools with more white children do relatively better than those in schools with fewer whites?

Question 4: Did children from higher social class backgrounds progress less than those from lower social class backgrounds?

In order to answer these questions a random sample was drawn from among students who were in the second, third, or fourth grade in 1975 and who had taken five subsequent fall achievement tests in reading and math (through 1979). Because the study focused on the mainstream of public school students, three groups were omitted: (1) students who failed and repeated a grade, (2) students who were assigned to special education classes, and (3) children who entered or left the Metro schools during the five-year period. In sum, the study centers on the performance of typical students who spent five years (1975–79) in the public schools of Davidson County.

The test results are reported in stanine (standard of nine) scores. The distribution of achievement is divided into nine categories, and a score of 5 is defined as the national average level of achievement for each grade level each year. Figure 3 shows the percentage of students in the test publisher's national sample who scored within each stanine.

Table 10 shows the average test scores for students in the sample used in this study.[5] The average scores for both reading and math in 1975 were far below the averages for the nation (5 being the national average). The averages went up in small increments through 1979, when they were much closer to the national norm.

In order to answer our four questions, a simple method was developed to identify students whose relative performance between 1975 and 1979 (1) increased, (2) decreased, or (3) remained the same. The

Figure 3. Normal Distribution of Test Scores

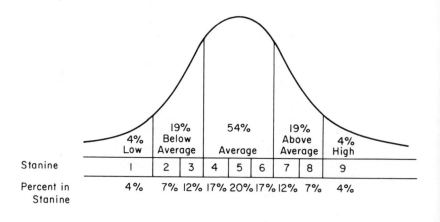

Stanine	1	2	3	4	5	6	7	8	9

4% Low | 19% Below Average | 54% Average | 19% Above Average | 4% High

Percent in Stanine: 4%   7% 12% 17% 20% 17% 12% 7%   4%

5. The sample's average test scores are between .1 and .2 stanine scores below the average reported for the system as a whole.

Table 10: *Average Test Scores for Students in the Sample (in stanine scores)*

Year	1975	1976	1977	1978	1979
Reading	3.93	4.12	4.26	4.37	4.50
Math	3.82	3.93	4.03	4.13	4.28

1975 score of each student was compared to his 1979 score and the difference calculated. For example, if a student had a stanine score of 4 in 1975 and a score of 7 in 1979, he had *increased* his score by +3, indicating that he had made an enormous improvement in achievement compared to the national level of achievement for students in his grade level.

Table 11 shows the cross-tabulation of the Nashville students' 1975 and 1979 reading scores. The percentages between the diagonal lines represent students whose relative scores remained the same in the two years. The percentages above-right of the diagonals represent students whose 1979 scores were higher than their 1975 scores. Those below-left show students whose relative positions fell.

Table 11 suggests why so many people complained about busing's impact on academic achievement. Many children fell in terms of relative achievement while the system's average was rising. The feelings of individual parents were affected more by their own child's scores than by those of the "typical" child in Metro.

The first line on Table 11 shows that 233 students (11 percent) had a reading achievement score of 1 in 1975. These were very low achievers. Only 16% of these very low achievers had a score of 1 in 1979, however. The vast majority had improved their position substantially. The same pattern was found for other low-achieving groups. Of 231 students who scored 2 in 1975, 22 percent remained in the same category in 1979, 8 percent fell in relative achievement, but fully 70 percent increased.

A problem on the other end of the achievement scale caused great concern among middle-class parents of early high-achieving students. Many children with scores of 7, 8, or 9 in 1975 actually fell from these lofty heights towards the national average. In 1975, 72 children (3 percent) had a reading achievement test score of 9; this score placed them in the top 4 percent nationally. However, less than half (43 percent) of these still had a score of 9 in 1979.

For many parents witnessing the decline in their child's relative achievement, this phenomenon meant the schools were neglecting early high achievers and catering to low achievers. Busing, it appeared, affected their children. They took little comfort from the

Table 11: Relationship of 1975 Reading Scores to 1979 Reading Scores

1975 SCORE	1979 SCORE									TOTAL %	N =	MARGINAL %
	1	2	3	4	5	6	7	8	9			
1	16	29	34	15	4	1	1	0	0	101%	(233)	11%
2	8	22	33	24	9	3	0	0	0	99%	(231)	11%
3	6	14	25	32	17	5	1	0	0	100%	(400)	19%
4	1	3	10	32	32	18	3	1	1	100%	(428)	20%
5	0	1	3	10	34	36	12	3	0	100%	(333)	16%
6	0	0	1	6	17	39	22	8	8	100%	(246)	12%
7	1	0	0	1	6	30	28	15	19	100%	(146)	7%
8	0	0	0	0	3	16	31	22	28	100%	(58)	3%
9	0	0	0	0	0	17	18	22	43	100%	(72)	3%
N =	(86)	(190)	(313)	(400)	(400)	(386)	(186)	(88)	(98)		N = 2147	
MARGINAL %	4%	9%	15%	19%	19%	18%	9%	4%	5%			100%

system-wide results which showed more children with high scores in 1979 than in 1975. They were not reassured to know that their child's place as a high achiever was taken by someone who had improved his score between 1975 and 1979. It is an irony, perhaps, that parents of students who did better in 1979 than in 1975 were less vocal than those whose children fell in achievement. No one seemed publicly to argue that busing raised the scores of their children, but when the scores fell busing was often publicly labeled the culprit.

In a very real sense the precision of the test score reports given to parents created a serious problem for the schools. On the face of it, the schools did appear to be neglecting early high-achieving children in an attempt to bring up the bottom end of the achievement distribution. But there is another explanation which was not widely understood. This explanation centered on the *instability of the measurement* itself.

The Metro schools used nationally standardized achievement tests. These tests are widely used and greatly respected as valid and reliable estimators of student achievement. Nonetheless, they are not perfect scales of measurement. The test scores of an individual student are an *estimate* of his level of achievement. Educational psychologists recognized this, but parents did not. Moreover, the estimate is less accurate at the extreme high end of the achievement range, particularly in group tests. For example, the subtest on mathematical computation may involve 20 items. If a child gets all 20 correct on the achievement test his score would be reported as the 96th percentile. But, if he missed one item, his score might fall to the 80th percentile. Very few items are used to discriminate among the levels of high achievement on these tests. An incorrect answer on one item might indicate that the child has not grasped the material being tested by the item. And one year a lucky guess on a difficult item might propel a score significantly upwards; the next year a similar item, answered incorrectly, would bring the composite score down to a true estimate of the child's level of achievement.

Measurement instability is to be expected on achievement tests, particularly on the subtests and in the early grades. Yet too often parents saw the bouncing scores as a true reflection of their children's educational achievements and of the quality of the schools. Parents of children whose scores fell or were erratic became anxious and often blamed the changes on a supposed relationship between busing and educational quality.

Achievement test score reliability was not an issue for individual families only. Psychometric assumptions underlying Metro's average test scores affected the whole community. The tests Metro used were "normed" for a *spring* test schedule, but Metro gave the tests in the *fall* of each year. The fall "norms" were derived by a linear interpolation technique on the basis of a ten-month school year which assumed one month growth for the summer. This practice underestimated the real achievement of Metro students. Metro was not as far from the national norm as its published figures indicated. When Metro began a spring test schedule in 1979, results showed that in many grades Nashville students were above the national norms for the first time in history. "At every grade level, Nashville public school children outperformed the norm groups from other large cities by a substantial margin."[6]

Findings

Since the focus of this chapter is on test scores and desegregation, in the following discussion the sample results were broken into two groups: black and white. This was done to determine if the effect of critical factors was similar for students of each race. The size of the sample varied from question to question, but generally speaking, data were obtained for 1,400 white students and 750 black students, making the sample size approximately 2,150.

Question 1: Did the number of different schools the child attended affect his chances of improving his test scores?

One issue often addressed in the desegregation discussion was the effect of changing schools on students. While not all of the concern about changing schools centered on the child's academic success, it was often mentioned in public discourse. Parents argued that changing schools was emotionally and academically disruptive for the child.

The desegregation plan required children to change schools one or two times in their years of elementary education, and additional changes were scheduled for the junior and senior high years. Families voluntarily relocated within the county, too, but presumably the effects of changing schools on children were the same. Hence, the measure used in this analysis was the number of schools a child attended in five years, regardless of the reason for school change.

Among white children there were no appreciable differences among those who moved one, two, three, or four times in five years in terms of success on reading or math tests. Tables 12 (reading) and 13

6. Metropolitan Public Schools, "Report on Standardized Testing," (May 1980, mimeographed).

(math) show that over 50 percent of the white children in each category achieved higher scores in 1979 than they did in 1975.

Black children showed the same results. Table 14 presents the findings for reading tests, and Table 15 gives those for math exams. Differences between the two are insignificant, and differences between black and white are minor. The strength of the relationship between the number of schools attended and the change in test scores between 1975 and 1979 is near zero (gamma = .06). These findings show that the number of schools children attended in five years had no systematic effect on their performance relative to achievement tests.

Question 2: Did children in the non-court-ordered area improve more than those in the court-ordered area?

No question about busing is more central to the debate on educational effects than this one. But the relative improvement in white student reading (Table 16) and math (Table 17) test scores was not a function of the number of years the child spent in schools involved with court-ordered busing. For example, of the white children who spent 5 years in court-ordered schools, 55 (47 + 8) percent improved their reading test scores (Table 16) in the five-year period; of those who spent *none* of their time in such schools, 56 (47 + 9) percent improved their scores. The students in the non-court-ordered area for five years are only slightly more likely to achieve higher math scores than those in the court-ordered area for five years: 54 (43 + 11)

Table 12: *White Students: Relationship Between Number of Schools Attended and Changes in Reading Achievement Test Scores Between 1975 and 1979*

NUMBER OF SCHOOLS	3 TO 6 STANINE DECLINE	1 TO 2 DECLINE	NO CHANGE	1 TO 2 INCREASE	3 TO 6 INCREASE	TOTAL
One	0	13	33	43	10	99% (30)
Two	0	14	28	54	4	100% (225)
Three	1	15	30	47	8	101% (417)
Four	2	16	27	47	8	100% (554)
Five	4	23	24	40	10	101% (170)

prob. = .04   N = 1396
gamma = −.05

Table 13: *White Students: Relationship Between Number of Schools Attended and Changes in Math Achievement Test Scores Between 1975 and 1979*

NUMBER OF SCHOOLS	3 TO 6 STANINE DECLINE	1 TO 2 NO DECLINE	NO CHANGE	1 TO 2 INCREASE	3 TO 6 INCREASE	TOTAL
One	0	14	25	57	4	100% (28)
Two	3	24	27	42	5	101% (205)
Three	3	22	26	44	5	99% (317)
Four	2	19	24	45	9	99% (496)
Five	1	28	21	38	12	100% (157)

prob. = .23 N = 1203
gamma = .05

Table 14: *Black Students: Relationship Between Number of Schools Attended and Changes in Reading Achievement Test Scores Between 1975 and 1979*

NUMBER OF SCHOOLS	3 TO 6 STANINE DECLINE	1 TO 2 NO DECLINE	NO CHANGE	1 TO 2 INCREASE	3 TO 6 INCREASE	TOTAL
One	4	15	40	35	6	100% (52)
Two	0	17	29	49	6	101% (247)
Three	1	19	31	42	7	100% (304)
Four	2	25	28	42	4	101% (130)
Five	(0)	(3)	(3)	(8)	(0)	(14)

prob. =   .26 N = 733
gamma = −.06

percent in Table 17 versus 48 (42 + 6) percent improved their standing.

Very few black students were in the non-court-ordered area, but as far as can be seen from the sample (see Tables 18 and 19), there was no difference in relative achievement gains between those in the court-ordered and non-court-ordered areas.

Table 15: *Black Students: Relationship Between Number of Schools Attended and Changes in Math Achievement Test Scores Between 1975 and 1979*

NUMBER OF SCHOOLS	3 TO 6 STANINE DECLINE	1 TO 2 DECLINE	NO CHANGE	1 TO 2 INCREASE	3 TO 6 INCREASE	TOTAL
One	2	17	26	49	6	100% (47)
Two	0	16	22	57	6	101% (217)
Three	2	18	31	42	7	99% (260)
Four	4	12	28	46	10	100% (116)
Five	(0)	(5)	(2)	(6)	(0)	(13)

prob. = .04 N = 640
gamma = .06

Table 16: *White Students: Relationship Between Years in Court-Ordered Schools and Changes in Reading Achievement Test Scores*

YEARS	3 TO 6 STANINE DECREASE	1 TO 2 DECREASE	NO CHANGE	1 TO 2 INCREASE	3 TO 6 INCREASE	TOTAL
5	0	16	29	47	8	100% (640)
4	1	13	23	54	9	100% (79)
3	4	15	28	46	8	101% (76)
2	2	13	35	46	4	100% (98)
1	1	17	31	46	6	101% (132)
0	3	18	23	47	9	100% (371)

prob. = .13 N = 1396

The findings show that for both black and white students there is no important difference in the relative gains made by students in court-ordered and non-court-ordered schools.

Question 3: Did the percentage of students of the opposite race in a student's grade level affect his academic improvement?

Table 17: *White Students: Relationship Between Years in Court-Ordered Schools and Changes in Math Achievement Test Scores*

YEARS	3 TO 6 STANINE DECREASE	1 TO 2 DECREASE	NO CHANGE	1 TO 2 INCREASE	3 TO 6 INCREASE	TOTAL
5	3	23	26	42	6	100% (557)
4	4	22	27	42	6	101% (74)
3	1	11	26	53	10	101% (74)
2	1	22	17	51	9	100% (88)
1	2	28	24	42	5	101% (123)
0	2	20	24	43	11	100% (339)

prob. = .04   N = 1255
gamma = .08

Table 18: *Black Students: Relationship Between Years in Court-Ordered Schools and Changes in Reading Achievement Test Scores*

YEARS	3 TO 6 STANINE DECREASE	1 TO 2 DECREASE	NO CHANGE	1 TO 2 INCREASE	3 TO 6 INCREASE	TOTAL
5	0	20	30	43	6	99% (616)
4	4	7	34	49	7	101% (77)
3	0	23	27	41	9	100% (22)
2 or less	0	19	25	53	3	100% (32)

prob. = .52   N = 747

The racial composition of classrooms was a concern of parents of both races. In private, if not in public, some white parents complained that their children were being shortchanged in school because teachers spent too much time with black students. Some black parents complained that their children were emotionally and intellectually confused when they were compelled to leave their neighborhoods in the early grades in service to a busing plan that nearly always put them in the minority. Black children, they argued, did not

Table 19: *Black Students: Relationship Between Years in Court-Ordered Schools and Changes in Math Achievement Test Scores*

Years	3 to 6 Stanine Decrease	1 to 2 Decrease	No Change	1 to 2 Increase	3 to 6 Increase	Total
5	2	17	28	46	6	102% (536)
4	3	10	17	64	6	100% (69)
3	0	22	17	50	11	100% (18)
2 or less	0	10	27	50	13	100% (30)

prob. = .24   N = 653

need to be in a majority white setting to learn, and moreover, always being in a minority had done the children real harm.

In order to examine the effects of racial ratios on achievement, an average percent black was calculated for each grade in each school, and each student was assigned a racial composition score depending on the school he or she attended. The scores for the five years were summed and an average taken. The final score on this variable, then, was the average percentage of the other race each child experienced for the five years.

The distribution of achievement for four levels of racial experience is presented in Table 20 for reading scores and Table 21 for math scores of white children. These tables indicate that the percentage of white students who improved their scores was about the same regardless of the percentage black in their classes during the five years. Of the white children who had an average 20 percent or less black student ratio in their classes 54 (47 + 7) percent increased their reading achievement scores; while among those who experienced 40 percent or more black children in their classes, 57 (46 + 11) percent increased their reading score—an insubstantial difference. The same pattern held true for math scores as well.

There is no relationship between racial experience and reading (Table 22) or math (Table 23) achievement scores for black students either. Among black children who were a part of schools in which they were on average in a 30 percent or less minority, 54 (49 + 5) percent increased their scores in reading. Among those who found themselves on average in classes 40 percent or more black, 49 percent (43 + 6 in Table 22) raised their reading achievement scores. In math the pattern was similar (see Table 23).

Table 20: *White Students: Relationship Between Average Proportion Black and Changes in Reading Achievement Test Scores Between 1975 and 1979*

PERCENT BLACK	3 TO 6 STANINE DECREASE	1 TO 2 DECREASE	No CHANGE	1 TO 2 INCREASE	3 TO 6 INCREASE	TOTAL
0-20%	3	18	27	47	7	100% (688)
20-30%	1	14	28	50	7	100% (182)
30-40%	0	16	30	48	7	101% (263)
40% +	0	13	29	46	11	99% (263)

prob. = .03 N = 1396
gamma = .07

Table 21: *White Students: Relationship Between Average Proportion Black and Changes in Math Achievement Test Scores Between 1975 and 1979*

PERCENT BLACK	3 TO 6 STANINE DECREASE	1 TO 2 DECREASE	No CHANGE	1 TO 2 INCREASE	3 TO 6 INCREASE	TOTAL
0-20%	2	22	23	43	9	99% (631)
20-30%	3	24	27	41	6	101% (162)
30-40%	3	20	28	43	6	100% (241)
40% +	2	21	24	47	6	100% (221)

prob. = .46 N = 1255

From these results it seems clear that the racial composition of classes had little if any impact upon the performance of students on reading and math achievement tests.

Question 4: Did the social class of students affect the likelihood of their raising their achievement test scores?

In order to answer this question, the median family income was determined for neighborhoods. The child was assigned an income figure based on the census profile for the school zone where he lived. There was no method available for determining the actual family

Table 22: *Black Students: Relationship Between Average Proportion Black and Changes in Reading Achievement Test Scores Between 1975 and 1979*

PERCENT BLACK	3 TO 6 STANINE DECREASE	1 TO 2 DECREASE	NO CHANGE	1 TO 2 INCREASE	3 TO 6 INCREASE	TOTAL
0-30%	1	19	26	49	5	100% (78)
30-40%	1	19	29	46	6	101% (188)
40% +	1	20	32	43	6	100% (481)

prob. = .73   N = 747

Table 23: *Black Students: Relationship Between Average Proportion Black and Changes in Math Achievement Test Scores Between 1975 and 1979*

PERCENT BLACK	3 TO 6 STANINE DECREASE	1 TO 2 DECREASE	NO CHANGE	1 TO 2 INCREASE	3 TO 6 INCREASE	TOTAL
0-30%	3	12	31	47	7	100% (68)
30-40%	1	15	27	49	8	100% (169)
40% +	2	18	26	48	7	101% (653)

Prob. = .80   N = 890

income of students. So neighborhoods where the median family income (based on 1970 census data) was $8,000 or less were called "low"; those between $8,000 and $10,000 "mod-low"; those between $10,000 and $12,000 "mod-high"; and those above $12,000 "high."

The social class of children is generally related to the skills they initially bring to school. For this sample the income factor is moderately and positively related to the *level* of the student's performance on the achievement tests in 1975. Higher income areas produce higher-achieving students. This is true for both black and white students, and the relationship is seen in Table 24 for reading scores and Table 25 for math scores.

For whites, social class effects on change in reading test scores is shown in Table 26, and the same relationship for math achievement scores is presented in Table 27. The proportion of students increasing

Table 24: *Relationship Between Median Neighborhood Family Income and the 1975 Reading Achievement Test Scores*

INCOME	STANINE SCORE					
	1	2–3	4–6	7–8	9	TOTAL
Low	20	37	38	4	1	100% (796)
Mod-Low	9	32	49	8	3	101% (652)
Mod-High	5	22	54	14	5	101% (671)
High	7	17	48	19	10	101% (155)

prob. = .0000 N = 2274
gamma = .35

Table 25: *Relationship Between Median Neighborhood Family Income and 1975 Math Achievement Test Scores*

INCOME	STANINE SCORE					
	1	2–3	4–6	7–8	9	TOTAL
Low	16	41	39	4	0	100% (697)
Mod-Low	9	37	46	7	1	100% (581)
Mod-High	3	24	57	15	1	100% (624)
High	5	22	55	13	4	99% (150)

prob. = .0000 N = 2052
gamma = .29

their scores after 1975 is not related to income at a statistically significant level. The same findings apply to black students for both reading (Table 28) and math (Table 29) scores.

For both white and black students, the percentage increasing their scores was substantial and similar in magnitude, regardless of the income level of the neighborhood from which they came.

Summary

The average achievement test scores of Metro students in the sample increased substantially but incrementally during the

Table 26: *White Students: Relationship Between Median Neighborhood Family Income and Changes in Reading Achievement Test Scores Between 1975 and 1979*

INCOME	3 TO 6 DECREASE	1 TO 2 DECREASE	No CHANGE	1 TO 2 INCREASE	3 TO 6 INCREASE	TOTAL
Low	0	15	25	51	10	101% (241)
Mod-Low	2	18	25	46	9	100% (426)
Mod-High	1	16	29	47	6	99% (598)
High	1	13	34	46	7	101% (131)

prob. = .34   N = 1296

Table 27: *White Students: Relationship Between Median Neighborhood Family Income and Changes in Math Achievement Test Scores Between 1975 and 1979*

INCOME	3 TO 6 DECREASE	1 TO 2 DECREASE	No CHANGE	1 TO 2 INCREASE	3 TO 6 INCREASE	TOTAL
Low	2	23	23	44	8	100% (201)
Mod-Low	4	21	27	42	7	101% (385)
Mod-High	2	23	26	42	8	101% (546)
High	2	21	16	51	10	100% (123)

prob. = .15   N = 1255

1975–79 period. To the extent that this rise in achievement test scores reflected a real increase in student academic performance, it indicated that the quality of education in Metro public schools steadily improved relative to the national norm. Nashvillians could take pride in the efforts of children and teachers in the system. Yet few of them did.

There is no evidence in this study that the busing plan, under which the schools operated since 1971, was a deterrent to improved performance on nationally standardized reading and math achievement tests.

To sum up:

Table 28: *Black Students: Relationship Between Median Neighborhood Family Income and Changes in Reading Achievement Test Scores Between 1975 and 1979*

INCOME	3 TO 6 DECREASE	1 TO 2 DECREASE	No CHANGE	1 TO 2 INCREASE	3 TO 6 INCREASE	TOTAL
Low	1	20	30	43	7	101% (514)
Mod-Low	2	19	28	49	4	102% (189)
Mod-High	0	13	40	42	5	98% (38)
High	(0)	(1)	(3)	(2)	(0)	(6)

prob. = .74 N = 747

Table 29: *Black Students: Relationship Between Median Neighborhood Family Income and Changes in Math Achievement Test Scores Between 1975 and 1979*

INCOME	3 TO 6 DECREASE	1 TO 2 DECREASE	No CHANGE	1 TO 2 INCREASE	3 TO 6 INCREASE	TOTAL
Low	2	17	27	47	7	100% (445)
Mod-Low	2	17	26	50	5	100% (164)
Mod-High	0	13	26	47	13	99% (38)
High	(0)	(0)	(2)	(4)	(0)	(6)

prob. = .86 N = 653

- The number of schools students attended was not related to their success on the tests.
- Attendance in court-ordered schools was just as likely to stimulate improved scores as attendance in non-court-ordered schools.
- The percentage of students of the opposite race in a student's grade was not related to his performance on the tests.
- The social class background of students had no bearing on their propensity to improve their test performance.

Conclusions

These findings show that busing had no meaningful negative effect on the academic achievement of Metro's school children. Indeed, the rising achievement scores of most children over the years suggest that the constant pressure on teachers, stimulated by the stresses of busing, may have been a factor in the improved scores. Many people in the schools and in the community struggled to make sure that children learned as much as possible. Schools were encouraged to develop a variety of programs to meet children's individual needs; individualized learning programs and ability groupings were authorized and bore fruit.

The general improvement in academic achievement escaped the attention of most parents. Approximately 20 percent of the children in the schools fell in relative achievement; their scores were lower in 1979 than they wre in 1975. This decline was not systematically related to aspects of the busing plan, but parents often blamed busing for their children's decline in relative achievement. A continuing chorus of complaints was heard in both black and white communities.

Busing was intended to redistribute educational benefits and respect among children. Black children were to be the principal beneficiaries of the policy. Did busing accomplish this goal? Black children's academic achievement test scores did improve, but overall the gap between the average achievement test scores of blacks and whites remained substantial after years of busing. The generally lower achievement of black children meant that many continued to be stigmatized, though now within desegregated schools. Many black leaders began to wonder if busing was worth the price, at least as the policy was being implemented in Nashville. Busing had not ended many of the inequalities between the two races in the city.

CHAPTER SEVEN

White Flight: A Continuing Pattern

"What most people don't realize is that a gradual loss of students over an extended period of time can result in the school population being cut in half," observed Ray Osborne, a man who well understood the effects of declining student populations. From the beginning of court-ordered desegregation in 1971 he was responsible for monitoring the racial balance in the Metro schools. "If you lose only 5 percent of your students a year, in ten years nearly 40 percent of your student population will be gone."

During the years following the implementation of busing in Nashville, there was a substantial decline in the number of white students attending public schools. Before busing began, in June 1971, there were 66,393 white students in the Metro Public Schools. In June 1979, eight years later, there were 44,295—a decline of 22,098 white students. A burning question in the debate about busing was to what extent this decline resulted from "white flight" rather than "normal" outmigration or declining white births.

To answer this question, one must compare *actual* white enrollments after 1971, and the level of enrollments *expected* in the absence of court-ordered busing. The best way to estimate the expected white enrollments after 1971 is to examine the pattern of white enrollments in the years immediately before busing became an issue. By examining the retention rates of the pre-busing period, we can establish the patterns of white enrollment that would have continued had it not been for the introduction of busing for desegregation. The retention rate is simply the percentage of students in a given age group who move from one grade to the next grade each year. During the years before busing some white children left the public schools. Families may have sought escape from desegregated neighborhood schools, or they may have been attracted by the amenities offered in other schools or settings. White families moved from public to private schools or to adjacent counties for a variety of reasons, but they did not move because of busing; it had not yet become part of the public agenda. The loss of white children during the 1967–70 period can be considered the "normal" migration out of the public schools.[1]

Two patterns of normal outmigration must be established if we are to develop expectations for the 1970s. First, we must establish the public schools' retention rates for the interval between birth and first grade; and second we must calculate the retention rates from grade to grade once the children were enrolled in the Metro schools.

In 1963 7,081 white children were born to parents living in Davidson County; in 1969, six years later, 6,452 white children entered the first grade in the Metro public schools. Thus, the initial retention rate for this cohort (age group) was 91 percent. Overall, the public schools attracted 88.9 percent of the total number of white children born to Nashville residents when they came to school age in the years 1967–70. This figure becomes the expected retention rate for the 1970s in the birth to first grade interval.

Similar retention rates were calculated for each cohort as it moved from grade to grade in the Metro schools during the 1967–70 base period. During these years the total number of white students in a particular grade one year did not equal the total number of the next grade the following year. For example, in 1967 there were 6,286 students in first grade, but in 1968 there were only 5,927 (94 percent) in second grade. Six percent of the white students had left Metro schools. Retention rates were calculated between each two grade levels for the years 1967–70. These rates show that many whites were leaving Metro schools before busing began; they reveal "normal" outmigration. The reasons people left the public schools varied. During the 1960s many families moved to nearby counties in search of lower taxes, better housing, and more land. Families put their children in private schools in search of something special. But whatever the reasons for withdrawing their children from Metro schools, it was not because of busing.

Table 30 shows the percentage of each age cohort which we would have expected to be in the public schools in the 1970s, based on the patterns established in the late 1960s. A major diagonal crosses Table 30. Above the diagonal the figures represent the percentage of white children born to county residents whom we could reasonably have expected to stay in the public schools. As we have seen, 89 percent

1. Families who left the public schools in the late 1960s because of the fear that busing might come to Nashville are included in the "normal" outmigration from the public schools. White flight is defined as the percentage of white families who left the public schools in the 1970s above the level we would have expected based on the enrollment patterns of the late 1960s. Hence, our estimation of white flight is actually a conservative one; it probably *underestimates* white flight from desegregation.

Table 30: Expected Percentage of Each White Cohort Continuing in the Public Schools (Continuation Rates, Base 1967–1970)

RETENTION RATE	GRADE	1970–71 AGE/GRADE COHORT	1971–72 100% (6391)	1972–73 100% (5958)	1973–74 100% (5638)	1974–75 100% (5600)	1975–76 100% (5880)	1976–77 100% (6036)	1977–78 100% (5785)	1978–79 100% (5334)
(.889)	1	100% (6088)	89%	89%	89%	89%	89%	89%	89%	89%
(.937)	2	100% (5848)	94%	83%	83%	83%	83%	83%	83%	83%
(.972)	3	100% (5772)	97%	91%	81%	81%	81%	81%	81%	81%
(.981)	4	100% (5497)	98%	95%	89%	79%	79%	79%	79%	79%
(.985)	5	100% (5709)	99%	97%	94%	88%	78%	78%	78%	78%
(.981)	6	100% (5908)	98%	97%	95%	92%	86%	77%	77%	77%
(.968)	7	100% (5880)	97%	95%	94%	92%	89%	84%	74%	74%
(.974)	8	100% (5945)	97%	94%	92%	91%	89%	87%	81%	73%
(.992)	9	100% (5659)	99%	97%	94%	92%	90%	89%	86%	81%
(.941)	10	100% (5268)	94%	93%	91%	88%	86%	85%	83%	81%
(.914)	11	100% (4655)	91%	86%	85%	83%	80%	89%	78%	76%
(.923)	12	100% (4164)	92%	84%	79%	79%	77%	74%	73%	73%

normally attended public schools in first grade, and as Table 30 shows, only 73 percent of this cohort could be expected to be in the public schools by the eighth grade (the 1978–79 school year), based on the 1960s pattern. Below the major diagonal, the figures show the percentage of white students who remained in the public schools from among those who were already in the public schools in 1970. For children in the first grade in 1970–71, for example, only 94 percent would have remained for second grade the next year and only 81 percent would have remained by eighth grade (the 1977–78 school year), according to the patterns established before busing began.

The expected enrollment figures were compared to the actual enrollment in Metro schools to determine the magnitude of white flight from the school system due to busing. The actual calculations are not shown here, but Table 31 summarizes the results.

Table 31 gives the difference between the expected and actual pecentages of each cohort remaining in the public schools as each one passed from grade to grade during the period 1971–79. These percentages show both magnitude and patterns of white flight. The data show, for example, that there were 8 percent fewer white children in the first grade in 1971–72, the year busing began, than were expected; the percentage rose sharply to 13 percent for children entering the first grade in 1972–73. White flight between birth and first grade varied over the following years, reaching a high of 16 percent in 1976–77, but overall the public schools enrolled 14 percent fewer white children in first grade in the 1970s than they had in the late 1960s, even though the first grade under the busing plan was in white-neighborhood schools.

There was no sharp increase in white flight between the end of first grade and the end of fourth grade, although there were small incremetal losses for most cohorts. For example, among the 1974–75 first grade cohort there was some additional loss; 18 percent of the cohort had been lost to the public schools by the fourth grade in 1977–78.

A sharp increase in the level of white flight did occur, however, at the transition from fourth to fifth grade for almost every cohort. In the 1978–79 school year there were 20 percent fewer whites in the fifth and sixth grades than could have been expected based on pre-busing enrollment patterns. The high level of white flight at this point in the children's educational careers is directly related to the busing plan. The fifth and sixth grades were located in black-neighborhood schools, so for most white children attendance meant travel to downtown Nashville.

A careful examination of Table 31 shows that some white children

Table 31: *White Flight: Difference Between White Students Expected to Enroll and Those Who Actually Enrolled in the Public Schools for Each Cohort(%)*

GRADE	1971-72	1972-73	1973-74	1974-75	1975-76	1976-77	1977-78	1978-79	NUMBER LOST FROM COHORT	AVERAGE COHORT LOSS FOR THE GRADE LEVEL
1	-8	-13	-14	-14	-15	-16	-15	-14	(747)	-14
2	-6	-9	-10	-12	-13	-16	-16	-14	(810)	-12
3	-4	-7	-10	-11	-14	-15	-19	-17	(1026)	-12
4	-6	-8	-8	-12	-12	-15	-18	-19	(1117)	-12
5	-17	-15	-14	-14	-14	-15	-18	-20	(1120)	-16
6	-17	-17	-15	-15	-13	-16	-16	-20	(1128)	-16
7	-9	-11	-12	-12	-12	-12	-12	-13	(775)	-12
8	-4	-9	-9	-10	-10	-12	-11	-15	(959)	-10
9	-10	-11	-13	-11	-10	-13	-14	-14	(852)	-12
10	-6	-11	-11	-11	-8	-11	-12	-13	(760)	-10
11	-6	-10	-13	-11	-11	-13	-14	-8	(402)	-11
12	0	-11	-11	-18	-14	-16	-15	-16	(880)	-13
Number Lost from Cohort			(579)	(622)	(1070)	(832)	(945)	(856)		
Average Cohort Loss for the Year	-8	-11	-12	-13	-12	-14	-15	-15		

may have come back to the public schools after having abandoned them in the fifth grade. But overall the data reveal a clear pattern. The rate of white flight did not abate two or three years after busing began, as some experts had predicted it would; rather it continued at a high rate.[2] The average cohort lost 8 percent in 1971–72, 11 percent in 1972–73, and 15 percent in the last two years of the 1970s. By 1978–79, the public schools enrolled 15 percent fewer white children than would have been expected in the absence of busing. In general, early losses from the schools carried through all the grades.

The data in Table 31 reflect the overall loss of white students from the Metro public schools. As we know, however, only about two-thirds of the county's children were involved in the court-ordered busing plan. The outlying areas of the county were exempt from busing for desegregation. Hence, the losses from the *system*—to private schools or to other school districts in the metropolitan area—mask the highly localized levels and patterns of white flight. We would expect white flight to be greater among those areas most impacted by the busing plan.

Patterns of White Flight Within the School System

The aggregate patterns of white flight *from* the Metro public schools have been examined. *Within-system* white flight also occured—movement of white children from one school to another within the public school system when the pattern of movement was associated with aspects of the desegregation plan. Within-system white flight can be measured by applying the 1960s retention rates to the enrollment of individual schools. The focus here is only on the first six grades, since much of the white flight occured in these grades.

The 1971 desegregation scheme created three different types of elementary schools within the county. In the areas where busing for desegregation was not required, "neighborhood" Grade 1-6 schools were continued. Within the bused area, a few Grade 1–6 schools were permitted, either because they served naturally desegregated areas or because one-way (black to white) busing was deemed appropriate. Most of the bused area elementary grades were divided between Grade 1–4 schools in white neighborhood, and Grade 5–6 schools in mixed or black neighborhoods. The patterns of within-system white flight were clearly linked to these aspects of the busing plan.

2. Farley, "Is Coleman Right?" Giles, Cataldo, and Gatlin, "Is Coleman Right?" Orfield, "Is Coleman Right?"

As in the system level analysis, the retention rates were translated into the percentages of each cohort *expected* to continue in the public schools based on the 1967–71 base period. Table 32 shows this pattern of expected enrollment in percentage terms.

The percentage of white students who actually continued from first grade onward in each cohort in each school was then compared to the expected values, and an average cohort loss was calculated for each school. For simplicity in presentation, the school averages were themselves averaged to create a figure for the average loss suffered by schools of different types.

As can be seen from Table 33, an average of 11 percent of the white students who began first grade in desegregated Grade 1–4 schools in white areas had left those schools by the end of the fourth grade. These schols had been projected to be 15 to 35 percent black under the busing plan, but white flight in the birth to first grade interval and among those who did enroll in first grade meant that the percentage black in these schools quickly rose above the upper threshold of the court-ordered plan. Table 33 also reveals the impact of busing on the other two types of schools. The Grade 1–6 schools in the court-ordered area lost 3 percent of their white students between the end of the first and the end of the fourth grades. One-way busing of black children and desegregated neighborhoods seems to have prompted little white flight. Schools in the outlying areas of the county, those exempt from busing for desegregation, gained about 6 percent in each white cohort between 1971 and 1979 in the interval between first grade and the end of fourth grade. This set of findings confirms that the patterns of white flight that were established in the first year of busing were continuing, and that they were related to aspects of the desegregation plan.

Almost two of every three children in elementary schools in the county lived in the bused area. The vast majority of these children attended fifth and sixth grades in a black neighborhood school. Busing had a significant impact on whites at that point in their education. As Table 34 shows, 11 percent of the whites who had enrolled in desegregated schools in white areas in the first grade and stayed through fourth grade failed to transfer to the black downtown school for the fifth grade. Some of these families must have moved into Grade 1–6 schools in the court-ordered areas because at fifth grade the average cohort in those schools enrolled 2 percent more than expected, even though they were down 3 percent in the fourth grade. Once again, these data confirm a pattern of white flight from busing.

The evidence is stronger still when the racial characteristics of the neighborhood around the grade 5–6 schools are taken into account.

Table 32: Expected White Cohort Continuation (Read Diagonally)

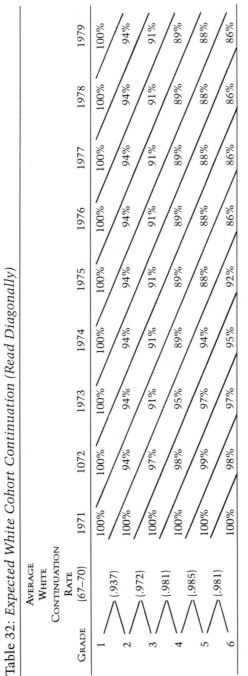

Grade	Average White Continuation Rate (67–70)	1971	1072	1973	1974	1975	1976	1977	1978	1979
1	(.937)	100%	100%	100%	100%	100%	100%	100%	100%	100%
2	(.972)	100%	94%	94%	94%	94%	94%	94%	94%	94%
3	(.981)	100%	97%	91%	91%	91%	91%	91%	91%	91%
4	(.985)	100%	98%	95%	89%	89%	89%	89%	89%	89%
5	(.981)	100%	99%	97%	94%	88%	88%	88%	88%	88%
6		100%	98%	97%	95%	92%	86%	86%	86%	86%

Table 33: *Average Percentage of White Cohort Losses, Above Expected Levels, Between Grades 1 and 4*

COURT-ORDERED 1–4	COURT-ORDERED 1–6	NON-COURT-ORDERED 1–6
Average −11%	Average −3%	Average +6%

Table 34: *Average Percentage of White Cohort Losses, Above Expected Levels, Between Grades 4 and 5*

COURT-ORDERED 1–4, 5–6 SCHOOLS	COURT-ORDERED 1–6 SCHOOLS	NOT COURT-ORDERED 1–6 SCHOOLS
Average −11%	Average +2%	Average +3%

Table 35 does this. For the few clusters which had Grade 5–6 centers in predominantly white areas (1970 census), there was little loss between fourth and fifth grades. As the neighborhood around the school increased in percentage black, the proportion of whites leaving the school (cluster) increased substantially. When the black population was less than 20 percent, on average there were only 2 percent fewer whites than expected. When the area around the fifth grade school was 80 to 100 percent black, the average white cohort was fully 18 percent lower than expected. This means that for every one hundred white children who were in desegregated white schools in first grade, eighteen left between fourth and fifth grades when they were scheduled to move to a Grade 5–6 center in a predominantly black area of town. Judging from Table 35, it is fair to observe that the "blacker" the neighborhood around the school, the greater the white loss suffered by the schools.

The pattern of gains and losses suggests that many whites leaving cluster schools between fourth and fifth grades moved to Grade 1–6 court-ordered or non-court-ordered schools. Others went to private schools or nearby counties. In any case, there was a net loss to desegregation, since those schools were largely white.

There is a class basis to this movement as well. Table 36 examines the loss between fourth and fifth grade from the perspective of the median family income of the predominantly white neighborhoods involved in clusters or the school zone itself in the case of Grade 1–6 schools (1970 census).

The average loss of whites from cluster areas where the median family income was $9,000 or less in 1970 was only 5 percent, but from cluster areas where the median family income was over $12,000 the average white flight was 19 percent between fourth and fifth grades.

Table 35: *Average Cohort Difference Between Actual Grade 4 Percent and Actual Grade 5 Percent Continuing, Controlling for Percent Black in Area Around the School*

	RACIAL MAKEUP (% BLACK)			
SCHOOL TYPE	0–20	21–50	51–74	75–100
Court-Ordered 1–4, 5–6	−2%	−5%	−14%	−18%
Court-Ordered 1–6	+2%	+3%		
Not Court-Ordered 1–6	+3%			

Table 36: *Average Cohort Difference Between Actual Grade 4 Percent and Actual Grade 5 Percent Continuing, Controlling for Median Family Income of Grade 1–4 Schools*

	MEDIAN FAMILY INCOME		
SCHOOL TYPE	BELOW $9,000	$9,000–$12,000	ABOVE $12,000
Court-Ordered 1–4, 5–6	−5%	−11%	−19%
Court-Ordered 1–6	+12%	−4%	−1%
Not-Court-Ordered 1–6	+7%	+3%	−1%

So far we have found a general decline in the percentage of white students continuing in public schools in the court-ordered clusters and more than expected growth in the non-court-ordered areas. The pattern of flight was associated with the proportion black in the neighborhood around the school and with the median income level of the whites assigned to the cluster schools.

A comparison of the general level of white cohort losses at the sixth grade permits us to discover the combined effect of (a) losses from court-ordered schools and (b) the net pattern of gain or loss for non-court-ordered schools. Since income and proportion black in the neighborhood have been found to be significantly related to white losses over time, these factors have been used as control variables in the final table.

Table 37 is the final summary table. It shows the average cohort loss at the sixth grade for the three types of schools, controlling for income and "blackness" of the area around the school. As can be seen, the greatest losses beyond those expected (based on 1967–70 retention rates) are to be found in clusters associated with a high

Table 37: *Average Difference Between Expected and Actual Proportions at Grade 6, Controlling for Percent Black in the Neighborhood Around the School and for Median Family Income of the Paired White School Zone*

SCHOOL TYPE	NEIGHBORHOOD 0–50% BLACK		
	BELOW $9,000	$9,000–$12,000	ABOVE $12,000
Court-Ordered 1–4, 5–6	−3%	−16%	−1%
Court-Ordered 1–6	−3%	−5%	−7%
Not Court-Ordered 1–6	−1%	+14%	+14%

SCHOOL TYPE	NEIGHBORHOOD 51–100% BLACK		
	BELOW $9,000	$9,000–$12,000	ABOVE $12,000
Court-Ordered 1–4, 5–6	−17%	−24%	−43%
Court-Ordered 1–6	—	—	—
Not Court-Ordered 1–6	—	—	—

proportion black in the neighborhood around the school and high income in the predominantly white areas assigned to the school. Two schools located in the black area of town illustrate these effects. Between Grades 1 and 6 the Wharton cluster lost an average of 49 percent and the John Early cluster 44 percent from among children who started in desegregated public schools at first grade. These were staggering losses.

In middle-income areas ($9,000 to $12,000 in the 1970 census) white children were removed at a very high rate if the Grade 5–6 center was in a predominantly black neighborhood. There was an average loss of 24 percent for schools of this type.

Cluster schools (court-ordered Grade 1–4, 5–6) which were in areas of white majority suffered very little white flight between 1971 and 1979 from among those students who actually enrolled in the public schools at first grade. Among the non-court-ordered schools there was a pattern of substantial growth; on average, the schools in predominantly white middle- and upper-income areas gained 14 percent above their expected enrollment. The findings from Table 37, then, reinforce results obtained in earlier tables.

The findings from our analysis of within-system white flight are clear:

1. There were moderate white losses in cluster schools between

Grades 1 and 4; the average white cohort loss was 11 percent more than expected. These were fully desegregated schools; hence, it appears that many whites accepted biracial classrooms with equanimity when the schools were in predominantly white neighborhoods.

2. There was an additional average loss of 11 percent between Grades 4 and 5 from white student cohorts enrolled in cluster schools; however, white flight was much greater than average when the Grade 5–6 school was in a predominantly black area (average cohort loss = 18 percent) or when the median family income in the predominantly white area zoned to the Grade 5–6 school was higher than average. For income areas averaging above $12,000 in 1979, the white flight from cluster schools averaged 19 percent (25 percent if predominantly white Robertson Academy is excluded from the list).

3. By the end of sixth grade the white losses were greatest in clusters where upper-income whites were to be bused into schools in predominantly black areas of the community. Income and race reinforced one another.

4. The losses suffered in court-ordered clusters between Grades 1–4, 5–6, or 1–6 are associated with gains of whites in non-court-ordered schools, despite the fact that many of those who withdrew from public schools went to private schools or relocated out of the county.

Private Schools and White Flight

During the 1960s there was a "natural" private school segment of the community. In 1969, for example, 9 percent of the county's children were enrolled in private schools at first grade. If we apply this percentage to white births in the county we can estimate the number of children who could have been expected to enroll for the first grade in private schools during the 1970s. Any differences we observe between expected and actual enrollments in private schools at the first grade level can be attributed to white flight from busing, since there was no other major new factor influencing parental choice between the late 1960s and the early 1970s.

Table 38 shows the proportion of the private schools' first grade enrollment which was not consistent with their normal pre-busing totals. In 1969, 9 percent of the county's children were in first grade in private schools. In 1970 there was a busing scare, and 115 children above the expected number enrolled in private schools. Thus, 15

Table 38: *Proportion of Private Schools' Grade 1 Above the Natural Private School Cohort in the Population*
(Base Year 1969)

WHITE BIRTHS:	1969 / 7081	1970 / 7110	1971 / 6391	1972 / 5958	1973 / 5638	1974 / 5600	1975 / 5880	1976 / 6036	1977 / 5785	1978 / 5334	1979 / 4968
	(.0898)										
Projected Natural Private School Cohort (1969 base)	636	639	575	535	506	502	527	541	518	478	445
Actual Private School Enrollment	636	751	879	890	892	935	1026	1139	1094	1053	1027
Students Entering From Public Schools	—	112	304	355	386	433	499	598	576	575	582
Proportion of Private Schools' First Grade From Public Schools Cohort		15%	35%	40%	43%	46%	49%	52%	53%	55%	57%

percent of the private schools' first grade enrollments that year can be linked to the threat of busing. By 1979, 57 percent of private schools' first grade students would not have been there if the pattern of the pre-busing years had continued.

Another way to display private schools' enrollment patterns is found in Table 39. In this table the base year for "normal" private school enrollment is 1970–71, the year before busing began. Using this year to project the expected private school enrollments creates the *lowest* estimate of white flight to private schools due to busing. In 1970–71, 11 percent of the county's first grade children were in private schools. The following year, when busing was implemented, 14 percent of the county's first graders were in private schools—3 percent more. In 1970–71, the private schools enrolled between 9 and 12 percent of the county's children in each grade level through seventh grade. In every case the following year they enrolled more whites than expected. At the fifth and sixth grade levels, for example, busing brought a sharp increase in private school enrollments: from 9 percent to 15 percent at fifth grade, and from 10 percent to 16 percent at sixth grade.

In 1978–79, 20 percent of the county's first grade students were in private schools. This was up from nine percent in 1969 and 11 percent in 1970. Once in private schools, children tended to stay there and to be joined by others. By 1978–79, between 18 and 22 percent of the county's students in Grades 1–7 were in private schools. Private schools had *doubled* their share of the school age population in less than ten years.

Acknowledgment

By 1979 both sides in the *Kelley* case recognized that the 1971 busing plan needed to be altered. Schools in the inner city were no longer racially balanced. And, because of the decline in enrollments due to white flight and fewer births, some schools needed to be closed. In outlying areas of the county, schools were exceeding capacity, but the 1971 court order forbade the Metropolitan School Board to build new schools or classrooms at existing schools there. During court proceedings in 1979, Federal District Court Judge Thomas Wiseman took a look at the issues and ordered that a new desegregation plan be developed for all of Davidson County. Resegregation of schools due to white flight was one of the major factors Wiseman cited in ordering the 1971 plan abandoned.

Because of the judge's interest, counsel for the Metropolitan School

Table 39: *Private School Enrollments as a Proportion of Age Cohort*

GRADE	BIRTH	1970–71 BASE YR.	1971–72 100% (6391)	1972–73 100% (5958)	1973–74 100% (5638)	1974–75 100% (5600)	1975–76 100% (5880)	1976–77 100% (6036)	1977–78 100% (5785)	1978–79 100% (5334)	COHORT GAIN OVER NATURAL PRIVATE SCHOOL BASE (70–71)
1	100% (7110)	11% (751)	14%	15%	16%	17%	17%	19%	19%	20%	+9% [N=480]
2	100% (7081)	10% (726)	13%	14%	15%	15%	17%	18%	19%	20%	+9% [N=521]
3	100% (7139)	10% (696)	12%	13%	15%	16%	16%	18%	17%	20%	+9% [N=543]
4	100% (7307)	9% (689)	13%	14%	14%	16%	17%	18%	18%	18%	+7% [N=412]
5	100% (7525)	9% (710)	15%	17%	17%	18%	19%	19%	21%	21%	+10% [N=560]
6	100% (7425)	10% (709)	16%	16%	18%	19%	18%	20%	20%	22%	+11% [N=620]
7	100% (7402)	12% (878)	16%	17%	17%	18%	19%	19%	20%	21%	+10% [N=596]
8		13%	13%	15%	16%	16%	17%	19%	19%	20%	+9% [N=575]
9				13%	14%	14%	14%	17%	17%	18%	+7% [N=53]
10					14%	13%	14%	14%	14%	17%	+7% [N=51]
11						12%	12%	13%	14%	16%	+6% [N=42]
12							12%	11%	13%	15%	+6% [N=41]
							0	+1	+4		[N=4494]

Cohort Gain Over Natural Private School Base

Board asked Professor Richard Pride to prepare a report and testify on white flight in Davidson County. The foregoing analysis constituted the report submitted to the school board and to the court in hearings during spring 1980.

Conclusions

White flight from the Metro public schools was a significant and continuing problem. The white middle class was leaving the court-ordered shools in substantial numbers, relocating children in non-court-ordered public schools, adjacent counties, and private schools. Traditionally, the white middle class had been the public schools' strongest ally; its members had supported the schools politically, financially, and, through countless hours of volunteer labor, personally. Without their strong support the public schools could slip into mediocrity or worse. In the magnitude and patterns of white flight there was another, more frightening prospect—that the community would develop a new dual school system along race and class lines, with a private system for the affluent and white and a public school system for the poor and black.

Why did whites flee the public schools? Because they were afraid. But of what were they afraid? Busing redistributed educational services and social status between blacks and whites and within each racial group. White parents feared that their children would suffer a loss in class or status if they remained in court-ordered public schools.

It is unlikely that poor educational services was the root cause of white flight. The textbooks, teachers, and buildings in the court-ordered schools were just as good as those elsewhere. The Wharton elementary school cluster experienced tremendous white flight; 43 percent of the white children who started school in the white neighborhood had left by sixth grade. Yet the schools embedded in this cluster (West Meade, Parmer, Crieve Hall, and Wharton) had strong faculties and their achievement test averages were above the national average. Indeed, at Wharton itself in 1980 the fifth grade average achievement test score was above the national sixth grade average. As we have seen, busing had no significant impact on the achievement of white children. Educational achievement is the ultimate service delivered by schools, and educational achievement increased for both white and black children during these years. Objectively, white flight could not have been caused by decreasing educational achievement in the schools.

Schools provide other services. Discipline is a service; people expect well-ordered classrooms in their schools. Discipline problems were not related to the level and pattern of white flight in the 1971–79 period, as far as we could determine. Moreover, if discipline had been a major problem, children's educational achievement would likely have declined, not increased, as it did. Some parents could argue that music or art classes were not provided in sufficient quality or quantity by the Metro schools after busing, whereas private schools did provide them. That would be a decline in educational services warranting "white flight," but it could not make economic sense. A family could buy a lot of private supplementary music and art instruction for less than it would cost to pay private school tuition or to move the family to another county. Any list of educational services provided by schools would not have found the Metro schools so disadvantaged that the magnitude and pattern of white flight could be explained on those grounds.

White flight seems more clearly related to status issues. Racial prejudice is an extreme manifestationn of a status differential; a prejudiced person clearly says, " 'We' are better than 'you,' and nothing will persuade me otherwise." Of course, a truly prejudiced person is always afraid that events might prove that "you" really are as good as "we" and is unwilling to risk that discovery. Surely some of the whites who fled the schools were racially prejudiced in just this way. Others, however, were not so much racists as afraid that in school their children would acquiire manners and values opposed to their own. White flight is directly related to three factors we have examined: (1) the "blackness" of the school, (2) the "blackness" of the neighborhood around the school, and (3) the ability of whites to pay to educate their children elsewhere. To many whites, the black culture represented values they abhored. The white middle-class values of self-discipline, hard work, real achievement, proper manners, and deserved merit were sacred. The black culture, as whites conceived of it, valued other things; otherwise, whites asked, why would there be so much violence, so many illegitimate children, and so many people on welfare in North Nashville? Busing could assimilate blacks to white cultural values, or it could assimilate whites to black cultural values. Many white parents, it seems, did not want to risk the latter. It was not the color of the skin that mattered; it was the values which skin color only symbolized. If blacks were like us, whites implied, there would be no problem. But black children issue from the black culture, and the black culture is not ours. We want our children to be reinforced in our values, not theirs. "Our" lifestyle and values are different from and better than "theirs." These were the messages conveyed by white flight. And many black leaders came to understand busing and the meaning of white flight in just these terms.

CHAPTER EIGHT

Public Attitudes about Busing and School Desegregation

*// T*he moral imperative and great hopes that gave momentum to desegregation efforts seem to have been replaced by a combination of pessimism and pragmatism. The old mythology held that children of all colors learning side by side would bring about the end of prejudice and would substantially undermine social inequalities. This faith has apparently given way to a new mythology, which holds that we have tried our best, but the costs of imposing desegregation on an unwilling community generally outweigh the benefits."[1] For Willis Hawley, a desegregation scholar of national standing, the old mythology promised too much, and the new mythology accepted too little. The experts pointed out that, given certain strategies and conditions, desegregation does achieve worthwhile goals in most places most of the time.[2] But these findings did not comfort most Nashvillians.

Instead, many of the city's white parents were converts of the new mythology, which held that the strains entailed in desegregating the schools were harmful to the educational system as a whole. Among black parents an initial enthusiasm for busing had given way to skepticism. The specific tenets of the new educational philosophy included the following: (1) desegregation doesn't enhance the academic achievement of minorities and indeed may impede the cognitive development of minorities and whites in many cases, (2) desegregation increases interracial conflict and prejudice, and (3) desegregation is harmful to the development of self-esteem, vocational aspirations, and racial identity of minorities. These beliefs, said Willis Hawley after his review of the scholarly literature, "are not demonstrably true." Indeed, the best studies showed just the opposite: black achievement was enhanced, race relations were im-

1. Hawley, "The New Mythology of School Desegregation" *Law and Contemporary Problems* 42:3.4 (Fall 1978), 214–33.

2. Hawley, "Equity and Quality in Education: Characteristics of Effective Desegregated Schools," in Hawley, ed., *Effective School Desegregation* (Beverly Hills, 1981), 297–308.

proved, and black self-esteem was strengthened by the school deseg-regation experience.[3]

Still, the new mythology had a firm grip on Nashville. If the populace believed the myth, then the actual consequences of that belief were as real as if the myth was established fact. One difficulty with the debate on busing is that the discussions have too rarely focused on the unfolding effects of the policy on public opinion in a community. In this chapter we present survey data from Nashville in order to evelop the ideological facets of the new mythology. Our data show that the general public, parents, and teachers were convinced that the costs of busing were high and the benefits incidental.

Throughout the 1960s and 1970s national poll results consistently showed that the majority of Americans believed "integration should be brought about gradually," and that black leaders were "pushing too hard" in their drive for social justice.[4] It is not surprising, given a history of such feelings, that the quest for interracial understanding through busing was never strongly supported. In Nashville, years of court-ordered busing stimulated community concern for issues such as quality education and school system stability. Survey findings suggest that the community believed the public schools were not doing a good job of educating the city's young children and that busing simply didn't work. By 1980, Nashville had lost confidence in its public schools.

Attitudes of the General Public in Nashville

An observer of busing has written that "the real concern of parents goes . . . to the perceived quality of schools."[5] Surveys of public opinion were made in Nashville between 1977 and 1981. These

---

3. "School Desegregation: Lessons of the First Twenty-Five Years, Parts I and II," *Law and Contemporary Problems* 42:3,4.

4. Survey Resarch Center, 1964, 1968, 1972 *National Election Studies* (Ann Arbor). In 1968 the SRC election survey revealed that 61 percent of the respondents believed that "civil rights leaders are pushing too fast" in the drive for social justice. In 1961 the Gallup Poll showed that 61 percent of respondents believed that "integration should be brought about gradually." In 1964 and 1970, 64 percent of the populace polled believed "racial integration should not be speeded up." George H. Gallup, "Gallup Poll of the Public's Attitudes Toward the Public Schools," *Phi Delta Kappan* 63(Sept. 1981), 33–47.

5. William L. Taylor, "Brown in Perspective," in Hawley, *Effective School Desegregation*, 15.

periodic samplings revealed that the community believed the quality of public schools was low and that busing had failed.

One indicator of school quality is the confidence that the public has in public school teachers. In the 1970s there was a growing sentiment that Nashville public school teachers were not as good as they should be. Questionnaires mailed to samples of registered voters in 1978, 1979, and 1980 asked whether teachers should take competency tests to demonstrate their knowledge of their subject matter. Although the question was worded differently in different years, the results were unambiguous; over 80 percent in all three surveys said "yes".[6]

In 1979 the mail survey asked, "As you look at your own elementary and high school education, is it your impression that children today get a better—or worse—education than you did?" Almost two in three (64 percent) respondents said today's children received a "worse" education than they had. In 1981, Keckley Market Research did a telephone survey of Nashville's general public. Keckley asked a similar question and found a similar result; 61 percent said "a worse education today." In a separate Keckley survey of Nashville's business elite, 71 percent said children today receive a "worse" education than they had.[7]

In 1979 and 1980 samples of registered voters were asked to evaluate the performance of the public schools on a rating scale. In 1979 only 15 percent of those answering the question said "good" or "excellent." In 1980 only 13 percent made those replies.

Clearly Nashvillians had a low opinion of the quality of their public schools, despite the fact that by 1980 Metro's average scores for nationally standardized achievement tests had risen to the nation-

6. In Oct. 1978, 1979, and 1980 random samples were drawn from lists of Davidson County registered votes, and 975, 788, and 915 respondents, respectively, received questionnaires in the three surveys. The return rates were 36, 41, and 42 percent. These surveys were intended to monitor the attitudes and behavior of voters. The self-selection process involved in returning mail questionnaires operates in the same way as electoral turnout: the most interested and involved citizens participate in both. Sample sizes are as follows: 1978 mailed questionnaire, 324 respondents; 1979, 323 respondents; 1980, 364 respondents. In 1981 a random sample of 429 members of the general public were interviewed by telephone. Random-digit dialing was used to select households. These studies were carried out as class projects under the supervision of Richard A. Pride. In Aug. 1981 a telephone survey on education was done by Keckley Market Research, a private firm using a random selection process; Keckley's report was based on 385 respondents drawn from Davidson County.

7. The business elite was composed of 175 leaders in the community who were owners or managers of a business and who held membership in the Nashville Area Chamber of Commerce. Of this sample, 87 percent were male, 51 percent made $50,000 or more, and 24 percent had a graduate or professional degree.

QUESTION: *How good a job are the public schools doing in educating Nashville's young people?*

	1979 (percent)	1980 (percent)
Excellent	2	1
Good	13	12
Fair	42	44
Poor	34	32
Don't Know	9	11
Total	100	100

al average and were higher than those of comparable cities. By that time support for public education had badly eroded, and it seemed it would continue to do so.

Nashvillians rated their public schools much lower than other Americans rated theirs. In 1981 telephone surveys of the Nashville general public were conducted by Keckley and by Richard Pride. These surveys asked people to grade schools on the quality of their work, just as students were graded. The results of this rating confirmed Nashville's generally negative evaluation of its public schools. A similar scale was employed by the Gallup poll in its yearly national survey on education.[8] Results from these surveys are compared below.

In Gallup's 1974 poll, 48 percent of the national sample gave the

QUESTION: *Students are often given the grades A, B, C, D, and FAIL to denote quality of their work. Suppose the public schools themselves, in this community, were graded in the same way. What grade would you give the public schools here—A, B, C, D, or FAIL? (Results in percent)*

	Gallup '74	Gallup '81	Keckley '81	Pride '81
A	18	9	4	4
B	30	27	13	18
C	21	34	34	39
D	6	13	15	17
FAIL	5	7	8	4
Don't Know	20	10	26	17
Total	100	100	100	100

8. Gallup Opinion Surveys, "Thirteenth Annual Survey of the Public's Attitudes Toward the Public Schools" (Princeton, N.J., Spring 1981).

public schools a rating of A or B. Nationally, this favorable rating dropped to 36 percent in 1981. As both the Keckley and Pride surveys showed, in 1981 only about 20 percent of Nashville's general public rated local schools that highly.

In Keckley's 1981 survey of business leaders, respondents were asked if they sent (or would send) their children to public or private schools. Fully 75 percent of Nashville's business elite said they wanted "private" education for their children. When asked why, they consistently replied that better education and discipline were to be found in private schools.

These Nashville findings were consistent with national poll results. Gallup's 1981 survey asked respondents why there had been such a growth in private church-related schools in recent years. The three most popular answers to this "open-ended" question were: (1) poor educational standards in the public schools, (2) integration, forced busing, and racial problems, and (3) greater discipline characterized private schools.[9] In sum, Gallup Poll respondents expressed little confidence in the public schools. For the first time in the nation's history, many adults considered themselves better educated than young people.

Private education, on the other hand, had a positive image among the general public. In our 1981 Nashville telephone survey we asked respondents without children whether they would put their children in public or private schools. About 60 percent said they preferred private schools. We asked respondents to grade the performance of private schools in Nashville just as they had earlier evaluated public schools. Fully 60 percent of those answering the question gave the private schools a grade of A or B, whereas only 22 percent rated the public schools that high.

As reasons for the support for private schools are explored in another chapter, here it will suffice to say that the general public evaluated the public schools quite negatively. There was strong sentiment in favor of private education.

The general populace had also concluded that busing was a failure. In the 1978 survey of registered voters, respondents were asked "whether court-ordered busing for desegregation helped blacks and whites get along better." Almost three in four respondents (72 percent) said "no." The same question was put to respondents in the 1979 survey, and this time 79 percent said busing did not help the two races understand one another.

In our 1981 telephone survey of the general public, we asked,

9. Ibid., 5.

"Some people favor busing children in order to desegregate the public schools . . . others are opposed to busing for racial desegregation . . . What is your opinion?" Fully 80 percent said that they opposed busing. Keckley's telephone survey of the general public, made the same year, asked a question about problems facing the public schools. Busing was the most frequently given reply, even though that answer was not listed among the options given to respondents. Lack of discipline was the next most important issue cited by both business leaders and the general public.

A large majority of Nashvillians, then, were unhappy with their public schools at the end of the 1970s. The typical citizen, it seemed, rated the quality of the public schools as very low, certainly as worse than when he was in school. These feelings were not restricted to Nashville. A 1980 report by the U.S. Department of Education and the National Science Foundation stated that most Americans were moving toward "virtual scientific and technological illiteracy."[10] The 1980s marked the nadir of a sixteen-year decline in Scholastic Aptitude Test (SAT) scores for students going to college. In April 1983 the National Commission on Excellence in Education issued a report ominously entitled "A Nation at Risk." The widely quoted findings cited a "rising tide of mediocrity" in the educational system.[11] No wonder, then, that most Nashville respondents wanted teachers tested for competency in the subject matter for which they were responsible.

Parent's Attitudes

It is clear that the general public believed there was something ailing education, but did parents of school children share these sentiments? Parents should be better informed about schools than the general public. They are closer to children, teachers, and classroom activities. If children are learning, and if desegregation is working, parents should be among the first to know the good news.

To answer the question of whether parents' beliefs differ sharply from those of the general public, the authors surveyed parents of Metro school children in November 1980.[12] Parents, we found, did evaluate the quality of the schools much more favorably than did the

10. *New York Times*, Oct. 23, 1981.
11. *Washington Post*, Apr. 23, 1983.
12. In Nov. 1980 questionnaires were mailed to a random sample of 1,000 parents of Metro school children. The return rate was 30 percent (303); 18 percent of the respondents were black, which is close to the adult population ratio of Davidson County.

public at large, but they still were worried about the quality of education and about school busing. We also found some significant differences between white and black parents.

Parents were asked to rate the quality of education their children received, as well as that available to other children.

QUESTION: *How would you rate the overall quality of education your child has received in Metro schools?*

	White Parents (percent)	Black Parents (percent)	
Excellent	9	11	
Good	40	54	
Fair	36	32	
Poor	15	4	
	100	100	
	(N=247)	(N=56)	prob.=.0781

QUESTION: *How would you rate the overall quality of education most children have received in Metro schools in recent years?*

	White Parents (percent)	Black Parents (percent)	
Excellent	1	7	
Good	30	38	
Fair	51	47	
Poor	17	7	
Total	99	99	
	(N=247)	(N=56)	prob.=.0125

There is a striking contrast between the responses to these two questions. Almost half of the white parents (49 percent) and two-thirds of the black parents (65 percent) said their children received an "excellent" or "good" education in the Metro schools. This rating is substantially higher than that given by the general public. However, when parents were asked to assess the quality of education *other* children received in Metro, they were less positive in their evaluation. Only 31 perent of the white parents and 45 percent of the black parents said other children received an "excellent" or "good" education. As we have seen, only 13 to 15 percent of the general public rated public education at this level. This pattern of response suggests (a) that the closer the respondent was to the particular child-school relationship, the more favorably the schools were evaluated; and (b) that the race of the respondent altered his perception of the schools.

By 1980 the issue of competency testing for high school graduation was being widely discussed. Many people believed that low standards, an absence of discipline, and "social promotions" had reduced the quality of education in Metro schools. In our survey we asked about competency tests.

QUESTION: *Should students be required to pass a competency test before they can receive a graduate diploma from high school?*

	White Parents (percent)	Black Parents (percent)
Yes	74	48
No	15	22
Undecided	11	30
Total	100	100
	(N = 247)	(N = 56) prob. = .0003

Fully three in four white parents (74 percent) and almost half of the black parents (48 percent) said that they favored competency testing. In effect, they were saying that they wanted a way to judge the quality of both high school graduates and the schools, and a way to hold both accountable.

As a social policy, busing was meant to end racial separation in the schools. Desegregation through busing, it is argued, would enhance the educational achievement of blacks without damaging the educational achievement of whites. Both races would learn to accept the other without racial prejudice. These ideas, so firmly established by social science research, were not, however, widely accepted by Nashville parents. When we asked about busing's impact on educational achievement, most white parents and a majority of black parents said desegregation damaged achievement.

QUESTION: *Has busing children for desegregation in Nashville hurt the educational development of black children, white children, neither group, or both groups?*

	White Parents (percent)	Black Parents (percent)
Hurt black children	0	15
Hurt white children	7	4
Hurt neither group	12	42
Hurt both black & white	81	39
Total	100	100
	(N = 247)	(N = 56) prob. = .0000

Only 12 percent of white parents said desegregation hurt neither black or white children's educational achievement. Most (81 percent) said busing hurt both black and white children. Black parents did not approach consensus; only 42 percent said neither group was hurt by busing.

The same pattern appeared when parents were asked to assess race relations. Two of every three white parents (66 percent) said busing had not "improved the understanding and acceptance blacks and whites have of one another." Only 45 percent of the black parents agreed that busing had helped. Significantly, a majority (27 + 29 = 56 percent) of the black parents were unsure of busing's positive effects on social development of children.

QUESTION: *Has busing improved the understanding and acceptance blacks and whites have of one another?*

	White Parents (percent)	Black Parents (percent)	
Yes	15	45	
No	66	27	
Not sure	19	29	
	100	101	
	(N = 247)	(N = 56)	prob. = .0000

While busing was not credited with a significant improvement in attitude, manifest racial conflict between children seemed not to be an issue. In a separate question, only 17 percent of the whites and 15 percent of the blacks said their child had ever had "a problem in dealing with children of another race at school."

Racial balance—the idea that every school should be a microcosm of the larger community—was the guiding principle of busing in Nashville and other cities. When we asked parents about this idea, sharp differences between the two races emerged. Almost seven in every ten black parents (68 percent) thought that racial balance was a good idea, but among white parents only two in every ten (23 percent) thought so.

These response patterns are revealing. White parents said that busing hurts the educational development of children, even though analysis of test scores indicates this is not so. They said that busing had not improved race relations, even though very few children had had a problem dealing with children of another race. Finally, by rejecting racial balance in schools, white parents repudiated the assimilationist thrust of busing itself. Even those white families who

QUESTION: *In principle, do you think it is a good idea or a bad idea for children to go to schools that have about the same proportion of blacks and whites as generally exists in the Nashville/Davidson County area?*

	White Parents (percent)	Black Parents (percent)	
Good idea	23	68	
Bad idea	36	5	
Not sure	41	27	
	100	100	
	(N = 247)	(N = 56)	prob. = .0000

had not fled to private schools or moved to neighboring counties longed for a different system of education. Such sentiments became evident when the issue of private schools was broached.

White parents, more than black parents, preferred private schooling for their children. Almost two of every three white parents said they would like to put their children in a private school if they could afford to do so. Only 38 percent of black parents said they would select private education if they could afford it.

QUESTION: *Would you put your child in a private school if you could afford to do so?*

	White Parents (percent)	Black Parents (percent)	
Yes	64	38	
No	26	55	
Not sure	10	7	
	100	100	
	(N = 247)	(N = 56)	prob. = .0001

QUESTION: *If we go back to neighborhood schools, do you think the community will support the schools more fully than it has in recent years?*

	White Parents (percent)	Black Parents (percent)	
Yes	90	42	
No	5	26	
Not Sure	6	33	
	99	101	
	(N = 247)	(N = 56)	prob. = .0000

White parents said that if busing were to end and "neighborhood" elementary schools were to return, the community would support the public schools enthusiastically. Fully 90 percent of the white parents expressed this view. Once again, black parents gave a mixed response. Still, there was more preference for neighborhood schools than for the alternative.

White parents, the survey showed, manifested a clearer pattern of responses than black parents. The typical white parent rated the quality of public schools somewhat lower than did the average black parent, although not so low as did the general public. The white parent wanted competency tests for high school graduation, believed that busing hurt educational achievement and did not help racial understanding, and would prefer a private education for his children. The white parent said that the public would support the schools if these resumed a "neighborhood" character.

There was no typical black parent response in the data, although majorities were to be found on some points. A majority of black parents rated the quality of the schools as "excellent" or "good," but a majority also said busing hurt achievement. Still, blacks favored racial balance in the schools. A majority of black respondents would not put their child in private school if they could afford it, but more than one-third would.

Teachers' Attitudes

Teachers are even closer to schools than parents. In November 1980 a survey was undertaken to probe the attitudes of teachers and to see if their views differed from those of the general public and parents.[13] Several questions were used to probe the attitudes of teachers towards desegregation.

An overwhelming majority of white teachers believed that the educational development of children was damaged by busing. Only 19 percent said that busing for desegregation hurt neither blacks nor whites. Almost half (48 percent) said that busing hurt both groups, while one-third said that busing hurt only white children's development. Only 1 percent of white teachers said black children alone were hurt by busing.

13. In Nov. 1980 questionnaires were mailed to the home of 1,000 randomly selected Metro classroom teachers; 40 percent returned questionnaires by the end of Dec. Blacks made up 14 percent of those who returned questionnaires, whereas they are approximately 20 percent of the Davidson County population.

QUESTION: *Has busing children for desegregation hurt the educational development of black children, white children, neither group or both groups?*

	White Teachers (percent)	Black Teachers (percent)
Hurt black children	1	37
Hurt white children	33	2
Hurt neither	19	46
Hurt both	48	15
Total	101	100
	(N = 345)	(N = 56) prob. = .0000

There was a significant difference between the responses of black and white teachers. Almost half (46 percent) of the black teachers who answered the question said busing hurt neither group, but another sizeable segment of black teachers (37 percent) said busing hurt black children's educational development. Altogether only 17 percent (2 + 15) of the black teachers believed that busing hurt white children, in sharp contrast to white teachers' views.

Other questions registered teachers' views toward achievement and other aspects of desegregation by asking them to compare their recent experience to the pre-busing situation.

QUESTION: *Has busing for desegregation improved the educational achievement of black youngsters?*

	White Teachers (percent)	Black Teachers (percent)
Yes	37	36
No	32	38
Not sure	32	26
Total	101	100
	(N = 345)	(N = 56) prob. = .4692

QUESTION: *Has busing for desegregation helped black and white children to understand and appreciate one another?*

	White Teachers (percent)	Black Teachers (percent)
Yes	41	79
No	33	2
Not sure	26	19
Total	100	100
	(N = 345)	(N = 56) prob. = .0000

As can be seen in answers to the first question, no majority of white or black teachers—only 37 percent of white teachers and 36 percent of black teachers in the sample—said that busing had improved black youngsters' educational achievement. Roughly one-third of both groups said busing had not improved black achievement.

Black teachers were much more likely to say that busing had improved race relations. Nearly eight of every ten (79 percent) said that busing had helped black and white children to understand and appreciate one another, whereas only 40 percent of the white teachers thought so. One-third of the white respondents said busing had *not* helped racial understanding.

Enhancing the self-esteem of black children was another goal of desegregation. According to many teachers, this objective had not been met. About 40 percent of each racial group said busing had not helped black self-esteem. Only 18 percent of white teachers and 28 percent of black teachers said that busing had helped black students to see themselves more positively.

QUESTION: *Has busing for desegregation enhanced the selfesteem of black children?*

	White Teachers (percent)	Black Teachers (percent)	
Yes	18	28	
No	40	39	
Not sure	42	33	
	100	100	
	(N = 345)	(N = 56)	prob. = .3171

One of the essential ideas underlying busing policy is that white students' educational achievement is not damaged by the process. Clearly, a great majority of the white teachers (68 percent) disagreed. Yet 78 percent of black teachers felt that white achievement was not damaged. Here again there was a striking difference in black and white teachers' evaluations of the busing policy.

QUESTION: *Has busing for desegregation hurt the educational achievement of white children?*

	White Teachers (percent)	Black Teachers (percent)	
Yes	68	3	
No	16	78	
Not sure	16	19	
	100	100	
	(N = 345)	(N = 56)	prob. = .0000

In brief, then, white teachers believed that the educational achievement of white students was hurt by busing, but they were divided on the issues of whether busing enhanced racial understanding, black achievement or black self-esteem. Black teachers held that busing had not hurt white achievement and that it had helped racial understanding. Black teachers wre divided on whether or not black achievement and self-esteem had been improved by busing. Taking the data at face value, white Metro schoolteachers, like the general public and parents, seem to have judged busing a failure. For black teachers, busing was a mixed blessing.

Private Schools

"We were at a dinner party right before school started, and we listened to the other couples talking about the advantages of a private school," recalled one mother in a 1980 newspaper interview. "I realized how fortunate we were that we could afford to send our children—I mean, we wouldn't have to dig ditches to be able to afford it . . . if all the good people leave the public schools they may go down."[14] In the estimation of many white Nashville parents, "all the good people" had already abandoned the public schools. Busing had shaken their faith in the public education system.

The coincidence of private school openings and desegregation mandates is amazing. Seventeen of Davidson County's forty-three private schools, or nearly 40 percent, were founded after 1969. Private school enrollment in the county almost doubled during the decade of the 1970s. A report by Metro schools' Department of Research and Evaluation indicated that 7,923 students were attending private schools in 1969, but 14,882 were registered in fall 1979. This phenomenal growth (see Table 40) came in spite of declining white birth rates.

There was an especially large jump in private school enrollment in 1971, the first year of busing. This increase came in the grade levels most affected by the desegregation plan. Fifth-grade enrollment in private schools jumped by 57 percent, and sixth-grade by a whopping 73 percent. Many parents withdrew their children from public high schools as well; freshman through senior classes at private schools grew an average of 18 percent in 1971. Table 41 shows private school enrollments by grade level two years prior to busing and two years after busing. The large increases in 1971 were followed by moderate growth in the years after busing.

14. *Tennessean*, Aug. 3, 1980.

Table 40: *Davidson Country Private School Enrollment 1969–1979*

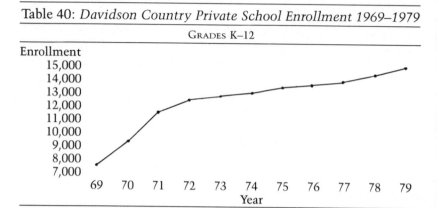

GRADES K–12

Parents give various reasons for placing their children in private schools: a longing for religious instruction, a desire for discipline in the classroom, and a concern about educational quality. But their basic convictions revolve around one idea—parents want a homogeneous setting for their children; they want to control the values to which their children are exposed. Parents concerned about the lack of prayer in the classroom might put their child in a Christian school. The children in another family which values learning achievement might attend a school with a demanding curriculum. But in both cases the fundamental explanation for the private school choice is the same: parents want to choose the sorts of ideas and cultural values taught to their children.

At one time this choice of social values was made with the purchase of a home in a specific location with an attendant neighborhood school. Busing changed this situation. The desegregation plan dictated where children would go to school, and parents no longer could choose the environment within which their children would learn and play. The private school system allowed parents to reassert their own values in education. Private schools provided teachers, curricula and an educational philosophy which puts parents' minds at ease.

On August 31, 1981, another new private school opened its doors to Nashville's children. Like a number of other private facilities, this one had a religious affiliation. "We have five teachers and . . . they will be Christian people." The school curriculum pledged itself to traditional values. "This is the only opportunity for your child to be educated in an environment that fosters growth; an awareness of the positive self that exists within all of us and true appreciation for

Table 41: *Davidson County Private School Enrollment by Grade Level, 1969–1973*

Year	K	1	2	3	4	5	6	7	8	9	10	11	12	Total
1969	296	636	595	550	588	601	636	741	721	679	642	614	644	7943
1970	325	751	726	696	689	710	709	878	853	764	683	638	607	9029
1971	393	879	897	871	923	1115	1229	1151	994	1007	811	742	643	11655
1972	423	890	907	956	986	1180	1178	1296	1111	998	913	837	730	12405
1973	472	892	902	968	1028	1236	1291	1243	1221	1011	1017	908	786	12975

Source: Tennessee Department of Education, "Private School Enrollment in Tennessee" Nashville, 1980.

others." What made the opening of the Temple Academy unique was that all 110 students enrolled there were black. In fact, the school was the only academy in Nashville owned and operated by blacks.[15]

It is too facile to say that racial antipathy alone explains private school enrollments. Private schools exist to alleviate the concerns parents, both black and white, have about the ideals and values promulgated by the public school system. Each private facility is careful to cultivate a certain image and to communicate that ideal to a prospective student's parents. Mothers and fathers worried about educational quality, for instance, are reassured by a principal who recites the large percentage of the school's graduating class currently enrolled in college. An important role is played by those school alumni who attribute their career achievements to some character trait engendered by the school. An example is this quote which appeared in the Nashville *Tennessean* shortly before school began in fall 1980. "I can honestly say that I believe I wouldn't be in Vanderbilt Law School now if it hadn't been for MBA (Montgomery Bell Academy)," said Dewey Branstetter, entering his final year of law school.[16] School reputations are maintained and enhanced by such comments, whether they are spoken over a neighbor's backyard fence, at a social function, or to a reporter.

Private schools have been amazingly successful in convincing parents that educational opportunities available in their classrooms are superior to those available in Metro schools. No wonder that so many parents with school-age children preferred private school education and would enroll their children if they had the money. Among business leaders the preference was even stronger, as we have seen, and the reason they most frequently gave for their feeling was that their children would receive a better education.[17]

In some instances the claim for better education seems clear. The city's long-established prep schools do an outstanding job of preparing selected students for admission to top colleges and universities throughout the country. Students from Montgomery Bell Academy and Harpeth Hall, two of Nashville's best regarded private schools, have a "very high" acceptance rate at Vanderbilt University, according to William L. Campbell, former director of Vanderbilt's undergraduate admissions. Still, the majority of students from these schools end up at state universities.

Newer and smaller private academies often struggle to supply the

15. Ibid., Aug. 2, 1981.
16. Ibid., Aug. 1, 1980.
17. These figures are from the Pride and Keckley surveys of opinions about education in Nashville.

simple basics to their students. Sixteen of Davidson County's forty-three private schools are operated without state approval. State accreditation is not necessary for a school to function, but it does mean that a school adheres to minimum regulations approved by the Tennessee Board of Education for public facilities. In some cases failure to seek state approval is intentional. University School, for instance, does not seek state approval because "you have to use textbooks from an approved list and require certain classes."[18] For University School, the freedom to develop innovative approaches to learning with unique textbook assignments is more important than state certification.

For most private schools the problems are more fundamental. Tuition charges of $1,000 to $2,500 per year fail to cover all the services the school offers. As a result teachers and students often share janitorial tasks at private facilities. Libraries and curriculum choices are limited. Many of the academies "temporarily" use church Sunday School classrooms until they can raise enough money to build an appropriate building. Parents put up with these inadequacies because the schools promote values they believe in. Parents are willing to forego the amenities available in public schools in order to have a voice in the values taught to their children. The drawbacks of schools without hot lunches, organized sports programs, and wide curriculum choices are less important than the friendships, moral teaching, and status associations available in the private schools.

Evangelistic churches, with their simple doctrine based on a literal translation of the Bible, are the most frequent sponsors of new schools. The fears that prompt the growth of Christian schools are related to various unsavory aspects of the modern world, including "the end of old fashioned patriotism, the new view of America's role in the world, the changing attitude toward authority and leaders, shrinking church attendance, rising divorce rates, acceptance of premarital sex, dirty movies, public nudity, foul language, the loosening of constraint and custom, abortion, crime, drugs, erosion of the work ethic, textbooks that question old values and old heroes, and the countless other manifestations of a new view of themselves that many Americans are now entertaining."[19]

A common concern among parents whose children attend these schools is that American society is disintegrating because it has forsaken traditional Christian values. Such ideals are ones many people want to see retained and taught to children. Only private

18. *Tennessean*, Aug. 11, 1980.
19. David Nevin and Robet E. Bills, *The Schools That Fear Built* (Washington, D.C., 1976), 19.

schools offer the Christian alternative. It may be true, as Christopher Lasch has said, that "the Protestant virtues no longer excite enthusiasm;" but many parents are still sufficiently interested in such values to pay handsome private tuition so that their children may receive moral instruction.[20] The Reverend Jerry Falwell of Lynchburg, Virginia, has been quoted as saying that, "somewhere in the United States there are three Christian schools opening every day."[21] There are those who disagree with Falwell's math, but few would dispute the implications of his prediction. If present trends continue, the year 2000 will witness enrollment in private Christian schools exceeding that of the public schools.

Conclusion

The community has invested heavily in the policy of desegregating the public schools through busing. Busing was begun in Nashville-Davidson County because racial isolation continued in neighborhood schools even after the dual school system had been abandoned. From the legal viewpoint, racial isolation of school children was suspect in any circumstance, regardless of community feelings.

Social science research had indicted segregation as the culprit behind racial stereotyping. Black children judged themselves and black culture to be inferior to white children and white culture. Black children's educational achievement, a product of low self-esteem, was much lower than desired. Research set new expectations: mixing white and black children through busing could end racial stereotyping, enhance black self-esteem, and raise black achievement without damaging white achievement.

By 1980 many white Nashvillians had concluded that busing had mixed students of the two races but accomplished little else. Busing, the lament continued, hurt educational achievement of both white and black children, did not improve racial understanding or acceptance, and exacerbated the problem of educational quality. These beliefs, according to the best scholarly literature, were part of a "new mythology" unsupported by the facts.

The black community was divided by its experience of busing. For some, the early promises had been fulfilled; they supported the policy. For others, busing had more than anything delivered new

20. Christopher Lasch, *The Culture of Narcissism* (New York, 1978), 53.
21. *Tennessean*, Aug. 4, 1980.

insults. There was no agreement that busing helped black student self-esteem and achievement.

Education was part of a larger social system, and that system fostered the "in group" and "out group" values of segregation. The schools supported a given system of social status, and blacks consitituted an inferior caste in that system. Status politics implies a gap between those who are defined as dissolute and those who are accorded a measure of respectability. Respect is a cultural variable, and educational training—like how one dresses, where one lives, and what table manners one uses—bespeaks social acceptability.

Status groups in society operate with ideals of acceptable behavior. Certain groups contrast their actions and beliefs with those of other segments of society whose status is beneath their own. The rhetoric of status politics, however, rarely reflects this prejudice of respectability; instead, the in-group emphasizes some trait evinced by the out-group. For example, Gusfield's analysis of the Temperance Movement suggests that members of the Women's Christian Temperance League (WCTL) expressed their prejudice against Irish and Italian Catholic groups not by ethnic slurs, but by saying that alcohol was sinful and ruined families. Abstinence was made a symbol of "acceptable behavior," while drinking was defined as immoral; no self-respecting Protestant would ever imbibe. It was the Catholics' lifestyle which made them outcasts in Yankee eyes. The prejudicial attack was not direct; subtle status attitudes were based instead on a lifestyle characteristic.[22]

Private versus public school education is one manifestation of status in-group versus out-group sentiment. As we have seen in the previous chapter, the Metro public schools do a good job of teaching children. We believe that the real issue in private school enrollments is not educational quality, but subcultural values—social status values. Parents are willing to pay tuition for their children to see to it that their communal values are protected. Private education is part of a lifestyle which functions to support a system of social status with in-group and out-group loyalties. Private school attendance is a sign that one does indeed occupy the social position claimed.

Not many people in Nashville knew about the research summarized by Willis Hawley which pointed to the continuing successes of desegregation. Nor would many have agreed that their beliefs constituted a "new mythology." The community had not wanted desegregation through busing, and after a decade of experi-

22. Gusfield, *Symbolic Crusade.*

ence, most people were eager to pronounce it a failure. Accounts of busing failure were legion; personal stories told by friends and acquaintances carried more weight than scholarly reassurances.

Social science has established certain findings about school desegregation: (1) desegregation does not diminish white educational achievement, (2) it enhances black educational achievement and self-esteem, and (3) it improves race relations. We do not argue that those who hold opposite views are racially prejudiced. But to the extent that contrary attitudes are present, then busing has failed in terms of attitude or social change. If teachers are more supportive of busing's goals than are parents, and parents are more supportive than the general public, then the dynamic of social change underlying busing can be said to be working. If the members of the community most closely associated with busing are opposed to it and its goals, then we can conclude that it has failed.

The information gleaned from these surveys of the general public, parents, and teachers can lead only to very general conclusions about attitudes and their changing distributions. But after nine years of busing, it was difficult to see much change in public sentiment. Substantial majorities of the general public and the white parent samples opposed busing and said it did not help blacks and whites accept one another more fully. Substantial majorities of both groups preferred private over public education. Yet parents evaluated the public schools much more positively than did the public at large. White parents did not differ sharply from white teachers; only 12 percent of parents and 19 percent of teachers said busing had not hurt the achievement of either black or white children.

Busing in Nashville seems not to have brought about the hoped-for attitude change. School desegregation through busing has not yet, it seems, succeeded in engendering a more positive belief system in a great many people, especially those closest to the schools. To judge from the survey data, the prevailing sentiment in Nashville indicates that, as measured by the attitude change expected to follow from its implementation, busing has failed.

This conclusion may be premature, however. The data may be too crude and their time-frame too short to yield reliable judgments. More important, perhaps, the data in the surveys was not broken out by actual experience with busing. Only the teachers survey retrieved information which allowed us to compare teachers in court-ordered schools with those in the non-bused sector of the county.

The profile of community beliefs sketched in this chapter only began to describe the real situation. The great mass of public sentiment lay beyond the reach of surveys. Still, at the end of the 1970s the crisis of confidence in public education had reached significant proportions. The quest for new directions took on a new urgency. In the first years of the 1980s, local citizens would turn down a Metro tax increase to fund the public schools, approve a referendum establishing an elected (rather than appointed) school board, and push for a resolution to a pending desegregation suit. These events are explored in the next section.

Part III

Like any redistributive policy, busing was controversial. But perhaps it was doubly so because it sought to redistribute both class and status benefits within an institution that bridged the societal and communal aspects of people's lives. Most white people said they accepted the abstract ideal of racial equality, but the concrete reality of busing threatened their values and their expectations for their children. A primitive calculus of fear dictated individual and collective responses. For parents who felt secure about their children's ultimate success in the social and intellectual hierarchies of desegregated schools, busing was an opportunity to demonstrate without real loss their commitment to the goal of racial equality. For other less secure white parents, busing was seen as a real threat to their own and their children's relative standing in the community. If parents feared that their children would suffer a loss of educational achievement or social status, then to remove them from the public schools was an obvious step.

Our public opinion surveys showed that Nashville whites believed that busing hurt the educational achievement of children. Yet studies of achievement test scores, both locally and nationally, indicated that busing did not lessen academic achievement among whites. In fact, some of the schools with the greatest white flight from busing had test scores among the highest in Nashville. Despite the rhetoric about busing's impact on academic achievement, the patterns of white flight in Nashville suggested that the racial composition of the school, and of the neighborhood around the school, were the most telling indicators of fear among whites. Whites fled black area schools as much as black children. In this way they signaled their disapproval of the black community and its culture. Many white parents did not want to be seen—by themselves or by others, including their children—as acquiescing in cultural values manifested by the black community as they viewed it. The accumulated data suggest that many whites felt that their lifestyle and the values it subsumed were put at risk by busing.

Busing for racial balance was an assimilationist policy. Black children were to be brought from their isolated position of socio-economic inferiority into the mainstream of American life. But this plan could work only if the dominant culture and its institutions actually absorbed blacks. And assimilation was resisted by white and black reactions to busing. To the extent that whites fled the schools, assimilation—and the redistribution of class and status benefits it promised—would not take place. As private schools clearly became new elite domains within the educational status hierarchy, the elusive equality sought by blacks and by the courts for blacks became ever more remote. Blacks could achieve equality only relative to the whites who remained in the public schools.

Busing held out a great promise. Schools would no longer be "black" or "white" but instead "ours." Everyone would share equally in the community's educational resources. The educational gap between blacks and whites would be erased along with racial stigma. For a great many black children, the reality came close to the promise. But for many black leaders, busing and its attendant assimilation ideal were a one-way street. Busing for racial balance was yet another form of white cultural hegemony; blacks were being forced to give up more than they got. Busing was more of a burden than an opportunity.

The busing plan in Nashville closed many schools in black neighborhoods. Black children were bused into white areas for the first four years of school, and the junior high and senior high schools were largely in white areas. Black children were to be forever in the racial minority even in the few schools which remained in the black neighborhoods. And the gap between black and white achievement remained after years of busing. Schools were dominated by whites and their white culture—that was what assimilation meant, and that was what busing promoted. Many articulate black spokesmen felt that the black community had sacrificed its communal institution, the neighborhood school, and they regretted the loss. Busing, as defined in the 1971 plan, they said, was paternalistic, unfair, even racist.

In Part III the conflict of subcultural values emerges at center stage. As we shall see, black leaders increasingly came to reject the assimilationist assumptions of busing and to insist on a multi-cultural approach which would raise the black culture and its symbols to equality with others in a multi-cultural society. Among whites, conflict sharpened between those who insisted on reaching for the promises of assimilation and those who were willing to legitimize the separatist impulses within both races.

CHAPTER NINE

Blacks Against the Plan

" A s a minister, and as a theologian, I believe God has created us all to live together as brothers," said the Reverend Amos Jones in late 1979. "But really, I think this [countywide busing] would not benefit us." The scene was a familiar one, a black minister invoking the civil rights mantle of brotherhood to comment on black-white relations. What was new was Jones' conclusion: "I think it would exacerbate the situation even more if our children had to populate [white] schools. . . . That would further reduce the population in the schools for which we are concerned. I think it would not be to our advantage." Jones was turning away from the integration ethic born in the civil rights crusade. He was stating a new position, one which came to dominate the Nashville school debate.

In the late 1960s the Kerner Commission had ominously concluded that America was in danger of developing into two cultures— one black and one white—that would be endlessly at war. The national experiment of busing children can be seen as an attempt to heal this enduring division. If black and white children could attend the same schools, perhaps then, in the next generation, the two cultures would have merged into one, color-blind and consensual.

Nashville was one of the first cities to experience busing for desegregation, and many in the white community protested its coming. Either they did not share the great vision, or they feared that their children would suffer in the experiment. But protest against busing was not limited to the white community. Blacks, too, attacked the plan and its implementation. The Reverend Mr. Jones aptly summarized their sentiments. " . . . the trend since the 1971 desegregation order has been to discontinue, dismantle, and destroy schools in black neighborhoods and use black children to integrate schools in white neighborhoods."[1]

Busing placed a burden on black children and on the black community. Black Nashvillians were no longer interested in having access to formerly white schools; their new concern was with securing

1. *Tennessean*, Dec. 5, 1979.

the future of black ones. Now busing's quest moved from equality of services to equality of cultures and their symbols. More and more, blacks felt that busing called upon them to sacrifice their children to the majority white culture and its institutions. The historic struggle for civil rights and equal educational opportunity was not to end in a color blind application of law, but in a color-conscious protection of black schools.

The next three chapters show the chain of events which culminated in the district court's decision to abandon busing. These chapters trace the emerging alliance of North Nashville blacks and suburban whites. Both groups argued for neighborhood schools and limited busing; though they were culturally antagonistic they made common cause with one another. Before this story can be told, two actors in the drama whose decisions would shape the course of education in Nashville must be introduced.

In fall 1980 a joke about Avon Williams, longtime attorney for black desegregation case plaintiffs, made the rounds of Nashville's white civic clubs. It seems that attorney Williams died and went to heaven. But Saint Peter said there was no more room in heaven and sent Williams to the other place. When he arrived in Hades, the Devil told Williams that it was full. To resolve this situation, the Devil and Saint Peter held a conference and decided "to bus Avon Williams back and forth between heaven and hell for eternity."

Nothing grated on the white sensibility as much as the persistent militancy of Avon Nyanza Williams, Jr. It was "Avon" who argued for busing and at the same time enrolled his children in the private Nashville University School. To some he was a selfish hypocrite who cared only for the half-million-dollar legal fee he was sure to collect from the school board when the Metro desegregation case was settled. To others he was a modern champion of social justice. To all he was a man to be reckoned with.

Williams was born on the freezing cold morning of December 22, 1921. He was educated in the Knoxville public schools and graduated in 1940 from Johnson C. Smith University in Charlotte, North Carolina. Seven years later he received an LL.B. degree from Boston University School of Law, then took an LL.M. degree one year after that. He returned to Knoxville and was admitted to the Tennessee Bar in April 1948. Five years later he moved his practice to Nashville, where he was associated with Z. Alexander Looby. He entered the *Kelley v. Metropolitan School Board* case in August 1955, almost 24 years before Judge Wiseman reopened the case.

Thomas A. Wiseman, Jr., elevated to the federal bench on August 25, 1978, became the fifth federal judge since 1955 to hear the *Kelley* case. Wiseman had been educated in the public schools of his home town, Tullahoma, Tennessee, and received his undergraduate and legal education at Vanderbilt University. Two aspects of Wiseman's background became especially important as the case unfolded. First, Judge Wiseman had had children in Nashville's public schools during the implementation of the 1971 busing decree and so had personally witnessed the struggle to make busing work. Second, Wiseman was accustomed to political compromise, having been active in the Democratic party and in state government. He had served as state treasurer and state representative before failing in a 1974 bid for the Democratic gubernatorial nomination. As a public figure, Wiseman was a liberal Democrat in the tradition of former U.S. Senators Estes Kefauver and Albert Gore, Sr. The success of public education in Nashville and a resolution of the issues raised in the desegregation process were among Judge Wiseman's top priorities when he became federal judge.

The Long Range Plan

During the 1971–72 school year, the Metropolitan Nashville-Davidson County Board of Education (the school board) and the senior staff of the Metro school system were completely preoccupied with implementing the busing plan. But as soon as it was possible, they turned their attention to the development of a long-range plan for the school system. The requirements of the 1971 court order, demographic projections, and the recommendations of the Building and School Improvement Study (BASIS) conditioned their thinking.

BASIS, with its comprehensive high school concept, was developed by the board as a long-range planning document for the public schools of Davidson County. The plan was developed in phases and was to be implemented in phases. The board had a successful comprehensive high school model in McGavock High School, which opened in 1971. The plan called for immediate expansion of Stratford, Glencliff, Overton, Hillsboro, and Hillwood High Schools into comprehensive status. Whites Creek Comprehensive High School was to be constructed as a new facility in the northwestern sector of the county. This new school had been approved by the district court in its 1971 order. Maplewood High School would be expanded later. The court would have to approve the construction of a new Madison-Goodlettsville High School and the expansion of Bellevue, Antioch, and Dupont High Schools because they lay in areas of the county where the 1971 order had forbidden construction. There would be twelve comprehensive high schools in all; seven of them could be functioning in the 1978–79 school year. Each would be desegregated; the percentage black would range from 16 to 43 percent. Seven traditional high schools would be closed: in the city itself, Cohn, East, North, and Pearl; in the suburbs, Goodlettsville, Madison, and Joelton. Hume-Fogg, an established and strictly vocational open-zone high school, would continue. Table 42 shows the high school plan developed by the board.

The plans for the comprehensive high schools were largely completed by 1974, and construction on most of the additions began in 1976. Planning for elementary and junior high schools had to wait until the geographical zoning plan for the comprehensive high schools was settled.

In November 1976 the Metro staff issued two alternative plans for the lower grades which were congruent with its recommended high school zoning plan. The two elementary plans were very different. Plan A was based on a county-wide desegregation concept; it called for extensive zone changes and the inclusion of schools hitherto excluded from busing for desegregation. Plan B continued the division of the county into bused and non-bused sectors and projected more limited changes in attendance zones. In both plans ten to twelve elementary schools were to be closed; those scheduled for closure in the two plans differed, but in both plans most were in the inner city and inner suburbs. Both plans continued to use clustering of schools as the principal mechanism for desegregation; in Grades

Table 42: *1976 Secondary Education Plan*

| | STATUS | CAPACITY | PROJECTED ENROLLM | |
			TOTAL	(% BLA
McGavock	In Place	2900	2870	(19.9
Whites Creek	New-Under Construction	2000	2086	(33.4
Stratford	Expansion Underway	1600	1814	(23.4
Glencliff	Expansion Underway	2000	1891	(20.4
Overton	Expansion Underway	2000	1695	(23.3
Hillsboro	Expansion Underway	1600	1574	(43.3
Hillwood	Expansion Underway	1800	1950	(25.5
Maplewood	Expansion Planned	—	1958	(37.7
Bellevue	Expansion Required	1225	1507	(30.6
Goodlettsville–Madison	New Facility To be Constructed	2500	—	(25.8
DuPont	Expansion Required	850	1879	(16.0
Antioch	Expansion Required	1100	1859	(16.3

Note: Hume-Fogg School would continue as a special vocational facility. Seven traditional h schools would be closed: Cohn, East, North, and Pearl in the city, and Goodlettsville, Madi and Joelton in the suburbs.

1–4 blacks would be bused out, and in Grades 5–6 whites would be bused in. Both plans tried to improve "pupil articulation." Too often in the 1971 plan, students who began school together in Grade 1 would be split up as they progressed through the grades; friendship patterns were broken. Under both proposed plans, but especially in Plan A, most children would stay together in Grades 1–12.

The high school plan and the two elementary school plans were developed without much systematic input from the community. Most citizens active in school affairs were consumed during these years with the demands put upon children and teachers by the massive changes resulting from the implementation of the 1971 busing plan. But when the plans were made public in November 1976, community reaction was intense, immediate, and parochial.

Citizens Advisory Committees (CACs) had been established in each school in 1971 to serve as a forum and communications conduit for the individual school and for the system as a whole. The CACs held meetings to discuss the alternative plans, and later the board heard from CAC chairmen and other citizens.

During winter 1976–77 groups of parents and teachers appealed and agitated for their special interests. The patrons of schools scheduled for closing were particularly active; they sought to counter the claims of others and to cannibalize adjacent school zones in a vain attempt to stay open.

In the public generally, there were three main types of sentiment. First, people who lived in the non-court-ordered area argued in favor of Plan B because it continued to exempt their children from busing. Second, among the inner suburbs white parents favored Plan A. These people, and especially their leaders who represented the liberal professional sector of the community, argued that the whole county should bear the burden of busing. They were especially alarmed by Plan B because it encouraged continued white flight from their schools. They wanted Plan A adopted in order to recapture those who had fled to the more distant suburbs. Third, leaders of the black community saw the two plans in a different light. For them the burden of busing still fell disproportionately on black children and the black community. Their small children were to be bused out of their neighborhoods, and Pearl High School was to be closed.

Pearl High School

The focal point of black frustrations was the proposed closing of Pearl High School. Pearl was the last high school in the black com-

munity and had tremendous symbolic value. It had been designed by
a black architect and built by black contractors during the "separate-
but-equal" period. Black leaders argued that closing Pearl would rip
the heart out of the North Nashville community.

Under the board's plan Pearl-area students were to be included in
the Hillsboro and Hillwood Comprehensive High Schools. Hillsboro
and Hillwood were located in middle-class white areas of the southwestern section of the county. Both schools had been expanded from
traditional to comprehensive programs. Each came equipped with
large vocational wings to house about twenty additional programs.

Before the busing decree, Pearl had had over 1,200 students, all
black, in Grades 10–12. The 1971 desegregation plan projected that
565 blacks (38 percent) and 908 whites (62 percent) would make up
the student body in a newly drawn school zone. When the plan was
implemented, however, only 350 whites attended. Seventy-one percent of the white students assigned to Pearl had fled. White families
put their children in private schools, moved from the new Pearl zone,
or transferred to another school. From 1971–72 on, the proportion of
white students at Pearl continued to decrease. In 1976–77 whites
made up only 25 percent of Pearl's population.[2]

The longrange plan called for Pearl to be closed, and Hillsboro and
Hillwood would be ready to accept the Pearl students in fall 1978. The
issue of Pearl High School's fate came to a head in fall and winter
1977. The Board of Education met to discuss closing Pearl, and black
community leaders and black board members rose to protest its
impending demise. Why, black leaders asked, should their school be
closed? It was central to the life of the black community. It had
trained the emerging leaders of the black community for decades.
Why couldn't Pearl be made into a comprehensive school?

On the other side, board and administrative staff members recited
the facts as they saw them. The longrange plan and the court had
approved comprehensive educational facilities along Briley Parkway,
not downtown. The building had been constructed in 1936 on just six
acres of land near the L&N Railroad. There wasn't enough land to
meet the ten-acre state requirement for a comprehensive school. The
programs black children needed were at Hillsboro and Hillwood. In
any case, it was too late; additions to Hillsboro and Hillwood were
almost complete and had been designed to take in the Pearl students.
Besides, they argued, white students could be attracted back to the
public schools, if they were not zoned to Pearl.

2. Metropolitan Board of Education, "Ten Year Analysis of Enrollment Patterns"
(Nov. 1979, mimeographed).

The debate was emotionally loaded on both sides. In the end, the board decided not to close Pearl. It could continue as it was. That year, 1977–78, there were 492 blacks and 100 whites enrolled at Pearl. That year, too, there was a significant increase in white requests to transfer. In anticipation of the completion of the Hillsboro and Hillwood projects, eighty-five whites zoned to Pearl were given transfers, almost all on a "subject matter" basis. The following year, 1978–79, there were only twenty white students left at Pearl.

White students transferring from Pearl were not avoiding desegregated schools; both Hillwood and Hillsboro were desegregated institutions (about 30 percent black). But were these white students *escaping from a majority black school in a black community,* or were they truly *seeking educational programs not available at Pearl?* The answer to this question became a central issue in the court hearings of July and August 1979.

Student Transfer Policy

Back in August 1971, just before the busing plan was first to take effect, the school board had established a student transfer policy.[3] Under the board's policy, there were several categories of justifiable requests to transfer at the high school level. Serious emotional or medical problems, if documented by professionals, were acceptable reasons, as was the imminent relocation of the family. There was one category, however, which had greater potential for abuse; this was the "subject matter" transfer. If a course (or program) was not available at the assigned school, a transfer could be obtained to a school having the course and available space. Transfers had to be approved by the principal of the sending and receiving schools and by a transfer committee.

White students sought to transfer from Pearl right from the beginning. Between the 1971–72 and 1977–78 academic years, 390 white students sought transfers. Eighty percent of these requests were granted. Of those, almost eighty percent were subject matter transfers.[4] Since very few black students sought transfers, the effect of the transfer policy was to diminish the proportion of white students at Pearl.

The ease with which white students secured transfers from Pearl was particularly galling to black community leaders. They saw in this

3. Section IV(F)(4), Student Transfer Policy #5119.
4. Exhibit #92, Detailed Summary of Pearl-Related Transfer Requests.

a willingness on the part of school officials to undermine the school, the black community, and desegregation. Pearl would be a stable desegregated school if programs designed to meet the needs of all students were established there, they argued.

In 1978, when the board decided not to close Pearl and other traditional high schools, it still felt strongly that students who wished should be able to attend comprehensive high schools, and Subject matter transfers to a comprehensive high school were retained. Later, the board decided to modify its student transfer policy. Section IV (G) (2) which laid out the grounds for subject matter transfers, was amended in March 1979, to say that "students assigned to a non-comprehensive high school have the right to attend their appropriate optional comprehensive high schools." The board felt justified in its action, based on the logic of its longrange plan, the increased number of student requests to transfer, and a state law which mandated transfer from traditional high schools to high schools with vocational programs funded by state money.

Emerging Conflict and Paralysis

The debate in 1977–78 over the fate of Pearl presaged the struggle which ultimately led to court action in 1979 and to a new desegregation plan in 1980.

In 1971 whites had resisted busing under the slogan, "Preserve our Neighborhood School." Now, blacks took up the cry. In doing so, they energized communal sentiment in Bellevue, Cohn, and Joelton— other communities where traditional high schools were to be closed under the board's plan. In both North Nashville and outlying communities, the claims were the same: our school has a good educational program; it has tremendous support from teachers, students, and parents; it is the heart of our community. We don't mind desegregation, people would argue, but let "them" come to us.

A common unstated theme underlay the public argument. "This is our turf. Our values and traditions shall prevail. . . . Let them pay homage to us." Instrumental values and the rational calculations implicit in the board's plans and policies were subordinated to cultural symbolism. This conclusion was inescapable. Even when black students at Pearl had the option of attending Hillsboro and Hillwood comprehensive high schools, with their magnificent vocational programs so needed by black students, fewer than 5 percent of Pearl's native children were lured away. Communal loyalty proved as strong among blacks as among whites.

Early in 1978 the board found itself caught between instrumental
and subcultural values. For sound reasons it had favored comprehensive high schools and initiated a longrange construction program
based on educational programs and demographic trends. It had developed new zoning plans and submitted them to the community for
discussion. But though it had done all these things, no consensus had
emerged. The community was divided, and black spokesmen were
especially angry. Faced with this conflict, the board decided to table
its rezoning plans and instead adopted a limited interim rezoning
plan for the 1978–79 school year, in anticipation of the opening of the
new Whites Creek Comprehensive High School and the vocational
wings of five other high schools. In the interim plan the traditional
high schools which had been scheduled to close—most notably,
Pearl—were permitted to remain open.

The board capitulated in the face of the community's factionalism
and of its own uncertainty and internal division. But the issues raised
by the board in its construction and rezoning plans had not been
resolved, only postponed. The court would once again step in to shape
the future of Nashville's public schools.

The issues which brought Metro schools into court in 1979 actually had their origins in the 1971 busing plan and the court order
establishing it as much as in the board's subsequent construction and
rezoning plans. It was the HEW busing plan and the court order itself
which had determined how the costs of busing would be shared. Since
the ultimate goal had been to integrate blacks into white society, the
plan had established that blacks would be in a minority in each
school, commensurate with their proportion in the county's general
population. To achieve this proportion, black students were bused
out of their neighborhoods more than whites were bused out of theirs.
At the lower grades whites stayed in their neighborhoods four of the
first six years and blacks only two. The court had accepted Briley
Parkway (extended) as the appropriate location for comprehensive
high schools. This ruling had encouraged the board to close inner city
high schools, robbing the black community of services and symbols.
Moreover, the 1971 court order had left a large suburban sector of the
county outside the area of the busing plan; thus, the court had
encouraged white flight.

Court Proceedings

Judge Gray, of the Fifth District Court, took over the Nashville
desegregation case in August 1971; it lay before his court until his

retirement due to serious illness in 1978. During the years when the case was before him, Judge Gray took no action on various petitions made by both the defendant and the plaintiffs in the case. In August 1978, following appointment of Thomas Wiseman to the federal bench, the plaintiffs petitioned the court for relief, and the judge agreed to reopen *Kelley et al. v. Metropolitan County Board of Education*. The plaintiffs alleged that construction and expansion of schools in predominantly white areas, the closure of formerly black schools in the inner city, the institution of the optional transfer policy, and the failure of defendants to increase black-white faculty ratios were violations of the 1971 order.[5]

Judge Wisemen held pretrial conferences with the parties to the case in spring 1979, at which time he divided the case into four phases:

Phase 1: Historical recapitulation of school integration since 1971; construction requests by the Metro Board of Education.

Phase 2: Consideration of matters related to the racial mix of staff and faculty.

Phase 3: Consideration of petitions for contempt.

Phase 4: The matter of attorneys' fees.

Phase One of the hearings began on June 26, 1979, and continued through July 6. Step by step school officials justified their actions and plans. They testified that the comprehensive high school concept had been adopted by the board before 1971, and in the 1971 court order the court had explicitly recognized the intent to build comprehensive high schools. That court order, they said, had indicated that comprehensive high schools should be located along Briley Parkway between the white and black populations. The order had also accepted the board's plan to build Whites Creek High School in northwestern Davidson County. The board, the officials said, had asked the court in 1973 and again in 1976 to approve its construction program, including the expansion of Hillsboro, Hillwood, Bellevue, Glencliff, Stratford and Maplewood High Schools. The board had proceeded to build its comprehensive high schools when the court failed to act. It had felt justified in doing so, they said, because the 1971 court order did not proscribe building additional facilities in the area in which busing was in force. Moreover, the comprehensive high schools were educationally sound and fully desegregated. The board proposed building a new comprehensive high school to serve Madison and Goodlettsville in the northeast quadrant of the county. Since this was

5. Motions summarized in Court's Memorandum Opinion of Aug. 27, 1979.

in the area where the 1971 court order forbade new facilities, the board now requested court approval of its plan.

At the elementary and junior high school levels, the school officials pointed out, there had been a few minor changes, but the 1971 plan was basically still in place. The plan, however, was now inadequate, they argued. Migration of population from inner suburbs to outlying areas of the county had led to marked overcrowding in schools outside the 1971 bused area, and new classrooms were needed in these sections. Migration, coupled with a declining birth rate, had left many of the schools within the bused area underpopulated. As many as ten elementary schools needed to be closed, they said, and they sought the court's permission to close them. Moreover, the desegregation of schools within the court-ordered area was problematic. The 1971 plan set out a range of 15 to 35 percent minority in each school, but that range was no longer applicable. Many schools within the desegregation area were now over 50 percent black. Zone changes were necessary to reestablish a range around 32 percent black, the current minority proportion in the system.

A general theme emerged from the testimony of school officials: the board had complied faithfully with the 1971 court order; the comprehensive high schools were designed to provide a fuller range of programs for students and to be fully desegregated; demographic changes beyond the board's control made adjustments to the 1971 plan necessary.

In cross-examination of school officials and in presenting his own witnesses, Avon Williams, counsel for the plaintiffs, sought to portray the board's actions and plans, as well as parts of the 1971 court order itself, as violations of the Constitution because they retained vestiges of the forbidden dual school system.

Williams attacked the board's longrange plan. His main contention was that the board's actions had systematically undercut schools in the black community. He forced school officials to make damaging admissions. The high schools expanded to comprehensive status were all in the white community, as was the school planned for the Madison-Goodlettsville area, while schools in the black community had been closed (e.g. North) or were scheduled to be closed (e.g. Pearl). If Pearl, Cohn, and East were closed as planned, there would be no high school in or near the black community. Black children, already bused out of their neighborhoods for four of the first six grades, were now to be bused out all of their remaining years, if the board's plan were accepted. There was no reason for schools in the black community to stand empty, Williams reasoned. The obvious solution, according to the plaintiffs' line of argument, was to maintain and reopen schools in the black community and to bus more whites in.

To strengthen his overall argument, Williams needed to show clear-cut, intentional action by the board which discriminated against the minority race. He believed such discrimination was evident in the board's student transfer policy, which permitted what appeared to be automatic transfers from Pearl. If white students transferred from Pearl because they sought educational programs at other schools, then the board's failure to establish those programs at Pearl was *prima facie* evidence of discriminatory conduct. On the other hand, if white students transferred from Pearl for racial reasons, the board's failure to stop them was a violation of the 1971 court order. In either case, the board, by its failure to act, had encouraged resegregation of Pearl.

Williams pointed to enrollment trends at Pearl and the relationship of the transfer process to the school's resegregation[6] (see Tables 43 and 44). Williams noted that from school year 1971–72 through 1977–78 the board's transfer policy required a review of each student's request to determine its legitimacy. During those years there had been a steadily increasing number of requests to transfer from Pearl, almost all from white students on the basis of subject matter, and most had been approved.

Williams maintained that these subject matter transfers simply showed that the board had not provided adequate programs at Pearl. The board's discriminatory posture had led to resegregation.

Table 43: *Racial Composition of Pearl High School*

	BLACK STUDENTS	% BLACK	WHITE STUDENTS	TOTAL STUDENTS
1970–71	1212	(100.0)	0	1212
1971–72	499	(62.9)	353	952
1972–73	603	(66.4)	305	908
1973–74	594	(68.4)	274	868
1974–75	558	(74.7)	188	746
1975–76	551	(72.5)	208	759
1976–77	551	(75.8)	175	726
1977–78	492	(83.1)	100	592
1978–79	*577	(96.6)	20	597
Projection				
1979–80	532	(96.6)	19	551

*9th Grade Added
Source: Exhibit #87

6. Exhibits #87 and #92.

Table 44: *Transfer Requests of White Students from Pearl High School*

	APPROVED	DENIED	% APPROVED
1971–72	18	8	69
1972–73	11	3	79
1973–74	22	2	92
1974–75	32	3	94
1975–76	37	13	74
1976–77	45	5	90
1977–78	85	2	98

Source: Exhibit #92

Williams also focused on Pearl's enrollment after Hillsboro and Hillwood had opened as comprehensive high schools in 1978. In academic year 1977–78, Williams said, there were one hundred whites at Pearl. The two following years there were only twenty. Pearl had become 96.6 percent black. White students had transferred to the comprehensive high schools in overwhelming numbers. By building comprehensive facilities at Hillsboro and Hillwood and by adopting a virtually automatic transfer policy, the board had resegregated Pearl. This was clear evidence of racially discriminatory conduct by the board, Williams concluded.

Judge Wiseman was moved by Williams' argument. On July 2, he enjoined the board from further implementation of the optional transfer policy. Students who had used the optional transfer provision were to be reassigned to their former schools. The transfer problem was thus moved out of court for a time, but the issue would return and dominate the court proceedings in August.

Having dealt with the transfer policy, the court focused on the large question of what, in light of the board's longrange plan and the shifting demographic patterns, to do about revising the 1971 plan.

In comments and questions from the bench, Judge Wiseman signalled his thoughts. He seemed supportive of Avon Williams' line of argument, remarking, "The question that is occurring to this court is whether or not . . . the school board should build additional buildings to accommodate that white flight in the suburban areas, or bring those children into existing adequate school buildings that you now have."[7]

When school officials suggested that busing white children back into town might simply stimulate another wave of flight and further

7. Excerpts, Transcript of Proceedings, U.S. District Court, July 3, 1979.

erode support for the schools, Judge Wiseman made it clear that he was not going to let public sentiment affect his ruling and that he was not interested in why people moved where they did. Wiseman was, however, interested in a cost-benefit approach: "I am convinced Davidson County is made up of law abiding citizens. I think the experience in 1971 has proven that. Let's talk about what is feasible from a transportation standpoint, economical standpoint, from a utilization of existing buildings standpoint, and not try to psychoanalyze the population of Nashville as to whether or not they will or will not support that or abide by the Court's Order."[8]

True to the views expressed from the bench during the hearings, Judge Wiseman made two findings of fact at the close of August. First, the perimeter line of busing drawn by the court in 1971 had encouraged white flight to the suburbs. As a result, inner city schools were becoming progressively resegregated; the projected ideal ratio of 15 to 35 percent black population in each school was becoming increasingly difficult to meet; and school facilities outside the court-ordered perimeter were becoming increasingly inadequate to accomodate their growing student bodies. Secondly, the resegregation, resulting from the good faith efforts of the school board to implement the court order, amounted to *de jure* segregation.

Since the court order had been guilty of stimulating resegregation, Judge Wiseman felt compelled to reexamine the remedy fashioned in 1971. Accordingly, he directed the board to reconsider its entire plan. In doing so, the board was to assume no parameters earlier established by the court in the Nashville case, but was to seek simply to achieve a unitary school system for the *whole* of Davidson County. In developing the plan the board was "to consider the maximum utilization of existing buildings (specifically those in the inner city); economic factors of transportation; and any other factors which would impact upon the ultimate objective of a quality educational opportunity for all the children in Davidson County through a unitary school system."

The court was advised that compliance with the order would take a considerable length of time, and in fact it took the entire fall of 1979. The results were not seen until new hearings in spring 1980. These hearings were to replay the same issues with more elaborate evidence and were to end in a remarkably new desegregation plan.

At the end of the hearings, Judge Wiseman had come close to finding the board in full compliance with the 1971 court order. But, Wiseman said, the 1971 order itself had been flawed. The order and

8. Ibid.

the board's implementation of the order constituted a *de jure* violation. Wiseman justified the court's continuing interest in the case by
citing a passage from the Supreme Court's 1968 decision in *Greene v.
School Bd. of New Kent County*, (1968).:

> The obligation of the district courts, as it always has been, is to assess the
> effectiveness of a proposed plan in achieving desegregation. There is no
> universal answer to complex problems of desegregation; there is obviously
> no one plan that will do the job in every case. The matter must be assessed
> in light of the circumstances present and the options available in each
> instance . . . Moreover, whatever plan is adopted will require evaluation in
> practice, and the court should retain jurisdiction until it is clear that state-
> imposed segregation has been completely removed.

The school board had not escaped unscathed from Wiseman's
court. His patience and goodwill had been sorely tested by the issue of
student transfers from Pearl.

Transfers and White Flight

From the moment the judge enjoined use of the optional transfer
policy in July 1979 until the hearings resumed in late August, school
officials were preoccupied with the question of what to do with the
862 students who had transferred from traditional high schools under
the optional transfer policy.

At the school board's first meeting after the July hearings, it rescinded the optional transfer policy. Director of Education Dr. Elbert
Brooks summarized the effect by saying that "students who had
made these automatic transfers would be reassigned to their original
zoned school but would be permitted to request a transfer in order to
take a particular program or subject not offered at the students'
assigned school." He was asserting that the subject matter transfer
policy established by the board in 1971 would continue in effect
despite the end of the optional transfer provision. Dr. Brooks created a
transfer committee to review the anticipated applications and sent
letters to the students affected by the change.

Within two weeks three hundred subject matter transfer requests
were made by white students newly reassigned to Pearl. This fact did
not escape the eye of Avon Williams. When the hearings resumed in
August, the transfer of students from Pearl dominated the agenda. A
recent plaintiff motion for contempt was considered first. Williams
presented evidence to prove his claim that resegregation of Pearl
continued in spite of the court's injunction. At the time this informa-

tion was obtained, 326 whites had been granted new subject matter transfers and another 78 were pending approval. Williams maintained that the subject matter transfers recently granted had not been monitored adequately; a student would simply state that he or she wanted a course not found at Pearl, and no effort was made to determine if the request was educationally valid given the student's history and manifest interests.

The result of this process had been to take Pearl from racial balance back to a predominance of blacks.[9]

	Assigned to Pearl Zone	After Transfer	After Pending Transfers
White	532 (52%)	206 (30%)	128 (23%)
Other	36 (3%)	24 (4%)	20 (3%)
Black	461 (45%)	445 (66%)	428 (74%)

After the motion for contempt was filed in August, school officials became more thorough in trying to determine if a student's transfer request was genuine. They matched each student's preregistration course schedule with his subsequent subject matter transfer request. When the courses specified on the transfer request did not match the preregistration schedule, there was a *prima facie* indication that students had chosen courses in the August transfer request *only* because they were not offered at Pearl.

When this cross-check was made on August 16 in response to the contempt motion, the results showed that 266 (86 percent) of the 309 white students who had been granted transfers from Pearl were consistent or could not be shown to be inconsistent. However, 35 white students had obtained transfers in August despite the fact that the sending school had offered all of the courses they requested.

Avon Williams also faulted the board for not providing courses at Pearl which students had indicated they wanted to take at other schools. The board could prevent transfers if courses which over fifteen students requested could be established at Pearl. A preliminary survey of transfers from Pearl showed there were at least 38 requests for media arts, 34 for computer programming, and 22 for the vocational cluster.

Judge Wiseman scolded the director of education for the loose administration of the transfer policy following the July court order.

The Court finds that the school board policy for subject matter program transfers, although racially neutral on its face, by the manner in which it

9. Exhibit #98.

has been implemented and the inherent potential for abuse in its conceptualization, has a negative impact upon the desegregation efforts of the school board, and violates the spirit of the 1971 order, and the spirit of the order of this Court issued orally on July 2, 1979.[10]

Judge Wiseman did not, however, hold the board in contempt since the board had rescinded the optional transfer provision of its subject matter transfer policy. But the judge was not satisfied with the performance of school officials in this matter. He ordered the board to develop a set of procedures by which transfer applications could be judged to see if a change was valid for the educational objectives of the student or merely a subterfuge to escape a given school.

The board, Judge Wiseman ordered, had until September 7 to review all applications previously granted or pending. The review should include an interview with the student and his parents, as well as examination of the written recommendations of the sending and receiving principals and of the transfer committee. Appeals from a denial of transfer could be made to the director and the board.

During the next month the review process consumed hundreds of staff hours. System-wide, over 820 requests to transfer were acted upon by the transfer committee. In the end, 145 requests were denied, almost all from white students at Pearl.[11] Of the 123 Pearl students who were denied transfer, 96 appealed their denial to the director; he denied 62 of these. Of the 62 denied by the director, 34 appealed directly to the board. The board denied 19 of these. When the final tally was made, 74 Pearl students had been denied transfer, either because they had no educationally valid reason to take the course they said they wanted or because the course they had specified was now offered at Pearl. In an October 24 report to Dr. Brooks, school officials stated that only 17 of these 74 students were at Pearl. Some had moved; some had dropped out; some had gone to private schools. Others were simply not accounted for.[12]

School officials had found nine courses for which over fifteen white Pearl students had requested transfers. Some, such as Auto Body 1 and Data Processing, Pearl was not equipped to handle. For others no certified personnel were available.[13] Finally, though, the director established four of these courses at Pearl. As of October 23 only four

10. Memorandum of Opinion and Order, Aug. 25, 1979.

11. Memo to Dr. Brooks from Joseph Garritt re Transfer Request Summary, Oct. 4, 1979. Copy on file, Room 110 Metro Board of Education.

12. Memo to Dr. Brooks from Dr. Ed Binkley, re Summary of Pearl Zoned Students as of Oct. 24, 1979. Copy on file, Room 110 Metro Board of Education.

13. Memo to Lucille Nabors from Dr. Brooks, Aug. 25, 1979. Copy on file, Room 110 Metro Board of Education.

of the fifty-seven students who had requested these courses were then enrolled in them.[14]

The saga of student transfers from Pearl had ground to a close. In November 1979, there were sixty-eight whites at Pearl, up from twenty the previous year. Pearl remained 89 percent black. The review process had cost Metro $92,390.92 in salaries and supplies.

Conclusion

There had been an intense struggle over the school board's subject matter transfer policy because of its impact on one school—Pearl. Why did white students flee Pearl in such numbers and so persistently? Why did Avon Williams and the black community work so hard to keep the whites there? The answers to these questions shed light on the whole process of desegregation in Nashville.

Three reasons can be given for white students' flight from Pearl: (1) they truly wanted courses not available to them at Pearl, a traditional high school; (2) they did not want to be in a majority black school; or (3) there was something unique about Pearl to which they objected.

The data indicate that whites did not flee Pearl because of the exceptional attractiveness of comprehensive programs at Hillsboro or Hillwood. All but twenty of 356 white students zoned to Pearl took the automatic transfer to comprehensive high schools—a 94 percent transfer rate. From no other non-comprehensive high school was there anything approaching this rate of transfer. Only 22 percent of Joelton's white students transferred to Whites Creek Comprehensive High School, and less than 10 percent of the white students in other traditional high schools took advantage of the opportunity to transfer to comprehensive high schools. And in 1979, when courses were established at Pearl which white students had used as the basis of their transfer requests, only a few white students showed up.

It is unlikely that whites leaving Pearl were trying to escape black students. Desegregation of the school seems not to have been a factor in the flight from Pearl. When whites left Pearl, they moved to schools which were desegregated at rates approximating that of the general population: Glencliff, 30 percent black; Hillsboro, 33 percent; Hillwood, 29 percent; and Overton, 24 percent. This argument gains support from data in Table 45. Excluding Pearl, Cohn, and East, three city schools, all the whites who exercised their right to auto-

14. Memo to Lucille Nabors from Patty Harris, Oct. 25, 1979. Copy on file, Room 110 Board of Education.

Table 45: *1978–79 Optional Transfers*

	% BLACK IN SCHOOL	# OF WHITES TRANSFERING
From Pearl	83	
To Glencliff	30	34
To Hillsboro	33	35
To Hillwood	29	220
To Overton	24	1
From Cohn	32	
To Hillsboro	33	31
To Hillwood	29	35
From East	57	
To Stratford	31	10
From Goodlettsville	3	
To Whites Creek	57	68
From Madison	3	
To Whites Creek	57	46
To Maplewood	60	1
From Joelton	33	
To Whites Creek	57	149
From Antioch	3	
To Glencliff	30	62
From Apollo Jr. High	3	
To Glencliff	30	50
From Bellevue	12	
To Hillsboro	33	8
From DuPont	3	
To McGavock	23	37
From Neeleys Bend	5	
To Whites Creek	57	3
	Total	790

matic transfers in 1978–79 moved from schools with *lower* proportions black into schools with *higher* proportions black. Indeed, in the case of Joelton, Goodlettsville, and Madison, 263 students transferred into Whites Creek, a school that was majority black, leaving behind majority white institutions.

If Pearl whites were not rejecting black students and were not attracted to comprehensive education, what was the underlying cause of their discontent? It was the symbolic *blackness* of Pearl. Pearl stood in the black section of North Nashville, where historically it was lionized as the heart of the black community. Pearl was a symbol of the black culture for white students and parents as much as it was for blacks themselves. For whites, to go to Pearl was to acknowledge that black culture—its values, traditions, and institutions—was on a par with white culture. White students zoned to Pearl were mostly from middle- and upper-middle-class families, and for the white middle class, black cultural values were anathema. For them, Pearl, North Nashville, and the black culture together symbolized crime, violence, welfare, pregnancy, poverty, and antiwhite sentiment.

Why did the black community fight to keep Pearl open and viable? Because it was a symbol of the black heritage, community, and culture they were so proud of. If Pearl closed, it would mean the hegemony of white culture over black. White flight from Pearl, as from other schools in the inner city, was a continuing insult to black people; it was a reminder of white rejection of their institutions and their neighborhoods. The insult could be removed only when white people, and especially the school board, acknowledged the essential parity of black and white cultures.

For the leaders of the black community, the 1971 court order and the school board's longrange plan were predicated on a faulty and threatening notion—that blacks should be integrated into the white culture. For these leaders the struggle for racial equality had the goal of maintaining black pride, black institutions, and black culture in the face of this policy. They worked now to attain parity with the white culture, not to be submerged in it. As one black leader in 1980 put it, "Why give white children the concept that what's good is only good in their part of town?"[15]

15. DeLois Wilkinson, quoted in the *Banner*, Jan. 29, 1980.

CHAPTER TEN

The Burden of Busing

// **Y**ou are talking about experimenting with blacks like people experiment with animals," exclaimed school board member DeLois Wilkinson when shown yet another version of the Nashville desegregation plan. "It is imperative that we do not put the burden of the new plan on the inner city. . . ."[1] The question of "burden," or who should bear the costs of the integration of a racially separated society, had long been a central issue in the busing debate. In the early 1980s Nashville had to face this question yet again.

The massive withdrawal of white students from Pearl High School dominated the court's hearings during the dog days of July and August 1979. JudgeWiseman scolded the board for permitting the transfer of whites, and his bench order required school administrators to spend hundreds of hours reasessing the students' reasons for wanting to transfer. But though the transfer issue captured the headlines, the real problem was the original 1971 plan. The board believed that the plan was outdated and counterproductive. The black plaintiffs argued that it continued an historical abuse. So, on August 27, 1979, Judge Wiseman ordered the Metro School Board to "reconsider the entire plan, assuming no parameters heretofore ordered by the Court, but with the primary objective of the achievement of a unitary school system for the entirety of Davidson County."

There it was: Develop a new plan for the whole county. For many black leaders this was an opportunity to redress the inequities of busing, but a new plan was also potentially a threat. It could lead to still greater injustice. Whites similarly saw an opportunity and a challenge. Those already involved in busing saw a new plan as a chance to recapture the whites who had fled to outlying areas of the county to escape busing, as well as to strengthen the quality of instruction in the county.

Whites in outlying areas were angry and afraid. Busing for racial balance would involve them; they were now its target. They feared the possible effect on the quality of their schools and their suburban

1. *Tennessean,* Jan. 13, 1980.

lifestyles. These reactions were not farfetched. Judge Wiseman issued a directive that listed specific factors to be considered in the planning process: "Maximum utilization of existing buildings (specifically those in the inner city); economic factors of transportation costs and fuel economy; time and distance involved in transportation; and many other factors which would impact upon the ultimate objective of a quality educational opportunity for all children in Davidson County through a unitary school system."[2]

The development of a new desegregation plan, he said, "is a subject upon which the best minds available to the parties, including input from many well-motivated, thoughtful citizens of the community, should be sought and received."

A tentative planning process was approved in an October meeting of the board. The new plan would be drafted in four phases. In accordance with the court order, Phase One would focus on input from citizens. In Phase Two the board would develop specific criteria on which the plan would be grounded. By mid-December Phase Three would begin, at which time various committees would devise alternative plans. In late January the board would receive the alternative plans and approve one of them. Events were to mold these four phases of the planning process into an uneven stream of decisions affecting the ultimate distribution of costs associated with busing.

Where parents congregated, whether in schools, local CAC meetings, hallways, or homes, the "burden" of busing became a prime topic of conversation. Since 1971 the three major constellations of common interest had developed informally and now could be discerned readily among activists. Each group meant something different by the term, "the burden of busing."

For many blacks, the busing burden fell disproportionately on black people. The 1971 plan transported their children out of downtown neighborhoods and into white suburbs; it closed many schools in black neighborhoods, and others were likely to be closed. At the same time, schools in white neighborhoods were expanding. Black spokesmen complained about the quality of education their children received when they were bused to "white" schools and focused on the need for neighborhood schools of their own.

In contrast, whites in outlying areas of the county, whether longtime residents or recent escapees from the bused sector, largely opposed busing for desegregation. They felt they would be in jeopardy if the 1971 busing plan were revised. More busing was a reproach for

2. Judge Thomas Wiseman, Jr., from the bench, Aug. 27, 1979. Copy on file, Room 110 Board of Education.

their decision to locate in suburban havens with homogeneous "neighborhood" schools.

The whites who had participated in busing felt that they had paid costs which should have fallen on all whites in the county equally. They particularly resented those who had fled to private schools or to the outlying section of Davidson County. Spokesmen for this group believed in desegregation of the schools and society, but they wanted it on their own terms. They wanted each school to be a microcosm of the whole community. In such circumstances the middle-class values of discipline, respect, and achievement would prevail. Lower-class blacks would learn those values just as surely as spelling. As whites fled from the schools involved in busing, those who remained had grown increasingly anxious. If the white middle class would only stay in the schools during busing, everything would work. Disadvantaged blacks would learn more and be socialized to middle-class values, white achievement levels would remain high, and racism would diminish. But if the white flight continued, those whites who remained would suffer. Their children would not have the safety of majority; middle-class values and consequent academic achievement would be overwhelmed by lower-class black culture. Middle-class whites seemed threatened by the prospect of black majorities in the schools. They needed a county-wide busing plan to protect themselves and their values.

These views did not surface immediately as clear-cut policy options; they emerged over time. At first each group embraced conflicting ideas; the ultimate preferences were sharpened and ordered by subsequent events. We began by outlining the convictions of these three groups. In the remainder of the chapter we will see how these clusters of conflicting ideas were reflected in the decisions of the school board.

Phase One: Citizen Input

The school board held public hearings in November 1979 to receive input from citizens. Each speaker was asked to submit a written statement which addressed ten major issues associated with busing.[3] The atmosphere at these public hearings was emotionally charged

---

3. The ten issues were: definition of a unitary school district, quality of education, grade structures for the system, geographic areas to be included, appropriate ratios for racial balance, the question of burden, cost, time and distance considerations, fuel, and utilization of space.

but civil. During breaks conversations erupted among all varieties of partisans, as each sought to advance his or her cause.

Relatively few blacks spoke before the board, but those who did represented important groups in the black community. On November 15 Leo Lillard read a revealing statement on behalf of the Nashville Citywide Neighborhood Coalition and the Pearl High School Community Education Council. Lillard's diagnosis of the racial problem was a familiar one: systematic white racism. But his proffered prescription was not more integration, but rather black control of black community schools, especially Pearl. "First we want it known that we are not opposed to any other parent group—so long as that group is not advocating . . . the further dismantling of schools in the African-American communities." Lillard, and presumably the groups he represented, wanted economic compensation and black cultural separatism. With such a request, blacks were not attacking whites in outlying areas of the county. Instead, they were opening the possibility of making common cause with them.

Lillard's second point reinforced the first. "To ask underpaid, under-budgeted, under-respected school faculty and parents to undo what the housing industry, banking enterprises, zoning boards, trade unions, corporate giants, judicial systems, etc., have done—and continue to do—is like asking me to fight a nuclear war with a napkin." Lillard articulated a sentiment common among the black leaders. For them, America was divided between the majority white culture, which had the power, and the minority black culture, which was its victim. Majority whites through their power elites kept blacks quiescent by dividing them, closing their schools, and denying them the institutional mechanisms necessary to redress this historical imbalance.

> I strongly urge the court that is ordering that we develop a unitary system to mandate that a unitary system be developed by/for mortgage companies, employment policies, police protection, insurance regulations, park services, judicial practices and zoning ordinances. The school system alone cannot create a unitary system with the "deck stacked" as it has been, is now, and may continue to be. But if the court is saying that the educational process over twelve (12) years should produce a citizenry that is dedicated and capable of attacking the originators of duality, then I think we must respond with creativity and determination to graduate agents of social change. However, I have a suspicion that is not what the power centers really expect.[4]

In the face of such injustices Lillard called for black separatism; in

---

4. Statement to Board of Education, Nov. 15, 1979. Copy on file, Room 110 Board of Education.

fact, the separatist theme was embedded in each of h
recommendations. His statement implied that black chil
emotionally abused and educationally neglected by biased
teachers. "The T.V. show 'White Shadow' with a white leader mir
the Metro decisions of who should be coaches, band directors, drama
teachers, and art directors." For this reason he recommended black
control for schools in the black community.

To create a nexus of school and community values, Lillard urged
the board to "give extra weight to the employment of a teacher
applicant who is asking for a school assignment in the zone in which
he or she lives." Lillard wanted institutionalized cross-cultural activities such as "Black History Week (not Brotherhood Week)" and
"to reopen closed public school buildings." Recommendation #17
was to upgrade and expand "Pearl High at its present campus into an
educational showcase, comprehensive high school, and community
service institution."

Lillard's statement contained other recommendations which,
taken alone, would not necessarily imply a conflict between the two
cultures. But the cumulative thrust of his comments was one inescapable contention—that black children would learn more if they
were both taught and socialized in the black community by black role
models. Black children and teachers alike needed active support
which could be found only in their own community.

Two other black groups submitted a joint statement. It was not as
argumentative as Lillard's, but its approach was similar. The Social
Action Committee of the Interdenominational Ministers' Fellowship
and the Education Committee of the North Nashville Community
Council recommended that Pearl High School be expanded through
the presence of a fine arts magnet program. The proposed racial ratio
was 75 percent black and 25 percent white. The school would have a
natural feeder pattern from other schools in the North Nashville
community, thus minimizing the need for busing.[5]

Surprisingly, the local NAACP did not offer much in the way of
commentary or recommendations for the new plan. Given that this
organization had been strongly pro-integration for decades, both nationally and locally, we may wonder if the new emphasis on cultural
dualism didn't cause internal division. In any case, Eileen Price,
chairman of the Education Committee of the NAACP, submitted a
statement to Dr. Brooks so that he could pass it to the board before it
was released to the press. The statement was noteworthy above all for
what it did not include.

5. Letter to Board of Education, Nov. 19, 1979. Copy on file, Room 110 Board of
Education.

,ue for opening more doors closed to blacks
ng for desegregation. It did not assert that
cially balanced. Instead, the NAACP paper
enhance black culture and self-esteem. It
personnel within the public school system be
an attitude adjustment education program for
more appropiate attitudes towards themselves
o boost self-esteem, the NAACP proposed that
ty students be provided a self-image and human
The importance of role models was stressed, and
the board to reduce the number of white teach-
ers in preau.... y black school populations and/or to increase the
number of black teachers in predominantly white school populations. Finally and most importantly, the NAACP called for the development of a "home education program" for preschoolers and first
graders; "because of the great hardship that busing imposes on this
age group we feel that this approach can immediately compensate for
the initial trauma and loss of identity perspective."[6]

Without saying so explicitly, the black leadership of Nashville was
in the process of abandoning busing. For almost ten years busing had
been the most visible and controversial policy in the blacks' quest for
equality. As they assessed the impact of that policy, black leaders
came increasingly to feel that the costs of busing had been too great.
When black youngsters were distributed across the county to meet
racial balance percentages, more was lost than was gained. Black
children, it seemed, suffered humiliations, lost confidence, failed to
learn as much or as quickly as they could, and all too often withdrew
into unproductive behavior.

The major problem for black leaders now was how to help black
children achieve their full potential and at the same time maintain
desegregated schools in a city characterized largely by segregated
housing patterns. The answer, it became increasingly clear, was for
blacks to regain control over schools in the black community, with
black teachers and principals and only enough whites zoned to the
schools to claim desegregated status. If there were not enough
whites—10, 15, or 20 percent—in the natural school zone, white
students could be bused in. Without explicitly embracing the attitudes of the outlying white communities, the black leaders' arguments now mirrored theirs.

At the November meetings, white spokesmen for the non-bused
outlying sections of the county took up most of the board's time.
Their message was clear: Give the blacks what they want, give them

6. NAACP statement, Nov. 27, 1979. Copy on file, Room 110 Board of Education.

their own schools, build them a new comprehensive high school if they want it, let them have a black history curriculum—just don't bus our children down there! We can take a few blacks in our schools, but busing is not good for children—theirs or ours.

These arguments, delivered in packed meetings, were couched in language which danced around the race issue. Busing takes too much time, costs too much, is unsafe. What is really important is neighborhood schools. Neighborhoods are at the heart of the community; if the community does not support the local school—and it won't if there is too much busing—the schools will be abandoned. As David Wilson, Goodlettsville, put it: "We . . . do not believe in the concept of busing to achieve racial balance, and contend that the neighborhood school is the best means of achieving a quality education."[7]

Like the blacks of North Nashville, suburban whites voiced a communal argument. The threat of white withdrawal over the issue of neighborhood schools was made directly by Joe Crockett at the first public hearing: ". . . if the adjustments are too sharp, if too long distances are involved . . . we believe it will do a great deal of damage ot our community. . . . large numbers of people will withdraw their children from Davidson County public schools.[8] Each speaker believed that the viability of his community rested on the dictates of the desegregation plan. Outlying whites argued that quality education was possible only if children were served by the local school. Parental support was a tangible factor in the calculus of quality.

Each child is entitled to a quality education—the best teachers, textbooks and facilities available to every child. But a quality education involves much more than these material things. The learning environment and parental support are just as important.

Ms. Margie Johnson
Madison Area Parent
Presented Nov. 19, 1979

Quality education and equal opportunity for everyone . . . (is) accomplished by community schools . . . made accessible to each by his or her choice and the parents involved. Quality education . . . can only be achieved in a proper environment where students can be receptive to learning. This is a primary requirement which cannot be made adequately in a forced environment or one in which the student cannot feel himself a part.

Guy Bates
Joelton Community
Presented Nov. 19, 1979

7. Statement to the Metro Board of Education, Nov. 19, 1979. Copy on file, Room 110 Board of Education.

8. Statement to the Metro Board of Education, Nov. 6, 1979. Copy on file, Room 110 Board of Education.

When we talk about a quality education, is there no place in quality education for a sense of pride in community, what we commonly call "community spirit." Is it not part of a good, sound education to have a community to be a part of, to have common aims and goals?

David Wilson
Goodlettsville Area Schools
Presented Nov. 19, 1979

The 1971 desegregation plan had established racial ratios for each school. The percentage black was to reflect the racial makeup of the larger community. Such a balanced approach was central to the logic of busing. But to whites who lived outside the bused area, racial ratios were a fearsome concept. "The black-white ratio of schools should not be important to this plan. . . . with open housing being the law of the land, all sections of the city are developing their desegregation schemes," wrote David Heffington.[9]

"Schools with artificially imposed ratios," said Dr. Jerry D. Westbrook of the Madison High School CAC, "do not achieve community support and often are a handicap to the total education process."[10]

The magnitude of the handicap was made clear by Dave Johnson of the Andrew Jackson PTA: "Ratios have little or no bearing on quality of education. . . . when ratios have been established in the past through forced busing, citizens have moved to other areas.[11]

Blacks had argued that the costs of busing fell disproportionately on them. Black children were bused for racial balance more than twice as often as white ones. Schools in downtown neighborhoods had been closed, or were scheduled to be. Blacks wanted minimum busing, and whatever busing had to be done had to be shared equally by the two races. Whites in the not-yet-bused areas, on the other hand, felt that the burden of busing was too much for anyone to bear. "In response to the burden issue, we suggest that busing is a burden to any child of any color."[12] Much of the criticism here focused on the debilitating effects of busing on school life. "Many families have children involved in extracurricular activities such as football, bas-

9. Letter to the Metro Board of Education. Copy on file, Room 110 Board of Education.

10. Statement to the Metro Board of Education, Nov. 27, 1979. Copy on file, Room 110 Board of Education.

11. Ibid.

12. Mrs. Etiole Beller, Union Hill CAC, statement to the Metro Board of Education, Nov. 27, 1979. Copy on file, Room 110 Board of Education.

ketball, soccer, gymnastics, band and scouting. . . . busing of children may cause many families to forego these activities."[13] Parents in the exempt suburbs simply wanted to end busing as a social policy.

White parents from the areas included in the 1971 busing plan comprised a third distinct group. By and large, they supported the integrationist philosophy. Not all were liberal politically, but they were liberal to the extent that they remained in the public schools while others left. These whites had lived with busing for some time, and in most cases they found the results palatable. They would cite statistics showing that the average reading and math scores of Metro students were on a par with private school results, and were above figures for large cities and the nation as a whole. And, they would note with pride that seven Nashville-Davidson County students in a Vanderbilt graduating class were elected to Phi Beta Kappa National Honor Society—one from a private school and six from Metro schools.[14]

The integrationist agenda included both desegregation and academic excellence. They believed that you could have both and had fought long and hard to make the 1971 plan work. They were activists; they attended all the meetings and became the cadre of organizational leaders and workers in their schools, including those schools in the black communty to which their children were transported. They came to resent the whites who fled the schools, yet agonized among themselves as to whether or not they should join the exodus.

This group's view of desegregation was rooted in the paradoxical emotions of anger at whites who had fled the public schools and anxiety at the prospect of being left behind. For them, desegregation would work only to the extent that blacks were exposed to, and absorbed into, the white middle-class culture. Blacks, they asserted, learned more and better in classrooms filled with hardworking, well-disciplined white children. However, if a critical mass of middle-class whites was not present in each class, then all children would lose, both educationally and socially. Busing was a burden that integrationist whites chose to bear. In many cases, the cost of private school tuition was no issue; they could afford to abandon the schools but did not. They wanted a better society and believe that busing could help to achieve it. But it could do so only if all whites participated equally. As far as the new desegregation plan was concerned, integrationists wanted to eliminate havens for white flight; they wanted county-wide busing. Their policy agenda called for the microcosm approach,

13. Dave Johnson, statement to the Metro Board of Education, Nov. 27, 1979. Copy on file, Room 110 Board of Education.
14. "Roundtable, 1980–1981." Copy on file, Room 110 Board of Education.

racial balance in each school, so that white middle-class values would dominate everywhere. Among these values was academic achievement; they wanted quality programs that were suited to the needs of each child and that would ensure that their children would not fall behind those in the private schools.

Unlike the outlying whites and North Nashville blacks, the integrationist whites did not argue for neighborhood schools as a prerequisite for quality education. However much they preferred the convenience and security of nearby schools, these whites thought that "neighborhood schools" were prohibited by the court order. Rather, they focused their attention on programs within the schools. A school could be anywhere, but it had to have accelerated as well as remedial programs. Ability grouping was acceptable as long as the schools were desegregated. "It is this very heterogeneity that requires . . . alternative educational programs be available within the system," said Leonard P. Alberstat of the West End–Natchez Trace––Woodlawn Parents Association.

A trademark of these whites, unlike non-bused whites and black leaders, was their insistence on racial balance in the schools. For white liberals, fragmentation into black and white subcultures was socially counterproductive. What was required, they argued, was a microcosm approach.

"Our black/white ratio is 42–45 percent, as opposed to the 25 percent projected by the original court order," said Richard Duncan of the Percy Priest CAC.[15] "All that we have asked this Board and Federal court to do is to reduce this ratio back down to the original projection."

As David Gibson of the Hillwood Parents Association stated, "A broad ratio such as 21 percent to 41 percent black to white is a meaningful, measurable guideline; it is not arbitrary. To have a predominantly black school is a step backward toward a dual system. This fact must be explained to the court."[16]

Sometimes the liberal whites were joined by blacks who shared Martin Luther King's integrationist vision. Paul Pierce, a confident, articulate black, said when he spoke, "Ratios are necessary . . . so that both races may experience human interrelationships. . . . this is of paramount importance if young persons are to mature, free from the prejudices that are transmitted as an integral part of parents' value

15. Richard Duncan, statement to the Metro Board of Education, Nov. 27, 1979. Copy on file, Room 110 Board of Education.
16. David Gibson statement to the Metro Board of Education, Nov. 19, 1979. Copy on file, Room 110 Board of Education.

systems."[17] What made this statement particularly poignant was that Pierce represented Hattie Cotton School. Hattie Cotton served a naturally integrated area and had a proud and productive biracial parents' group. Only a generation before, however, Hattie Cotton had been bombed by white racists.

In sum, the white integrationists who lived inside the 1971 busing zones believed that busing was a necessary evil. They might have preferred the comfort of neighborhood schools, but they also sought a desegregated society and were prepared to pursue busing toward that goal. They knew that it could work only if the rest of the whites supported the effort. Hence, they wanted a countywide busing plan including all whites, and in this quest they had hoped to be joined by blacks. But as the blacks' plan emerged, the white liberals became alarmed. Not only were their ideals being undercut, but their minority status in predominantly black schools might become institutionalized.

Although there were marked differences in the perspectives and recommendations of the three interest groups, there were also areas of agreement. Everyone who spoke out wanted quality public education. All wanted the schools to regain the broad community support that they had enjoyed in an earlier time. Everyone seemed to want stability and desired to have children attend only three or four schools in twelve years. All wanted children who started school together in Grade 1 to stay together through Grade 12. Everyone wanted naturally integrated areas excluded from any busing plan that might emerge from the board's deliberations.

Still, areas of conflict lurked beneath these agreements. Integrationist whites wanted a countywide plan, while outlying suburbanites wanted no expansion of the existing paired arrangements. Blacks wanted to limit busing as much as possible and to keep a majority black presence in downtown schools. "Educational quality" was a much-discussed ideal, but each group defined the term differently. For blacks, quality was synonymous with community control. Whites in the non-bused area defined it as a strengthened neighborhood school. And whites involved in busing saw quality as specific programs offered in schools reflecting the racial makeup of the community. These latent conflicts surfaced when the Metro School Board began to formulate a specific plan.

17. Testimony before the Metro Board of Education, Nov. 19, 1979. Copy on file, Room 110 Board of Education.

Phase Two: Criteria for the Plan

"I have drawn, by actual count in the last five years, 102 maps trying to find a way of improving the plan we have," said Metro school zoning director Ray Osborne. "This person is running out of ideas. . . . I can't find the answer to what the Court wants by myself. I need somebody to talk to."[18]

To relieve the tension that Osborne and others felt concerning the new plan, school administrators continued to receive testimony from concerned citizens. Public participation was essential if conflict was to be muted and the plan made acceptable to the community. On November 29 the board created a Joint Committee made up of the appointed Metro School Board and nine private citizens, one chosen by each board member from his or her respective district. The task of the Joint Committee was to discuss issues and establish criteria for the plan. Its recommendations would in turn be handed over to the school board, which, since it was the legally responsible agent, would make the final decision.

The Metropolitan Board of Education consisted of nine members appointed by the mayor from established geographical districts. In 1979, the board was made up of five men and four women—six whites and three blacks. These demographic characteristics, however, were not as important as the members' attitudes and values. In the debates over the new plan which consumed the board during that fall and winter, board members supported either the assimilationist-microcosm approach or the separatist–two cultures approach to school desegregation and race relations.

The *assimilationist-microcosm* group was committed to the integrationist assumptions of the liberal civil rights movement. This group included whites George Cate and Cynthia Morin and blacks Isaiah Creswell and Barbara Mann. In time, three of these four were caught between their personal values and the intensely-felt parochial interests of many of their neighbors. Cynthia Morin's district included bused and non-bused sectors, as well as two of the traditional high schools which were to be closed. Isaiah Creswell and Barbara Mann were black, and they were caught between their integrationist values and the new voices of black cultural equality.

The *separatist-two cultures* group included one black, DeLois Wilkinson, and four whites—Joseph Bottom, Troy Lynn, Ruby Major, and Ted Ridings. Three of the four whites represented outlying areas of the county. Everyone in this group wanted to preserve local communities.

18. *Banner*, Dec. 7, 1979.

Judge Wiseman had set aside two weeks in early March 1980 for hearings on the new plan, so time was precious. Once again the desegregation proposals would have to be drafted quickly. At study sessions in early December, the board heard staff members summarize the citizen input, especially as it bore on the issues of a unitary school district and quality education. Black leaders again addressed the board; this time the spokesman was the Reverend Amos Jones, chair of the Social Action Committee of the Interdenominational Ministers' Fellowship. Some themes were familiar, including the argument for expanding Pearl into a comprehensive high school and the disparaging view of busing. County-wide busing, Jones said, was a laudable goal but was "not high on our list of priorities." Placing black children in schools excluded from the 1971 plan would increase the burden on black children and accelerate the decline of inner city schools.[19]

On December 8 the Joint Committee met to begin the arduous task of establishing criteria for the plan. Briefly the politics of self-interest were submerged. The first criterion which was proposed required that all schools be included in a unitary desegregation plan; it was overwhelmingly adopted. Representatives from outlying areas recognized that this statement was required by the court, so they saved their comments until the specifics were to be elaborated.

The next three criteria were handled with similar dispatch. The frequent shuffling of children from school to school was an inconvenience mandated by the 1971 order. The committee's second criterion reduced the 1971 four-tier system to a three-tier one for Grades K–5, 6–8, and 9–12. The third criterion specified that no child should attend more than three schools if his residence did not change. The fourth criterion provided that groups of children who started school together in the first grade should stay together through the twelfth grade.

As long as the committee stuck to factors affecting stability, there was marked agreement. But when racial factors came into play, the interest constellations became evident. Representatives of outlying areas struck first. Troy Lynn, a board member from the outlying eastern portion of the county, moved that the plan establish a goal of 10 percent *either black or white* as a minimum minority presence in each school. His motion was quickly seconded by Charles R. Dorrier, a citizen committee member from the outlying Old Hickory area and a former member of the school board during the 1969–71 desegregation crisis.

19. Ibid., Dec. 5, 1979.

Sensing a majority in the committee, the outlying whites went farther. Ruby Major, a retired school teacher who represented the outlying eastern portion of the county on the board, seconded a Dorrier amendment which tied the racial composition of the *teaching staff* to the racial makeup of the student body. If the motion passed, schools in the outer rim would remain predominantly one-race institutions and schools in the inner city would once again become predominantly black.

The amended proposal would protect the outlying areas as much as possible, but it also appealed to the black separatist impulses of leaders from North Nashville. Despite legal questions raised by the board's lawyer, the motion was adopted by the Joint Committee seven to five.

The key issue of status politics had been joined. The Joint Committee had favored minimum desegregation; indeed, it had endorsed the idea of two separate cultures. The coalition of outlying whites and inner-city blacks had been formed out of mutual antipathy. It remained to be seen how the board would react. After a recess, the board met alone to consider the Joint Committee's recommendations. There was to be a surprise: the board quickly and overwhelmingly ratified the first four recommendations, but the vote on racial ratios crystalized factions on the board. Lower ratios favored community control. Higher percentages were more consistent with the original court order and were supported by integrationists of both races. When the vote was taken on the critical racial balance criterion, the board was split three to three. Isaiah Creswell, the elderly black board chairman from North Nashville, cast the deciding vote. There were gasps and moans from portions of the audience; Creswell had voted against the motion and so, apparently, against the expressed views of North Nashville's black leadership. The meeting adjourned, and the crucial issue of racial balance was left hanging.

The following day discussions were held within and between the three major interest groups. School staff and lawyers were consulted informally. When the Joint Committee met next, on December 10, Creswell took up the ratio issue immediately. He stated that the ratios of students and staff were separate issues and should not be combined. He had voted against the motion on that basis alone. Dorrier, as a principal spokesman for the outlying group, agreed to the separation of student and staff aspects of the plan. Student ratios were more important at this time, he said. With Dorrier again in the lead, an agreement was reached that specified a goal for the plan of an optimum 32 percent and a minimum 10 percent minority (*black or white)* student population in each school.[20] This new version of Criterion Four passed eleven to three.

The Joint Committee then went on to other things. Criteria were established easily because the major thrust of the plan had been charted. Barbara Mann, evidently worried that whites would not come to schools where they formed a small minority, proposed that a unique magnet program be established in any school with less than 20 percent white enrollment. The Joint Committee agreed, fourteen to one. The committee then voted to create as many naturally integrated school zones as possible (at least 32 percent minority black or white) and also to exclude these schools from busing.

The "burden of busing," which had been the focus of so much concern, received only perfunctory attention. The panel said the goal of the plan should be "to distribute the burden of busing as equitably as possible." If one had neighborhood schools, the burden of busing would not be very great. No-one offered an opinion about what "equitable" meant. The ambiguity here was to come back to haunt the board later.

The Joint Committee then took up the issue of school facilities. It unanimously said that the plan should consider how to use all existing school buildings, whether open or closed, to best conserve time, distance, and fuel. Priority consideration should be given to the use of existing facilities before construction of new buildings. These criteria satisfied both North Nashville black leaders and outlying whites. If schools were reopened in black neighborhoods, there would be less crosstown busing and greater racial identification with schools.

The Joint Committee adjourned, and after a recess the board met to ratify the Joint Committee's recommendations. This time there was no hitch. The board, almost without discussion, concurred on every recommendation and adjourned.

Phase Three: Consultants and Committees

The board had determined general criteria and goals for the new desegregation plan, and now it was time for various planning committees to elaborate upon these general ideas. In November, Brooks, the director of schools had asked the board to hire outside consultants to help prepare the new plan. At that time, the direction of the new

20. In the years since 1971, black enrollment in the Metro schools had increased from 25 percent to 32 percent.

plan was vague, and there was widespread resistance to the idea. By December the general criteria were in place, and when the issue of consultants came up again, the board approved three hirings. The principal consultant hired was Dr. Donald R. Waldrip, a former Cincinnati, Ohio, school superintendent who was president of a consulting firm specializing in school desegregation. In addition, two experts from the Desegregation Center at the University of Tennessee, Knoxville, were retained—Dr. Nathaniel A. Crippens, a retired black professor, and Dr. M. Everett Myer, a white associate professor.

Waldrip was to become a lightning rod for public anger. "He's going to take his check and go back to Cincinnati, and forget about us and the way he's messed up our lives," protested Marilyn Smith of the Richland Elementary School PTA.[21] Waldrip was nationally recognized as an advocate of magnet schools in desegregation planning. Although the planning committees were made up of administrators, principals, citizens, and board members, the consultants' opinions became most influential within the committees and were most often sought by the school board. Consultants knew how to work with numbers, maps, and planning priorities.

Waldrip, Myer, and Crippens had spent years drawing desegregation plans which used busing as the tool to end racial isolation. Their experience and values opposed "neighborhood schools," but this time, given the racial balance criterion adapted by the board, they were being asked to draw up a plan which reduced busing and favored racially identifiable schools.

Another consultant was brought in for two days to meet with the planning team: Dr. Robert Crain, a school desegregation scholar of national reputation from John Hopkins University. He, too, saw the board's criteria as favoring neighborhood schools at the expense of full desegregation. He, too, wondered if such a plan were wise. On December 15, in informal meetings with the planning committees and board members, Crain argued that Nashville had a successful record in desegregation, compared to most cities its size; to move away from the thrust of the 1971 plan, toward neighborhood schools, was a mistake. Crain reported research showing that it was in the early grades that desegregation was most effective in muting black and white racial sterotypes, and that black children gained most educationally if they were with whites in these years. He recommended that every school in the system be between 20 and 50 percent black. If a school was less than 20 percent black, black children felt alienated and performed poorly. But if it was more than 50 percent

21. *Banner*, Dec. 15, 1979.

black, whites would leave and the system would end up with predominantly one-race schools, warranting new court action. Busing was necessary for racial balance.

Crain also talked about Pearl High School. He said that the symbolism of the historically black high school was of immense importance: "If you don't maintain a black high school, a sense of deprivation, a grudge, will stay around for a long time." But Pearl, like every other school in the county, should be between 20 and 50 percent black.[22]

When asked about the burdens of busing, Crain betrayed a sense of impatience. He rose, took chalk in hand, and sketched out what was for him an inescapable conclusion: if desegregation was to work, blacks must bear the disproportionate share of its costs.

Crain was not alone in holding this conviction. Bill Wise and Donald Waldrip, too, had taken chalk to blackboard on other occasions to show why blacks had to shoulder a disproportionate burden in the racial balance model of desegregation. Let us look at the logic involved.

Assume that there are three Grade 1-6 elementary schools—two all white (Schools A and B), one all black (School C)—and 300 students in each school. In this system, as in Nashville, one-third of the students are black, and the two races are geographically separated. Consider three ways to approach desegregation of these schools.

Racial Balance Approach. The goal is that each school should end up roughly one-third black. To achieve this result, 200 white students are bused into School C and 200 blacks are bused out. This yields a new pattern, with 33 percent black in each school; each school remains at 300 students (see Figure 4).

There are two problems with this approach. First, as one can readily see, in the racial balance approach, two-thirds of the black students are bused out of their neighborhoods but only one-third of the whites are bused out of theirs. Second, *within* each race the burden is unequally distributed. If one tries to keep groups of children together—as the board said it would—then those children bused out of their neighborhoods for the first grade will be bused out for all six grades, whereas children who stay in their neighborhoods for first grade will remain there for all of their elementary education. One-third of the whites and two-thirds of the blacks take on the problems of busing for their respective races. This is clearly unfair, and it probably encourages instability. Busing is, in this system, based on

22. Ibid.

Figure 4: Racial Balance Approach

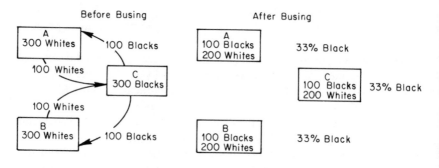

geographical areas, and a family can move a few blocks and be zoned into the neighborhood school.

Equal Percentage Approach. Suppose you choose to bus one-third of each race. The burden of busing is equal between the races, but this approach does not deal with the issue of fairness *within* each race. Moreover, it raises new problems. Here 100 blacks and 200 whites are bused out of their neighborhoods (see Figure 5). Twice as many whites as blacks are bused; whites will not like that. More importantly, though, the percentage black at School C is projected to be 50 percent. Though this is congenial to black citizens, such a high proportion of blacks will prompt a high rate of white flight from School C. Also, the total numbers of students in the three schools are no longer equal; Schools A and B have fallen to 250 students each, while School C's enrollment has risen to 400. Again, blacks may prefer this pattern, but whites will not. The question of closing School A or B may arise—a politically problematical issue. White flight will increase and with that, general support for the schools will diminish.

Low and Equal Numbers Approach. Yet another possibility is to bus a minimum and equal number of each race (see Figure 6). The problems of this approach are more extreme, although it reduces overall burden of busing. Suppose we bus only 100 of each race. The

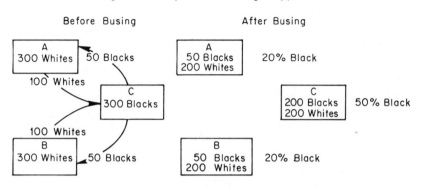

Figure 5: Equal Percentage Approach

problem of white flight becomes even more acute than in the equal percentage approach. In fact, white flight may quickly make School C a one-race institution. While this plan creates majority black schools and permits minimum busing of both races, the prospect of white flight and ultimate resegregation makes it unpalatable to the courts. It too impacts unequally on members of the same racial group.

Racial Balance, Split-Grades-Structures Approach. Many of the problems with the preceding approaches can be addressed by splitting grades among different schools (see Figure 7). In Grades 1–4 all children attend schools in the white area; in Grades 5–6 all children attend schools in the black area. No white is favored over another white; no black is favored over another black. The schools are racially balanced, microcosms of the community at large. This approach was the one chosen in 1971, and it was to be chosen again in 1980. But not without intense struggle!

A Turning Point

Behind the scenes, the consultants and planning teams worked at a frenetic pace trying to draw up a plan consistent with the board's

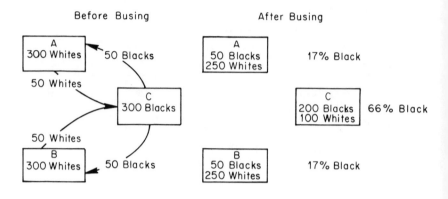

Figure 6: Low and Equal Numbers Approach

criteria. They were frustrated by two things: (1) the board had not decided what to do about high schools, particularly Pearl; and (2) the board's criteria would not lead to a stable desegregated school system. As Robert Crain noted, the citizens' input to the board and the board's subsequent planning criteria were consistent but misdirected. Crain wrote:

> It in effect means dividing the metropolitan area into two zones, one white and one black, with perhaps a boundary of integrated neighborhoods separating the two. . . . Such a plan would be easy to draw, but I think it would have very important consequences for Nashville and Davidson County. First, it would work much like a segregated school district in that schools would be identifiably black or identifiably white. Whites would be motivated to move out of the city and into the county. . . . The result would be a considerable increase in white flight. Since the plan would postpone most desegregation until middle school and high school, we could expect minority test scroes to go down instead of continuing to go up.[23]

Waldrip thought Pearl ought to be turned into a magnet school. He believed that the system could not be meaningfully desegregated

23. Letter from Crain to Donald Waldrip, Dec. 21, 1979.

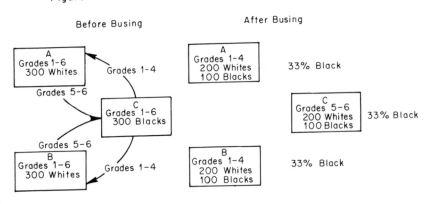

Figure 7: Racial-Balance Split-Grade Structures Approach

without an inclusive county-wide busing scheme. Waldrip was not alone in these views, but he was in a position to act on them effectively. He decided to confront the board with the issue of Pearl and the consequences of the board's desegregation criteria. Waldrip was no politician, but he was a skilled conjurer with maps and numbers. He would be ready.

Meanwhile, some board members were having second thoughts about what they had done. They were being pressed to consider the legal aspects of what they were proposing. Would predominantely one-race "neighborhood" schools be approved by the court?

On December 18 the Joint Committee and board met again. Pearl was at the top of the agenda. Robert Paslay and Cecil Harrell, experts from the Metropolitan Planning Commission, presented a report on the need for an inner-city high school. Given demographic trends and present facilities, they said, there was no need for Pearl, or neighboring Cohn High School to remain open. They believed that the Metro schools' longrange building plan, which projected the closing of Pearl and Cohn, was appropiate. The best they could suggest for Pearl was its use as a special-program magnet school. These statements prompted considerable discussion, but nothing was resolved.

The indecision reflected a very important development—the coalition of separatists was breaking down. Each side wanted to protect its traditional community high schools. But if the outlying whites voted with the blacks to keep Pearl open, what was to prevent Creswell and Wilkinson from subsequently joining with the integrationists— Cate, Morin, and Mann—in voting to close traditional white high schools? The reverse suspicion also wormed its way into consciousness. If the blacks voted with the outlying whites to protect the traditional high schools in the white's communities, would separatist whites then join the integrationists to defeat Pearl? Powerful emotions underlay the debate, but mistrust and the struggle for tactical advantage were more obvious now.

The Board failed to resolve its impasse over the future of high schools, so it turned its attention to a progress report from the desegregation planning team.

Donald Waldrip was prepared. Assuming the role of principal spokesman for the joint planning team, he began by summarizing the criteria previously adopted by the board: go to the edge of the county; involve all schools; use a three-tier system (1–5, 6–8, 9–12); equalize the burden; keep kids together as they moved through Grades 1–12; establish an optimum of 32 percent to a minimum of 10 percent minority (black or white) in each school; establish integrated school zones without busing where possible. The planning team, Waldrip said, had experimented with these criteria in an exercise using schools in the western sector of the county and found that they did not work. The criteria were in conflict when applied to the real world.

Using enrollment data and maps, Waldrip showed the problems inherent in the board's criteria. To meet even the minimum racial balance quota established by the board, some crosstown busing was necessary. And since the board had specified that children who started out together should stay together, those children who were bused out at kindergarten might well be bused out for seven years and possibly for their entire thirteen years of school—while other children living only a few blocks away would stay near home for virtually all of their schooling. This was very unfair to individual children. Waldrip said that a four-tier system (K–4, 5–6, 7–8, 9–12) would make possible a fairer distribution of the burden. Waldrip also pointed out that majority black schools prompted white flight. He wondered whether the court would accept this development.

Waldrip's presentation, nagging doubts about what the court would say, and lobbying of the board by the consultants bore fruit. George Cate, the board member assigned to work most closely with the planning team and one of the board members most committed to full desegregation, moved that the Joint Committee reconsider its criteria. His motion quickly passed. The Joint Committee and subsequently the board quickly altered their criteria to favor a four-tier system. Then the Joint Committee and board went further. They also revised the criterion on racial ratios. The new criterion said, "The goal of the plan shall be to provide an optimum of 32 percent *black* student ratios in each school, with a 20 percent deviation either way (12 to 52 percent black)." Blacks would once again be a minority in each school. In one sudden move, the separatists' criteria had been overturned.

The changes advocated by the consultants brought the board back to the basic ideals of the 1971 plan, albeit expanded now to the entire county. The major difference was that the 1971 plan had (1) specified a 25 percent optimum black enrollment with 10 percent allowable deviation and (2) placed all Grade 1–4 schools in white neighborhoods. The black community might in the new plan be able to keep some of its young people in their neighborhoods in the first four grades, but far fewer than it would have under the board's first set of criteria. Under the new criteria, as in the 1971 plan, blacks would be bused much more than whites, but the outlying whites were now to be included in busing more fully than would have been the case in 1971 or if the first set of criteria had prevailed.

The integrationist whites gained most by the revision. The outlying whites would now participate fully in busing, and the schools would approximate a microcosm of the larger community. The drive toward two cultures by the outlying whites and the inner-city blacks had been blunted.

Phase Four: Choosing a Plan

After the December 18 meeting at which the board changed its criteria, there was much grumbling by board members. Ted Ridings and DeLois Wilkinson especially seemed nonplussed, complaining about bringing in experts with theories but no real understanding of community needs.

Nevertheless, the planning team pushed on. The plan it was developing looked very much like the old 1971 plan. Waldrip and the planning team seemed comfortable with this design. The emerging plan was consistent with the advice of academic literature on successful desegregation: desegregate early grades for maximum benefit; permit no havens for white flight; and do not try to bus many whites downtown for they simply will not go.

What to do with Pearl and the other high schools in the county's southwestern sector remained a problem. But Waldrip had a solution to recommend. He was a strong advocate of magnet schools, especially as components of mandatory desegregation plans. He pressed his view at every opportunity. For him, the best solution was to close Pearl, Cohn, and Bellevue and then to establish an academic magnet high school at Pearl. His argument ran like this. There was great underutilization of the high school facilities in the southwestern sector, and the Bellevue, Cohn, and Pearl students could all be housed at Hillwood and Hillsboro (see Figure 8).

The vocational facilities most needed by Cohn and Pearl students were already waiting for them at the comprehensive high schools. If everyone attended Hillsboro and Hillwood, the racial composition of the schools would be perfectly on target. Pearl, as a building, could then house an open-zone academic magnet high school, rivaling in quality the most prestigious private schools in the area. Pearl, Waldrip argued, would not die but become a beacon of excellence for the entire county.

At the January 3 board meeting, Waldrip presented his new desegregation plan. He also presented a rough sketch of what would happen if Pearl were expanded or moved to a new larger site. The board offered questions and opinions, but again failed to deal with the issue. Latent conflict immobilized the board, and it adjourned.

Public reaction to Waldrip's plan was swift and intense. Busing was back at center stage in the continuing socio-political drama. This time school closures had upstaged racial ratios and grade structures as points of controversy. The day after Waldrip's presentation, the white community chanted its protests like the chorus of a Greek tragedy. Parents and other supporters of Cohn and Bellevue High Schools rallied to defend their schools in the same terms used by North Nashville spokesmen. If blacks could advocate neighborhood schools for community needs, so could they. The blacks had forsworn the moral high ground of integration, and now it was every community for itself.

The reaction in Bellevue was particularly well organized and virulent. Over 8,000 leaflets screaming "Save Our Schools" were printed and circulated. The flyers urged members of the Bellevue community to appear at the next board meeting to protest the closing of Bellevue High School and nearby Gower Elementary School.[24] Doug Underwood, publisher of the Bellevue community newspaper *Westview,* had fanned the flames of resistance all along. His favorite part of the U.S. Constitution was the Tenth Amendment: "The Powers not

24. *Banner,* Jan. 7, 1980.

Figure 8. Nashville High Schools

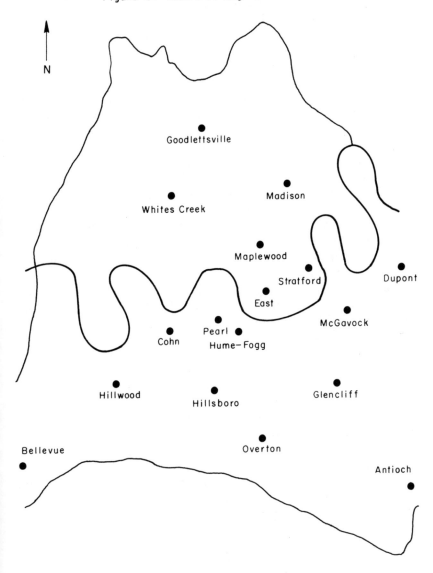

delegated to the United States by the Constitution are reserved to the States respectively, or to the people." Underwood saw the threat of federal government hegemony in busing, among many other things. Bellevue residents threatened to sponsor a petition to alter the Metro Charter to provide for and cause election of the school board if the presently appointed members closed their schools. The threat was not idle, for their efforts resulted in an elected board in 1982.

At the next meeting of the board, on January 7, 1980, the board was overwhelmed. A crowd estimated at between 1,500 and 2,000 people, most from Bellevue, sought access to a board room designed for 150. The board heard a series of parents and supporters of Pearl and Cohn argue against closing those schools; then Bellevue residents stormed in. The board was compelled to recess and reconvene later that night *at Bellevue.* When they arrived at Bellevue High School, members faced a sign-waving, shouting crowd of 2,000 partisans. The board heard Bellevue's spokesman describe the quality of their academic program, the central importance of the school to the community, and all the other familiar communal arguments. As a result of the Bellevue protest, the Board decided to take only written comments on the alternative plans in the future. The board was offended by Bellevue's efforts to intimidate it.

The board assembled on January 10 to make its fateful decision on high schools in the southwestern sector. Would it close Pearl, Bellevue, and Cohn? Waldrip outlined alternative plans developed by the planning team. None of them anticipated closing Hillsboro or Hillwood or keeping Pearl open. Pointed questions were asked by board members seeking to justify their positions. Couldn't Pearl and Cohn be joined in some way to create a racially balanced school in a contiguous zone? Wouldn't that leave existing facilities at Hillsboro and Hillwood underutilized? If Pearl were kept open, it would resegregate anyway, wouldn't it?

Sensing a moment of truth, DeLois Wilkinson sought to explain once again the affront to blacks if Pearl were closed. Hers was more than a cry for equal access to public institutions; it was an appeal for racial equity seen in historical dimension. She recalled for everyone the plight of blacks in search of an education. Early on, she said, whites had seen no need to educate blacks, "so Frederick Douglass and people like that had to steal their education." Then there were separate schools for blacks, but they were run by *white* people. And after that, blacks got "separate-but-equal" public education, but their schools were not equal. When desegregation started, whites said, "Let's give them equal schools," but blacks got busing instead. Still, blacks went where they were supposed to, but whites didn't. "So now we sit here proposing a desegregation plan—a unitary desegregation plan—to correct the racial imbalance which still exists. And most all these plans . . . put the burden of this new desegregation on the inner city and on the black community and on Pearl. It's not fair; it's not just . . . It's not ethical, and it's not humane, and it simply is not right."[25]

After Wilkinson's appeal, the board moved away from Pearl for a moment. They took up the pros and cons of closing Cohn. It served an older working-class area in West Nashville and was naturally desegregated. That community too wanted its school preserved. But it was an old facility, and its students needed the vocational programs waiting for them at Hillwood and Hillsboro.

The debate barely masked intense feelings all around, and no plan presented seemed to have majority support. Finally George Cate sought to move the board out of its stalemate. He said the board should consider a decision on one school, not one plan. From this assertion, he moved that "Pearl be made into an open-zone magnet for gifted students, Grades 7–12." Without saying so, he knew this to be the key issue. Cate's motion was seconded by Morin, the other white liberal integrationist. After an admonition to the audience to restrain itself, the board took a short recess. It had been deliberating for almost two hours.

Upon return, Ruby Major, one of the most consistent defenders of community schools, was the first to speak.

> There has to come change, and with change comes sometimes pain and differences of opinion. . . . But I do feel there is a definite need for an inner-city school and for a response to perhaps the guilt that we should feel in the fact that we are so long getting started on something that would focus upon the inner-city development, and I don't think there is anything better than Mr. Cate's motion, and Mrs. Morin's second, and I'd like to third it if you'd like to have such.[26]

Major, who had long argued that schools and their communities were and should be intimately related, cast her vote against the black community. An academic magnet school at Pearl was not a community school, hence it was not supported by North Nashvillians.

Barbara Mann, the black integrationist, spoke next. She was as calm and reasonable as DeLois Wilkinson was passionate and partisan. Mann would support an academic magnet at Pearl and another magnet at Cohn. The use of these schools, though in a new manner, saves their heritage, she said, and does support the inner city's effort to build a strong future for itself.

25. From tape transcripts, Jan. 10, 1980. Copy on file, Room 110 Board of Education.
26. Ibid.

Mann's statement brought forth another angry and anguished plea from Wilkinson:

> An academic magnet school would not meet the needs of a community school for North Nashville. A community school is supposed to relate to the community in which it resides. It's supposed to be an exchange between the community and the school, and if you have a highly academic magnet school which would house eventually the top 10 percent of the highest achieving students—gifted students—in Nashville, you will leave out the masses of the North Nashville population—the inner city population. You simply would not have the kind of relationship that the people of the inner city are asking for when they say they want a high school in their community. And there are some reasons for this. . . . We cannot ignore factors which led to cultural differences between the black community and in the white community. Not just cultural differences due to economic and socioeconomic factors—but also the fact that we have a cultural heritage in which we can be proud.[27]

To put an academic magnet at Pearl, Wilkinson said, would alienate the black community from its school and bear witness to the tyranny of the white culture.

She made a substitute motion in favor of a Pearl comprehensive/magnet high school, but it fell on deaf ears. When the vote was taken, Cate's motion was approved by both the Joint Committee and the board. Only Wilkinson and Creswell dissented.

Dr. Brooks congratulated the board on having made its most difficult decision. The board did not congratulate itself. Its members sat in resigned silence for a minute, each lost in private thoughts.

Ted Ridings leapt into the vacuum, moving that Bellevue remain open as a traditional community high school. His timing could not have been worse. The board had just voted against the expressed wishes of North Nashville; could it now allow itself to favor an outlying white area? The board got lost in tactical maneuvers as substitute motions were offered and amendments made. Each board member seemed to prefer a different configuration. Ridings wanted to leave Cohn open—it was naturally desegregated—and bus the Pearl blacks to Bellevue to desegregate it. Morin wanted to close Bellevue and Cohn as well as Pearl, sending their students to Hillwood and Hillsboro. Mann wanted Bellevue closed as a *quid pro quo* for Pearl, but she favored an alternative magnet high school at Cohn.

The board was finally brought back to the point by Barbara Mann, who moved that "Plan 1" be adopted. Cate seconded. Waldrip's Plan 1 closed Bellevue, Cohn, and Pearl, busing all students to Hillsboro and

27. Ibid.

Hillwood. But the motion failed. The three pro-integrationists (Cate, Morin, and Mann) voted for the plan. The four white outlying members (Major, Bottom, Lynn, and Ridings) voted against it. Creswell and Wilkinson, strong advocates for the black community, did not vote; they were protesting. If they voted for, they would sanction the closing of Pearl; if they voted against, they would side with the board members most insensitive to the black community.

The uneasy coalition of inner-city blacks and outlying whites had broken down. Both groups had favored "community schools" and decreased busing for both races. Now the outlying whites had voted to close Pearl, a black community school, but would not vote to close Bellevue and Cohn, white community schools. Naked self-interest stalked the room.

Plan 2 was immediately taken up. Waldrip's Plan 2 would close Pearl and Cohn but leave Bellevue open as a traditional high school desegregated by busing students from North Nashville. The advantages of this plan were discussed. Students might be permitted to choose which type of school they preferred—academic magnet (Pearl), traditional (Bellevue), or comprehensive (Hillsboro and Hillwood). A transfer policy could be worked out.

The Joint Committee still met with the board, although its members were less and less vocal. Joseph Cunningham, a citizen member from George Cate's area, refused to let secondary issues get in the way. For him, favorable racial ratios and alternative school programs were beside the point; the real issue was elemental fairness. One couldn't close Pearl and not close Bellevue. It was a moral choice. "The clear issue that we are talking about right now is who the hell are we willing to mess with—and what we are saying is it's O.K. to mess with poor black folks, and it is not all right to mess with more affluent white folks. And that's it. That's what that plan does. That's the only message it can carry."[28]

At that, Ruby Major was taken aback and made a rambling apology. "I'm sure I had no intention of imposing something on black people that was undesirable. I frankly thought we were making a privilege of the situation—one that was the best thing that had been offered in recent years to attract people to something very good."[29]

On Plan 2 only Ridings voted yes. Lynn, Bottom, and even Major could not now vote to keep Bellevue open. The symbolic dimension of the burden of busing hung squarely before the Board. Since blacks had made Pearl into a cultural symbol, the board knew whites would

28. Ibid.
29. Ibid.

not go there. If it were to continue open, it would surely resegregate, no matter what ratio was projected. The court would not accept this development, so Pearl had to be closed. But to close Pearl and not Bellevue was too much.

The board brought itself back to Plan 1. After little discussion a vote was taken. This time Plan 1 was adopted. Bellevue, Cohn, and Pearl were to be closed. Troy Lynn and Joseph Bottom—board members from the eastern part of the county—voted with the integrationists Cate, Morin, and Mann. Wilkinson and Creswell still did not vote. Only Ridings and Major voted against the plan.

Public reaction to the board's January 10 decision was predictable. Angry Bellevue residents swore they would put their children in private schools before they would see them bused to Hillwood or Hillsboro. Cohn supporters said they would join forces with Avon Williams and North Nashville blacks to fight the plan in court.[30]

The Elementary Schools Plan

Time. The board was under pressure to get its plan to the plaintiff and court by February 2, 1980. It could not delay.

On January 14 the board met to consider the desegregation plan for elementary schools. Waldrip again presented the options to the board. He pointed out that Judge Wiseman had been critical of the 1971 plan, especially those aspects which permitted havens for white flight and placed special hardships on small black children.

Waldrip asked the board to make key decisions which might constrain the plan. If every elementary school was to be desegregated, he said, it would involve long-distance busing. Students of both races would be involved, but outlying whites would be most affected, since it took much longer to fill a bus in the sparsely populated remote areas. Another critical question was whether or not Grades 1 and 2 were to be included in busing. Parents of both races had argued that small children should be kept near home for their first years of schooling, but desegregation had its greatest beneficial effects if it began early.

After considerable discussion, the pro-integration forces took the initiative. Mann moved and Morin seconded a motion "that Grades 1 and 2 be included in the desegregation plan." Bottom tried to undercut the motion through an amendment which would keep youngsters in Grades 1 and 2 in their neighborhood schools if busing involved

30. *Banner,* Jan. 11, 1980.

non-contiguous zones. His proposal lost; only the four outlying whites favored it, while black board members joined with the pro-busing integrationists Cate, Morin, and Mann. Ridings tried a similar move; he sought to exclude students in Grades 1 and 2 if they were to be bused more than thirty minutes. He said, "I'll predict to you that we'll see a lot more people drop out of the school system than we saw eight years ago, if we mandate that first and second graders cross the city to go to school."[31] Again Creswell and Wilkinson voted with Cate, Morin, and Mann to defeat the exclusion.

When the main motion—to include first and second graders in the desegregation plan—came up for a vote, there was a surprise. Wilkinson joined the outlying whites to defeat the motion. She said, "I find that my heart and my head are in opposition." Ultimately, she voted her heart. She wanted young black children to stay home.

The board continued to wrestle with questions of time and distance. Special exclusions did seem warranted. Harpeth Valley and Union Hill area students would be bused about seventy-five minutes each way, according to Waldrip's projection. But the board could not agree on a general rule governing exclusions that would satisfy a majority. William R. Willis, counsel for the board, said that until the board finally approved the plan, any board member could move to exclude any school from it. He cautioned, however, that the exclusion from the plan must have some solid rationale based in fact. The basis in fact could be a number of factors: time/distance, burden, health and safety, quality of education, or willingness of black or white parents to accept the action. In his opinion there was no constitutional requirement that every school in the county be integrated, but he suggested that if any schools were not to be, they should be named one by one, along with the reasons for each school's exclusion. Finally the board passed a motion including Grades 1 and 2 in the plan "subject to such exclusion as the board may deem necessary." It postponed exclusion decisions until Waldrip could gather more data.

When the board reconvened on January 19, Waldrip took up right where he left off. He reviewed the elementary, junior high, and high school plans and reported on busing times and distances. Waldrip showed that a thirty-minute limit would prevent some whites from being bused into the city from outlying areas, but it would not affect blacks at all. "By the time you pick up students in the outlying areas and take them to the closest school, you have used the thirty minutes. So you have to stop right there. In the inner city, it is possible to

31. *Tennessean,* Jan. 15, 1980.

pick up black students in five minutes and get to almost any school in the county within thirty minutes."[32]

Barbara Mann cited her concern that black children would be bused outward for six of their first eight years. Bobby Lovett, a citizen member of the Joint Committee, said that the whole plan was stacked against inner-city residents, particularly black children. Waldrip responded, pointing out that total time on the bus, was almost equal for the two races, for the reasons he had cited. Grade 5–6 schools were located in the inner city because larger buildings were available there. In naturally integrated areas, the planning team had created Grade 1–6 schools.

The debate ebbed and flowed as the board took up specific areas and special cases. In the end, Ridings and Bottom joined in moving "that first and second grade students will have the option of going to the nearest elementary school if the school to which they are zoned would require them to be bused over the thirty minutes from home to school." The Joint Committee rejected the motion, but the board went on to vote on the motion anyway. It passed five to two. Wilkinson again voted with the outlying whites—Major, Bottom, Ridings, and Lynn.

Ambivalence

The board elected to receive the completed but still tentative desegregation plan, with all its details, at a meeting on January 24. The meeting would be shown on WDCN-TV, the local public television station. Citizen reaction and comment would be received at a public hearing at East High School on January 26. The board would review the public reaction, make any revisions necessary, and vote on the final plan February 2.

The January 24 presentation went off as scheduled. Waldrip did most of the talking. After the meeting, it was the community's turn to respond. Citizen comments in the fall had been directed at the general criteria for the plan. Now, however, the comments dealt with the grievances of particular groups of parents, especially those whose schools were being closed or having grades reshuffled. Scores of individuals and groups submitted written statements or appeared at the open meeting on January 26. Anger ran deep, but there was one noticeable shift in public opinion since the fall. Many whites in the bused areas now spoke in favor of neighborhood schools.

The board's desegregation plan as a whole in fact embodied the

32. Board minutes, Jan. 19, 1980. Copy on file, Room 110 Board of Education.

arguments of the liberals of the white bused community. The outlying whites were now to be included in busing—they would bear their fair share of the burden—and the schools would have an assimilationist, microcosm character. But the white community within the bused area had undergone a change. The liberal leadership had lost its moral force in the face of black separatism.

No-one felt the ambivalence of the integrationists' victory more poignantly than John Egerton. Both as a citizen and as a reporter, Egerton had been at the forefront of the desegregation struggle. In 1970 he had been a leader in Concerned Citizens for Improved Schools, the citizens group which pushed for a county-wide assimilationist policy. As a writer, Egerton had achieved national recognition as a perceptive observer of the South and its travails. In an interview published by the Nashville *Banner*, Egerton expressed the feelings countless others had about the experience of desegregation.

> Although he still has a son in Hillsboro High School, he has kept a low profile in current desegregation discussions—not, he said, because he had abandoned integration as a goal, but because he is less sure now how to get there. "What seemed both fair and doable to me ten years ago no longer seems doable and I'm less certain it would be fair," Egerton said. "The older I get, the more convinced I am I don't have the answers I thought I had a few years ago."
>
> Egerton's confusion is mirrored by many other so-called "white liberals" as they have seen the once black and white issue of desegregation dissolve into shades of grey. "I think it was fairly clear the black community in Nashville was very close to being united in favor of across-the-board desegregation in 1971," Egerton said.
>
> "I don't think the black community is united now. And many whites who were willing to try that ten years ago are not willing to try it anymore. People's perceptions about the rewards and benefits of desegregation have changed."
>
> "Many blacks have come to resist the move to put a white majority in every school because it destroys black control over their institutions," he said. "They also are less willing to bus their children long distances to desegregate every white school."
>
> "Ten years ago, I would have bought that idea (of having a strict racial ratio in every school). Now, I don't know whether that would be equitable. If there is not going to be a stable white population in the school system, maybe there is no logic in trying for that when you know whites won't buy it."[33]

33. *Banner*, Jan. 17, 1980.

Pearl-Cohn Comprehensive High School

The board met again on January 29. The purpose of the meeting to reconsider the elementary school plan. The board had heard from parents and might need to make some changes. During the course of the discussions DeLois Wilkinson pointed out once again that there was no junior high school in North Nashville and that there ought to be. Her comments were a lament, but they prompted a chain reaction.

Ruby Major seemed to have been waiting for a chance to reopen the Pearl question. She said that the board had once before voted to build a comprehensive inner-city high school (on February 14, 1978), and it ought to follow through. Barbara Mann immediately moved that the board reconsider the Pearl decision, and the motion was overwhelmingly approved. The board asked for additional data about possible sites for a comprehensive high school in North Nashville and deferred judgment until a later time. In the meantime, members continued to discuss the elementary school plan both that day and at a January 31 meeting, making many small changes.

Clearly something important had happened in the past two weeks. Even liberal integrationists like Mann and Cate now wanted a comprehensive high school for North Nashville. When the new plan was seen as a whole, it was clear that its burden fell heavily on the black community. North Nashville had been left with no Grade 1–4 schools and no junior or senior high school, save the the proposed academic magnet at Pearl. This realization had prompted a reconsideration.

In haste, in the final hours before the plan was to be sent to Judge Wiseman, the board decided to construct a new comprehensive high school in North Nashville to be named Pearl-Cohn. It would be desegregated by including the working-class whites previously assigned to Cohn in a single contiguous zone with most of the Pearl area. Formerly powerful arguments were cast aside—that it would cost $12 to $15 million dollars for the facility, while the school budget was already strapped; that the school would duplicate programs already available at Hillsboro and Hillwood, leaving these schools underutilized; that the plan would resegregate the county's secondary schools.

Almost everyone was happy about this compromise. The board had given the black community something; and it had assuaged a lot of guilt. But not everyone rejoiced. Waldrip said that he thought the proposed school would resegregate, and Willis reminded the board that if it proceeded with Pearl-Cohn and the school did resegregate, its action would be construed as a continuing violation of the law. Morin objected to the new school on principle, and Lynn saw the new school as a redundant waste of taxpayers' money. The die-hard supporters of the traditional Pearl and Cohn Schools were not happy either, and, though they now lacked a voice on the board, they made up their minds to fight again later in court.

Waldrip had not entirely lost. The board voted to create an academic magnet at West End Junior High School for Grades 7–12.

Conclusion

The unitary school plan adopted by the board in 1980 was in large part a continuation of the 1971 plan. The principal difference between the two was that the 1980 plan involved the whole county in busing for desegregation, while the 1971 plan had not.

The school board had been caught between awful conflicting pressures. Clear majorities in the public and on the board preferred neighborhood schools, but the law required desegregation. Busing was onerous, but it was necessary because the courts required it.

The black community had complained that blacks bore more than their share of burdens under the 1971 plan. Their young children had been bused out of their neighborhoods for four of the first six grades. Their schools had been closed. They had fought for years to retain Pearl, the last of the black high schools. And the 1980 plan did not ease the burden on blacks. McCann remained the only primary school in a majority black area, but at least the board had elected to let first and second graders stay in the local area in two other schools. There was no junior high in North Nashville, and but for the reversal on Pearl there would have been no high school. The new plan closed four more elementary schools in the black community.

The outlying white area, under the 1980 plan, would have to share the problematical aspects of desegregation. This area retained its elementary schools, but these were now to be desegregated through busing. Blacks would comprise between 10 and 59 percent of students in schools that were previously exclusively white. Now, too, many outlying white children were to be bused into the city for Grades 5–6. Bellevue High School had been turned into a junior high.

The whites in the court-ordered area no longer felt that they bore the brunt of desegregation for all whites. The new plan closed several schools in their neighborhoods—those whose enrollments were small due to white flight and the declining birth rate—but in most cases the percentage black in the schools which were to remain open was projected to be lower than it was in 1978. The microcosm was to return in fact as well as theory.

The board had tried to distribute the burden of busing equally *within* each racial group, and it had been successful. But when the board tried to distribute the burden equally *between* the two groups, it failed. The board had decided that if a plan acceptable to both the community and the courts was to come forward at all, blacks had to be bused more than whites.

CHAPTER ELEVEN

The Court Rejects Busing

The Board's plan had hardly been announced when the voices of frustration and anger arose from North Nashville. "You still have majority white schools existing," said NAACP President Charles Kimbrough at a press conference early in February 1980; these schools were "still named after white people—some of them slave owners no doubt. . . . The director of schools and the school board. . . . are putting the burden of desegregation on the backs and brains of its most loyal citizens—the black parents and pupils."

Metro Council member Mansfield Douglas, a black from South Nashville, excoriated the board for not considering closing white high schools. "It makes as much sense to have a high school at Hillwood as to have it in Miami Beach. . . . the School Board added vocational programs in an area where residents like to send their children to private schools."[1] Kimbrough, Douglas, and PUSH President Richard Jackson supported the plans of Leo Lillard, a black consultant to the Metro Planning Commission, who was trying to develop a cluster plan which would allow the traditional high schools to remain open and allow blacks to retain majority status in their neighborhood schools.

Whites from Cohn, Bellevue, and Joelton also spoke out. They, too, supported the Lillard approach and ultimately joined him and others as a formal intervenor party to the lawsuit.

On February 29, three days before formal court hearings began, black members of the school board broke the news that they had filed a document with the court objecting to several features of the recently completed plan. They attacked the board for once again placing on blacks the largest sacrifices involved in desegregation. The board's plan, they said, unfairly permitted the construction of a new Madison-Goodlettsville Comprehensive High School while it closed Pearl; students from Madison and Goodlettsville could have been used to desegregate a renovated Pearl. Nor did the plan contain any provision for a junior high in North Nashville. Further, the plan

1. *Banner,* Feb. 6, 1980.

would bus black children out of their neighborhoods uniformly in Grades 1–4. The board's plan did not suggest closing Hillwood or Hillsboro, though equity demanded that those schools be closed and Pearl, Cohn, or Bellevue enriched.

The issues were not new, but the three black members of the board wanted to make sure they were not ignored. Ironically, Barbara Mann, who earlier had been caught between two sets of conflicting values, read the dissent to reporters. When asked whose side she was on, Mann replied, "I have to tell you it has been a very difficult thing to be a black member on this board. I have concerns about the board's responsibility to the total community, but I am concerned about black issues, too. So how do I resolve that? Sometimes it's like straddling a fence. I guess when it comes right down to it, I would have to say my position is closer to that of the plaintiffs."[2]

Board member Ted Ridings penned a nasty retort to Judge Wiseman. Ridings had not voted for the board's desegregation plan, but he said he had felt "honor bound" not to express public disagreement with it. "However, this same courtesy has not been observed by the three black members of this Board, even though they voted in favor of the overall plan."

Nathaniel Crippens, the black consultant on the desegregation planning team, also wrote to Wiseman. Fatigue, he said, had kept him from recognizing inequities in the board's plans, and now he too recommended that Pearl be kept open after 1983.

The protagonists in the board's struggle to come up with a desegregation plan were not the only ones to write to the court. Judge Wiseman indicated that he would welcome community reactions to the plan, and he got them. Over one hundred letters poured in during the court hearings; some came even before the hearings began.

Among them was a letter from David Gibson, a Hillwood parent. Unlike most writers, Gibson supported his argument with data. He had photocopied course enrollment records submitted to the Tennessee Department of Education by the Metro Schools. The records graphically showed the underutilization of Hillwood. Gibson, angry at Avon Williams and the new group of intervenors, maintained that comprehensive high schools were the most cost-effective means of desegregation at the high school level, and on those grounds he objected to efforts to keep Pearl open. But Gibson, like so many who wrote to the judge, had deeper complaints as well. He advised Judge Wiseman to be wary: "You will hear a lot about 'black heritage' as a reason to keep Pearl open. But the approximately 250 black students

2. *Tennessean,* Feb. 27, 1980.

at Hillwood will not agree that they have given up any of their 'black heritage' just because they go to school at Hillwood. Surely black heritage is not so fragile that it could be harmed by four years in a high school. The argument is childish . . ."

Gibson's letter is not so remarkable for the data he used to support his contentions or his lack of appreciation of black heritage as for his moral outrage. At some risk to himself, Gibson had made efforts to bring blacks into white institutions, but he could not bring himself to compel whites to pay homage to black symbols or institutions. Gibson was a southern white liberal for whom there was a boundary he would not cross:

> Judge, I grew up in a segregated Mississippi and spoke out against it in the mid-1950s when it was not popular to do so. As a result I was kicked out of the Masonic Lodge because I would not say that I believed in segregation. That was twenty-four years ago this month. Over twenty years ago I stood in line with black students from Fisk protesting the segregation of Nashville movie houses. We have come a long way from those days. Things may not be 100 percent perfect, yet some people are simply unreasonable and downright selfish in their demands. Over the years some of our friends have sent their children to private schools. I have been determined to support and be active in public schools because I believe in them; it is a good melting pot for rich and poor and white and black. But I am not trapped to where I have to send my daughters to public schools. I make over $60,000 a year and I can darn well afford to send my children to a private school. And now, for the first time in my life, I find myself seriously considering just that. If there is not a stop put to this Mickey Mouse process by which Avon Williams, representing one man, can waltz into court and put the whole school system in an upheaval every year or so, then I darn well will put my children into private schools. I'm tired. And why not, Avon Williams sent his children to private schools.[3]

The Plaintiff's Argument

Avon Williams filed his objections to the plan before the hearings opened.[4] As expected, he found the plan unfair. He objected to the closing of Pearl, arguing that it could be renovated and used in place of Pearl-Cohn, and to the closing or underutilization of other schools in the black community. He objected to the assignment of almost all Grade 1–4 black children to white area schools, contending that

3. Exhibit #185.
4. Objection of Plaintiffs to the Plan Submitted by Defendants in Response to Court's Memorandum of Aug. 27, 1979 (mimeographed).

whites could be bused into the inner city just as easily as blacks could be bused out. He objected to the notion that 12 to 52 percent black should be in each school; he felt that that idea perpetuated the historic attitude that blacks were inferior. He objected to the magnet school, arguing that it was a haven for whites trying to escape desegregation. He objected to one-way busing. He objected to many particulars, but all, taken together, summed up to one objection: the plan represented unequal treatment of black institutions and culture.

Attached to Williams' brief was a twenty-seven-page paper written by Dr. Hugh J. Scott, the plaintiffs' expert witness. Dr. Scott had been a teacher and administrator in the Detroit public schools and superintendent of schools for the District of Columbia; he was then dean at Hunter College, City University of New York. The views that he expressed in his written statement and later in his oral testimony had a profound impact on the court.[5] Dr. Scott provided an intellectual rationale for the feelings expressed more and more often by Nashville's black leaders.

Scott argued that black people had been and continued to be systematically and unconstitutionally injured by governmental policies. Slavery and Jim Crowism had violated their most basic rights. Because of these policies, black Americans were owed an enormous debt, and they must see that it was paid in currency truly beneficial to them. Busing, however, was not the right currency. Efforts to dismantle dual school systems through busing were wrongly designed, because busing assumed the "rightness of whiteness." Court desegregation decrees had forced blacks into white institutions and white culture, diminishing black institutions and black culture. Busing, as it was practiced in Nashville and elsewhere, insulted and injured black people.

Whites had always treated blacks as if they had no culture of their own or only an inferior culture. Blacks, said Scott, did not attack the dual school system because it created black schools, but because "separate but equal" implied cultural inferiority.

> Black Americans did not seek the elimination of segregated public schools because they believed that black schools by the very nature of their "blackness" were inferior and incapable of teaching black students to read and write. Segregated public schools were challenged in the courts by black Americans because they believed that racial segregation in education was founded on the premise of white superiority and black inferiority and

5. Dr. Hugh Scott, "A Black Perspective on Critical Social and Educational Factors Considered Pertinent to the Restructuring of Approaches to Desegregation in the Nashville-Davidson County Public Schools," Exhibit A (mimeographed).

because the separate but unequal schools for blacks denied equal educational opportunity to black students.[6]

The courts had overturned dual school systems and had created busing as a remedy for past wrongs. But as it had been practiced, busing continued to imply that black culture did not count for much and was not worth preserving. Moreover, Scott argued busing did not ensure that black children were better educated. Even in terms of basic educational skills, blacks could be better served by majority-black neighborhood schools.

> Proponents of school desegregation should not be entrapped and misguided by the false assumption that black children must attend school with white children in order for black children to acquire the basic skills at acceptable levels. School desegregation will not automatically guarantee a quality education for black students . . . Far too often, school desegregation has resulted in a large number of black students receiving "little more than a long bus ride." School desegregation will not erase the reality that quality education for a vast number of black students wll be achieved only when there is quality schooling for blacks in predominantly black schools.[7]

Equal educational opportunity did not mean that blacks had to be in the minority in every school. Blacks had as much right as whites to be in the majority in schools and to celebrate their own culture and institutions.[8] The debt owed blacks by white society could be paid by supporting black institutions and by allocating financial resources to establish programs which directly met students' educational needs. Scott advocated compensation, not busing.

> The concept of equal educational opportunity is critical to any meaningful desegregation plan, but if schools are ever to compensate for the delimiting factors of socioeconomic deprivation and rectify the massive condition of cumulative deficiencies in the basic skills in reading and mathematics, there must be more than an equal allocation of personnel and financial resources. The commitment must be to go beyond equality to what can be called equity in the provision of resources in order to provide the necessary compensatory services for students hindered by social and educational inequalities.[9]

Dr. Scott wanted compensation for historic injustices. More money, better programs, and a lower pupil-teacher ratio were part of the answer, but not the whole. Dr. Scott wanted black culture to be

6. Ibid., 6.
7. Ibid., 4.
8. Ibid., 8.
9. Ibid., 6.

raised to status equal to that of majority white culture, or, put another way, he wanted white culture reduced to the position of one culture among many. Scott recognized that public education inculcated values as well as facts and skills.

> Schools do far more than teach young people how to read and write. Society through education attempts to pass on the standards and ideals which society believes are good and necessary for the generations to come. . . . Culture is the unique achievement of a group that distinguishes it from other groups. Multi-cultural education deemphasizes the importance of homogeneity and places the emphasis on preserving and strengthening cultural differences. This concept rejects the ideal of the school as a "melting pot" to achieve cultural sameness. Multi-cultural education advocates that people have a right to their cultural past and to the freedom and privileges that are enjoyed by those in the dominant streams of our total culture.[10]

Scott argued that black children were made to feel inferior through busing. They could be brought to full achievement only when black cultural values were officially sanctioned in a multi-cultural setting. Blacks required black majority schools, staffed by black teachers and black administrators. It was not a matter of teaching competence but cultural experience: "Black parents ought to object strenuously to predominantly black schools being exclusively staffed by faculties that are majority white. . . . Black teachers by their inclusion in the black experience have an understanding of and sensitivity to the essence of the black culture that cannot be obtained from the white experience."[11]

Dr. Scott had raised his voice to support the drive toward black cultural ascendence so desired by North Nashville's black leaders. Black schools, black role models, and ample resources—those were the restitution blacks sought from their white debtors. Desegregation, for them, consisted of having just a few whites—perhaps 15 percent—in their schools. These whites would learn what blacks already knew—what it was like to pay homage to someone else's culture. Minority whites were to be held hostage, in a sense, until the historic debt had been repaid. Indeed, white flight should not be anticipated in crafting a new desegregation plan, but if whites fled from majority black schools, then the court should compel new whites to attend the school to assure the proper ratio.[12]

Never before had a federal district court judge been asked by black

10. Ibid., 12.
11. Ibid., 16.
12. Ibid., 11.

plaintiffs to establish so sweeping and novel a remedy for historic violations of black civil rights. The enforced decorum of Judge Wiseman's court proceedings was a far cry from the passionate give-and-take of school board meetings. But the stately flow of the arguments could not mute the silent hopes of all the participants. The school board brought forward a new busing plan, patterned on the racial-balance approach of *Swann*. But now this sweeping desegregation plan was being contested on the argument that *Swann* itself was based on a racist doctrine.

Plowing New Ground

Hearings in Federal District Court began on March 3, 1980. Visually the courtroom was dominated by giant maps hung on posts in front of the empty jury box. Ray Osborne, the Metro school zoning director, tediously explained each detail of the board's plan. A man of infinite patience and bone-weary gait, Osborne showed how each cluster conformed to the criteria set by the school board and the citizens' Joint Committee.

A pattern was established early. School officials would testify on some aspect of the plan. Then Williams would cross-examine, seeking to establish a pattern of unequal treatment of blacks, followed by Carrol Kilgore, the attorney representing the intervenors from the Bellevue, Cohn, Pearl, and Joelton areas. But throughout, Wiseman himself too probed and questioned, often more pointedly than the attorneys themselves. Wiseman questioned the time it took to bus whites from outlying areas and later had federal marshals drive him along bus routes to test the estimates presented by school officials. Wiseman first raised the issue of white flight as a cost of the plan and asked the schools' attorney to provide testimony on that phenomenon.[13] And Wiseman was the first to point out that busing was not the only remedy for past injustices, that other approaches were possible.

A turning point in the hearings came on March 11. Wiseman seemed to reach a tentative conclusion. He acknowledged that the school board's plan placed an enormous burden on young black children and wondered if more busing was a waste of resources that could better be used to help black youngsters in other ways.

Avon Williams was cross-examining Dr. Elbert Brooks on the educational consequences of busing large numbers of children out of

---

13. *Tennessean,* Mar. 8, 1980. *Banner,* Mar. 8, 1980.

their neighborhoods in Grades 1–4. Wiseman interrupted, "As I understand the law, transportation of children is a remedy to overcome past inequalities, but it is not the only remedy. It's a means to an end. The end is quality education for all children. I ask you, sir, as a professional, is there another remedy that might be more efficacious in achieving this end?"[14]

Brooks replied that unitary plan for the county seemed to require substantial busing. He didn't know any other way. "So to carry it out, Judge, we put a burden on students—a burden resented by many parents. It costs money, and with a finite budget inroads are made in the quality of educational programs."

Wiseman pressed ahead. He wanted school officials to think more broadly. "Given the choice of spending $2 million or $3 million to do that [busing] and spending it on lower pupil-teacher ratios in the inner city, better reading laboratories, remedial reading programs and more enrichment programs—given that choice as an educator, which would you take?" Brooks did not hesitate. The director of schools said he would prefer more and better programs to busing.

Observers of the proceedings were struck by Wiseman's sincere effort to grapple with the costs and benefits of busing. Increasingly they realized that Wiseman saw Nashville as a special case. It had tried busing, but the policy had not worked. A new racial-balance busing plan would not necessarily work either; it was simply more of the same.

The seminar continued the next day. Dr. Bill Wise, Metro assistant director of facilities and transportation, was on the stand. Wiseman, Wise, and Willis, the board's legal counsel, discussed the most effective and constitutionally permissible remedy for prior discrimination. Wise had been testifying on the number of pupils transported and the associated costs under the old and new plans, when Judge Wiseman interrupted once more.

You know, I think there is and perhaps has been—and perhaps the courts are as much to blame for this as the educators—a hangup on the means and an obscuring of the end. . . . We have nine years' experience in Nashville, and somebody ought to be able to say whether or not, and to what extent, [busing] has been efficacious in remedying the effects of prior discrimination. But, as you know, I have the sort of frustrated feeling sitting up here that we are spending an awful lot of time talking about the mechanics without talking about the underlying principle to which the mechanics are to apply.[15]

14. *Tennessean*, Mar. 12, 1980. *Banner*, Mar. 13, 1980.
15. *Tennessean*, Mar. 13, 1980.

The conversation lasted almost half an hour. Willis made it clear that he had not encouraged the school board to deal with the cost-benefit issues in relation to busing, because he had assumed that the law required racial balance. "It really comes down, does it not, your honor, to the extent to which you are constitutionally required to try to achieve a racial mixture in a given school. Until that fundamental question is answered, it is impossible for the school board . . . to really go any further."

Wiseman responded directly, "We might consider plowing some new ground, Mr. Willis. We might also consider laying the old aside if [it] has proved inadequate."

At Wiseman's remarks, Donald Waldrip threw his pencil to the table in frustration. Wiseman seemed ready to discard all Waldrip's plans and ideals. Waldrip's intuition was right, and from this point on witnesses were asked to think more broadly about desegregation remedies.

Expert Witnesses

The defendant school board brought three expert witnesses to the stand. Waldrip, the Cincinnati consultant, gave the first testimonial in support of the desegregation plan. When asked if he would choose busing over enhanced reading labs, remedial programs, and reduced pupil-teacher ratios, Waldrip, in contrast to Brooks, said he would favor busing. Waldrip cited scholarly research as the basis for his conviction that the educational benefits of early integration outweighed the effectiveness of remedial education programs. The "strongest part" of the desegregation plan, in his view, was its insistence "that very early in a child's career he is getting a desegregated education."[16]

Avon Williams' cross-examination of Waldrip threw into relief the contrast in the two men's attitudes about busing, given the lessons of experience. Waldrip advocated the orthodox desegregation position— that each school in the system should have a racial ratio which mirrored the black/white proportion in the system as a whole. Williams had once held this position, and at one point he said that in 1971 "You might well have been testifying for the plaintiffs." Yet this was not 1971, and ten years of busing had convinced Williams that his clients would not stand for more busing for racial balance. County-

16. Ibid., Mar. 18, 1980. *Banner,* Mar. 18, 1980.

wide busing was "subtly discriminatory" because it meant that only majority white schools were acceptable. The verbal duel between Williams and Waldrip illustrated the clash of two cultures and the new tenor of the black argument.

Williams: Isn't there something paternalistic in the concept of always having a white majority as optimum in this plan?

Waldrip: Blacks are in the minority in this society. They need to know how to operate in a situation in which they are in a minority.

Williams: When you allow the desegregation plan to take white flight into account, aren't you reinforcing the racist attitudes of some white people?

Waldrip: I don't think so.

Williams: But if you keep catering to white people to the obvious disadvantage of black people in the system, would this not make white people feel they are more sought after and more important?

Waldrip: You're saying because we consider white flight, we encourage prejudice. We don't. If you don't have white kids, you can't have integration.[17]

Spectators and judge were held spellbound as the verbal fencing continued, question and answer, thrust and parry. At one point Williams asked Waldrip if he remembered the famous doll experiments of Dr. Kenneth Clark, cited as evidence in the famous 1954 *Brown* decision. Waldrip indicated that he did recall that both black and white children chose the white doll as "best" and labeled the black doll "bad." Williams asked if such attitudes of white "self-adoration" didn't imply that black children of tender years shouldn't be bused into white suburbs. Waldrip responded, "Do I understand you to suggest that we [ought to] segregate young black children?"

Williams said that he did not favor a return to separate-but-equal schools. Instead, black plaintiffs were asking for "havens of black majority," so that both black and white children could learn that integration was not a one-way bus ride. Williams continued to push Waldrip: "If a black child is exposed to some of that racial prejudice and sees [that] he always goes to white neighborhoods and that no white children come to his neighborhood, are you prepared to say, as an educator, that that has no effect on his self-esteem?"

Waldrip responded, "I'm saying a first and second grade child doesn't think about those things. Other considerations, including the

17. *Tennessean*, Mar. 30, 1980.

desegregation of classrooms, are more important than the one you're raising, because it's irrelevant to small children."[18]

With this exchange Avon Williams smiled his tough sarcastic smile. Waldrip had admitted that the board's plan favored whites. If the self-esteem of black children was not damaged by being bused out, then the self-esteem of white children could not be damaged by busing them into black neighborhoods where they would be in the minority. In future arguments, Williams would ask that the transportation burden be shifted to whites. Waldrip anticipated Williams' demand and feared it. Resegregation was the only outcome he could foresee if whites were required to attend schools in the inner city in the early grades.

Jay Robinson, school superintendent in Charlotte-Mecklenburg County, North Carolina, was the next expert presenting evidence on behalf of the Metro School Board. Charlotte's desegregation plan, like Nashville's, attempted to establish a system-wide black-white ratio in every school, and Robinson testified that busing worked in his city. Black test scores had risen appreciably since busing began, and there was little white flight because all but one school in Charlotte was racially balanced. Judge Wiseman asked about this largely black school: what were its test scores like? "The children in Hidden Valley School are getting a good education," Robinson replied. Their test scores compared favorably to majority white schools in the system. "Then what's wrong with it?" asked Wiseman. Robinson replied that the black community considered it undesirable to have a predominantly black school. "The black community let us know the experience . . . didn't work, and they expect us to integrate it."

Next Robinson was asked about the burden of busing and the possibility of busing more whites into downtown schools. He replied that his experience indicated that such a plan was unworkable; whites would not send their children to inner-city schools in the early grades. In Charlotte, as in Metro, black children were bused toward suburbia in the early elementary years. "You have to make your school plan accomodate what the community will reasonably support," he said. But this reasoning did not satisfy the black plaintiffs. Avon Williams remarked to Robinson, "Your district, and this district, have developed plans that put more of a burden on black people and admittedly caters to the prejudices of white people."[19]

Judge Wiseman indicated that he wanted more evidence about

18. Ibid.
19. *Banner,* Mar. 22, 1980.

white flight. Counsel for the school board asked Dr. Richard A. Pride, a Vanderbilt University political scientist, to prepare a report on white flight in the county from 1971 to 1979. Dr. Pride had previously presented papers at academic meetings on first-year white flight in Nashville, Louisville, and Memphis. Judge Wiseman had read these, but he wanted more recent information.[20] Pride's testimony came late in the hearings, and the findings he brought to the court have been summarized in Chapter 7. Basically, Pride found white flight to be a significant problem in the implementation of the 1971 plan.[21]

Pride, Waldrip, and Robinson each testified to the value of a racial balance plan while acknowledging the hardships it placed on blacks. Each recognized that white flight had been taken into account in drawing up the plan. Like other white liberals, each one thought of himself as an ally of blacks in their struggle for equal opportunity, but now found the integrationist basis of his beliefs in question.

The Plaintiffs' Response

Plaintiffs' attorney Avon Williams continually attacked the school board's plan, arguing that blacks suffered disproportionately through school closings, years bused out of their neighborhoods, being always in the minority, and the closing of historic Pearl High School. Dr. Hugh Scott, whose beliefs supported Williams' argument, was the plaintiffs' expert witness. He criticized the board for relying solely on busing and racial balance in its plan.

The major assumptions underlying Scott's testimony were clear and consistent with the paper presented to the court earlier.[22] First, Scott emphasized the shame of black history; of all immigrant groups, blacks' treatment by whites was the worst. Black people had a never-ending struggle to prevent their complete subjugation as a race. The black experience in America conditioned them to approach proposals championed by white Americans with great caution. Second, Scott emphasized the role schools played in the battle for desegregation. Along with many other institutions, they had long operated on the assumption that there was a single American culture. Scott

20. Pride, "Patterns of White Flight: 1971–1979," report submitted to the Board of Education, Metropolitan Nashville-Davidson County Public Schools, Apr. 2, 1980 (mimeographed). Pride and Woodard, "Busing and White Flight: Implementation Plans in Three Southern Cities." Pride and Woodard, "Busing Plans and White Flight: Nashville and Louisville."

21. *Tennessean*, Apr. 25, 1980.

22. Exhibit #248.

emphasized social pluralism. Since the schools existed on public monies for public benefits, they had a heavy responsibility to promulgate those values that heighten a subgroup's self-awareness. For black Americans, quality education meant a commitment to the idea that "blackness" was not a regrettable human condition but rather a proud heritage.

These two convictions led to Scott's conclusion that black Americans shared a common set of values which distinguished them from other ethnic groups. School desegregation should demonstrate a respect for these differences. The premise that predominantly white schools are acceptable for black students while predominantly black schools are unacceptable for white students communicates a presumption of the "rightness of whiteness." Within the context of school desegregation, a rigid adherence to racial balance was counterproductive. The presence of predominantly black schools and even some all black schools does not infringe upon the right of black students to equal educational opportunity, Scott concluded.

Dr. Scott's testimony was a tour de force.[23] He was confident, articulate, and often scathing in his analysis of the school board's plan. But under cross-examination by Bill Willis, the board's experienced trial lawyer, Scott often seemed unfamiliar with Nashville and the proposed plan. Willis bludgeoned Scott, using his own language, and pressed him to make specific recommendations. Willis urged Scott to identify the schools in Davidson County which Scott thought should be 100 percent black. Scott responded by saying that he had given the criteria for decisions; the school board had only to use them. Asked how many all black schools he would advocate, Scott replied, "You could have any number," adding that he and Avon Williams disagreed on this point. Williams wanted no all black schools, while Scott would permit them. What was important to Scott was whether the students were achieving and whether closing the school would harm the students and their families unduly.

Willis aimed his cross-examination at the majority black schools proposal supported by both Williams and Scott. The board attorney asked what would happen if whites refused to participate in a busing plan with majority black schools. "Then I would assume you would take action to bus other whites in, just as you do blacks," Scott replied. When Willis said this might prove impractical, Scott explained his basic attitude about busing. "My concern with the plan . . . is ultimately, when whites refuse to participate, [you] put the burden on black students. . . . I am opposed to that." Willis re-

---

23. Transcript, 1–530. On file, District Court.

sponded by asking whether Scott believed in integration. "That is not what you are asking me," he replied. "You are putting a question: when whites refuse to take part in a public educational program, do you impose the burden on blacks? That is not desegregation, that is an imposition of inequity on blacks."

Scott's response touched an exposed nerve in school administrators and lawyers. They had often pondered this point among themselves. If whites left majority black schools and the system were required to zone another batch of whites to meet some minimum quota for such schools, white flight would inevitably accelerate and the spectre of a dual school system (public versus private) would fast become a reality. This line of reasoning was not lost on Judge Wiseman.

Scott insisted that many black youngsters, particularly those in the lower grades, needed to be in the supportive environment of neighborhood schools. Attorney Willis responded to this argument by reading a quotation which said in part, " . . . the inner core area in Nashville is a highly localized environment where learning is highly restricted."

Willis asked if Scott agreed "with the description that I just read to you about the destructive nature and repressive climate for young black children of the inner city area?" Scott paused, thinking the words might have been his own, then said that Nashville's inner city could not compare to the South Bronx. The statement might apply there but not in Nashville. Willis said he was delighted to hear that, for he had been quoting Merrill G. Herman, Scott's predecessor as expert witness for the plaintiffs, in the 1971 court hearings. Herman had been talking about Nashville at that time, and his remarks had been in support of busing for racial balance. In ten years two expert witnesses for the black plaintiffs had presented opposite arguments in the Nashville desegregation suit.

The Intervenors' Plan

At one point in his cross-examination of Dr. Scott, Willis raised the issue of school closures in white neighborhoods. Scott replied that there "doesn't seem to be any attachment to" such schools. The irony of this response brought a smile to Willis' face. "Have you met my friend Mr. Carrol Kilgore?" he asked.

Attorney Kilgore represented a group of citizens fighting to keep their schools open in the face of the latest school board plan. The intervenors were a loose coalition of mostly white parents opposing school closures in their areas. They proposed an alternative plan put together by a group of laymen from data supplied by the school board. The intervenors had divided the county into six "equity" clusters emanating from the central city like the blades of a fan. Within each cluster children would attend neighborhood elementary schools. The elementary schools in turn would feed middle schools in each cluster, where the intervenors were forced to use some noncontiguous zones to achieve even minimum desegregation. At the high school level each cluster would contain comprehensive and traditional high schools. The plan would retain Bellevue, Joelton, Cohn, Pearl, Antioch, East, DuPont, Madison, and Goodlettsville—the traditional high schools. Students could opt for either a traditional or a comprehensive high school education. The intervenors planned to use special magnet programs to desegregate the traditional high schools to a minimum 10% of either race.

The main problem with the intervenors' "equity" plan was the preponderance of one-race schools at all levels. Many of the schools in the plan did not meet the 10 percent threshold of "minority" students (black or white) which was to be the benchmark of desegregation. Though the intervenors hoped to attract "minority" students through special programs, they said that if, after a time, a school could not attract 10 percent of the other race, the school should be closed. Such a policy would create a built-in incentive for school supporters to work toward the 10 percent threshold.

The intervenors brought to the stand several witnesses, among them Dr. Walter Leonard, president of Fisk University, and Dr. Lou Beasley, a Pearl High School graduate and professor of social work at the University of Tennessee, Nashville. Leonard was one of Nashville's most prominent citizens. Fisk University had trained black leaders for generations, and everyone wanted to hear what he had to say.

Leonard opened his testimony by saying that in the ideal world each school should be a microcosm of the community, but his idea of microcosm was not proportional representation.[24] Each school would include a range of races and social classes. It was important to have some blacks in every predominantly white school and some whites in predominantly black schools. And it was educationally beneficial to whites to be in the minority in majority black schools, where they would learn that they are a minority in the world community. That they learn this was particularly important since the nation's major cities were majority black, both demographically and politically.

24. Transcript, 1–530. On file, District Court.

Majority black schools, Leonard went on, were very important to blacks. Only in black majority institutions were the leadership capabilities of young blacks brought to full potential, and only there were the history and culture of the black race in America preserved and glorified for black students. Unless there were identifiably black institutions in black communities, they would get the impression that their collective experience as a people was not important.

Before *Brown*, said Leonard, blacks were concerned about the unequal distribution of resources. Blacks thought there was nothing wrong with the learning ability of black children, if these children could just get the facilities and the environment in which to develop their capabilities. Blacks figured that the only way to get resources was to have their kids taken where the white children were or have white children brought to where black children were. But what blacks really wanted was access to the resources. That was the real issue in the 1950s, and that was the real issue still.

At the end of Leonard's testimony Judge Wiseman summarized the argument made:

> You suggested *Brown, Swann* and *Green* and other cases may have been misinterpreted to the extent that they have been read to require assimilation. It is not undemocratic and it does not violate equal protection of the laws to have a system that allows for recognition of and respect for differences in our society. Rigid adherence to racial ratios that is premised on the social goal of assimilation, which in the process demeans, diminishes, or neglects cultural and ethnic pride, as well as differences, it is not only constitutionally unrequired, but socially undesired. In view of the twenty-five-year experience with desegregation efforts, it is now far more important to concentrate on what happens at the end of the bus ride than upon the racial mix achieved. You would, therefore, recommend to the Board and to the Court that the plan include some schools which may be identified as black if this results from a natural geographic community assignment or freedom of choice on the part of students and parents rather than for reasons of maintaining segregation of the races.[25]

Judge Wiseman asked if this summary accurately reflected his testimony, and Dr. Leonard said it did.

Dr. Beasley had conducted research on stress in minority children. Racism, said Beasley, was a pervasive aspect of the black child's life. It was the top mental health problem of black people. It was very important that young children in their formative years *not* enter an environment that was alien to them. When a child was suddenly plunged into an environment dominated by those of another race, he

25. Ibid., 3458–3464.

could not perform normally; there needed to be a critical mass of others who were like him. Studies showed that when there was a high concentration of blacks in a school—say two-thirds—the self-esteem of black children in the situation was much higher than that of white children. Self-esteem was necessary for normal growth and development.

Dr. Beasley wanted the school board and the court to de-emphasize efforts to achieve racial balance in the schools in the lower grades. The closer the school environment was to the neighborhood environment, the better it was for the children. The 1971 plan, which took black children out of their neighborhoods in the early grades and put them in predominantly white suburban schools, was traumatic for their learning experience. The school system was a good place to prepare students to live in a multi-racial, multi-cultural situation, but that was best accomplished in the middle years.[26]

The Court Decision

Judge Wiseman's hearings had consumed sixteen days in March and nine days in April. Closing arguments were made on May 1 after more than one hundred hours of courtroom testimony. The hopes and fears of diverse community groups rested on this one man, who had to weigh the conflicting evidence and fashion a desegregation remedy.

If Wiseman accepted the school board's plan, he would endorse the assimilationist thrust of legal precedent. The board's plan, like *Swann* itself, made racial balance in pupil assignment the standard remedy to end racial separation in the schools and in society. But also as in *Swann*, under the board's plan, blacks would bear disproportionately the hardships of busing.

On the other hand, if Wiseman supported the plaintiffs' argument and reduced the blacks' burden, he would risk undermining the already waning community support of public education. The plaintiffs wanted more black community schools, and blacks and whites to be bused in equal proportions. To accede to this request would require busing more whites downtown; requiring that would probably result in more white flight and more empty classrooms. If Wiseman ruled in favor of the plaintiffs, he might truly create a new dual school system—one public, black, and poor; the other private, white, and middle-class.

On May 20, 1980, Judge Wiseman issued a bold opinion which

26. Ibid., 6581–6626.

departed from precedent. He escaped the horns of his dilemma by prescribing a new remedy for the historic violations of black rights. In order to bring blacks to the place they would have occupied if they had not been discriminated against, Wiseman rejected busing and mandated enhanced educational services. Implicitly he condoned cultural dualism and, in doing so, questioned the cultural assimilationist policy established by the Supreme Court.

Wiseman ordered the school board to come up with a new plan following the reasoning and guidelines of his sixty-page Memorandum Opinion. This carefully crafted document addressed the plaintiffs, intervenors, and school board one after the other.

The opinion began with a summary of the long history of the case, from 1955, when *Kelley* was first filed, through the 1980 hearings. Wiseman described the 1980 proposals in detail, then summarized the black plaintiffs' criticisms of the school board plan.

> The board plan and the 1971 plan are both premised upon a goal that the percentage of black students in each school represent the percentage of blacks in the county. This is justified upon the philosophy that each public school should be a microcosm of the community it serves and that it is necessary to use such a percentage mix in order to have enough blacks "to spread around," thereby achieving racial balance in all schools. . . . Plaintiffs insist: (1) the microcosm effect is practically impossible, (2) the "spreading around" effect is inherently disparately burdensome to blacks; and (3) the osmosis theory is invidiously racist and based upon assumed black inferiority. Plaintiffs assert that to contend that a black child can receive a quality education only in a white majority classroom is blatantly racist and paternalistic.[27]

The irony of such arguments was not lost on those who read the opinion. Ten years earlier the assimilationist theory had guided all desegregation decisions. But in 1980 these same proposals were criticized because they placed a disparate burden on black children, resulted in the closing of inner-city schools, and assumed a "rightness of whiteness." A tremendously important change had taken place during the past decade. Blacks no longer wanted busing.

"A dramatic role reversal has taken place," wrote Judge Wiseman. "Historically, black plaintiffs felt the necessity to be in a majority white school in order to be assured of equal distribution of educational funding." But such was no longer the case. In 1980 the "white majority of the school board, acting on the advice of a white desegregation expert, recommended to the Court *more* busing to achieve *more* racial balance. Equally contrary to earlier posture, the black

27. Memorandum Opinion, May 1, 1980, 32.

plaintiffs urge upon the Court *less* busing, and *more* neighborhood characteristics to the assignment plan, and the permissibility of majority black schools."[28]

The plaintiffs had not developed a plan of their own. When the hearings were half over Williams had indicated that the plaintiffs could put together a plan, but that it would take about six weeks. Wiseman said that was too long to wait. Williams had to be content with his criticisms of the school board plan and a list of revisions he might make to it. Wiseman listed Williams' recommendations in his opinion.[29]

1. An intervention program that addresses the needs of students who are deficient in the basic skills, especially when such students are bused to schools not in their immediate neighborhood;
2. A program at all schools that provides relevant educational experiences geared to helping students acquire an understanding of the life and culture of black Americans;
3. Programs and services that address the needs of students, black and white, who are achieving below the national norms in the basic skills areas;
4. A mechanism that insures that black students do indeed gain equitable access to the specialized programs offered in the comprehensive high schools;
5. A commitment to the maintenance of Pearl High School;
6. The concept that either whites or blacks can constitute the minority racial group;
7. The maintenance of the kindergarten and the primary grades as an integral educational unit;
8. A busing formula that does not shift black students in disproportionate numbers to white students;
9. A commitment not to dislocate black students disproportionately in the kindergarten and early grades;
10. An improved systemwide ratio of black teachers and black administrators;
11. A policy that permits a greater number of black teachers to be assigned to predominantly black schools.

The board had presented and defended a *Swann*-style racial balance desegregation plan. The plaintiffs were asking Judge Wiseman to go beyond *Swann* and make new law.

After summarizing the plaintiffs' objections, Wiseman evaluated the intervenor's plan. It was his opinion that this plan "emanated

28. Ibid.
29. Ibid., 33.

largely from a parochial desire to protect certain schools in certain communities." The judge found it impossible to justify such an approach; the proposed plan would lead to massive resegregation in almost all schools and grade levels. Aspects of the intervenor's plan did, however, influence Wiseman's proposals for fashioning a judicial remedy.

School desegregation cases are heard under a system of legal rules and doctrines known collectively as "equity law." These supplement common and statute law and supercede them when the latter prove inadequate for just settlement. Equity law permits the district court wide latitude in fashioning a remedy. The Supreme Court had never precisely defined what constituted a "unitary" school system, and Judge Wiseman intended to exercise his discretionary power to the full here. To justify his own approach, Wiseman cited legal precedent.

Four major cases provided guidelines for remedying the effects of school segregation. *Brown II* (1955) had required the destruction of racial barriers which excluded black children from attending schools with white children. After much delay, the Court outlawed "freedom of choice" plans and ordered school boards to "come forward with a plan that promises realistically to work, and promises realistically to work *now.*" In *Green v. County School Board* (1968) the Supreme Court emphasized the "now;" but Judge Wiseman cited Green for a different word. He emphasized "realistically." Throughout the hearings the judge had stressed pragmatism; the goal of desegregation was more important than the means of busing. In the third case, *Swann v. Charlotte–Mecklenburg Co. Board of Education* (1971), the Court had approved busing as a remedy for school desegregation. *Swann* was the last word on the subject in the south. In the North, however, the Court had gone further. In addition to busing, the Court emphasized the remedial (i.e. compensation) nature of judicial responsibility. In *Milliken v. Bradley* (Milliken I, 1974) the Supreme Court expanded the charge of federal courts to "restore the victims of discriminatory conduct to the position they would have occupied in the absence of such conduct." In *Milliken II* (1977) the Court specifically included remediation as a form of educational compensation designed to do this.

Wiseman took these cases to mean that his court must fashion a remedy for school discrimination that was effective. If busing was not effective, then other options, such as remedial education programs designed to benefit black children, were available. If, based on evidence he had heard, he concluded that busing was not effective, he would become the first federal judge to abandon busing in favor of another apporach in a school desegregation case. Though Wiseman recognized that he was taking a risky and uncharted path he concluded precisely that.

Judge Wiseman argued that remedies must be subjected to the traditional balancing tests required in a court of equity. "Effectiveness must be weighed against other available alternatives, and each alternative must be assessed in terms of its relative costs." Busing, he said, was only one alternative. *Swann* had been misinterpreted; it did not command a racial balance in each school, although courts had generally begun with the assumption that racial balance was essential. For Judge Wiseman, the achievement of racial ratios had mistakenly become the *end* of litigation of this type, rather than the means they had been conceived originally to be.

Wiseman's opinion evaluated the effects of busing. He wanted everyone, especially the appeals court, to know that his decision had been based on experience. This was a second-round busing case, and since the 1980 board plan was similar to the 1971 court-ordered plan, Wiseman was in a position to ask questions about the efficacy of busing.

> Were this Court addressing the situation in this county as it existed in 1971, there would be no alternative but to order the implementation of a plan that entailed school pairings, noncontiguous zoning, and substantial busing. Nothing in this opinion should reflect a diminution of the realization of the necessity of such an order in 1971 . . . It is only after nine years of zoning and busing to achieve a desegragated system and the changes that have taken place in the community and in the attitude manifested by the School Board that it is possible to reevaluate the efficacy of the remedy incorporated into the 1971 order.[30]

The new plan was weighed in the balance and found wanting. The costs of busing outweighed its benefits. Wiseman asked if the 1980 plan held out a realistic promise for the achievement of a unitary school system and found that it did not. First, he said, the racial balances established by the plan would not hold; white flight would result. He cited Pride's statement that trends indicated that 25 to 30 percent of the county's elementary-age children would be in private schools by the middle to late 1980s. Wiseman viewed this probability with alarm: "The spectre that haunts all of the parties in this case, the Court, and the community is a public school system populated by the poor and black,and a private school system serving the affluent and white." White flight was only partially due to remnants of racial prejudice, Wiseman held; testimony and letters sent to the board and the court made clear that flight also reflected a widespread belief that

30. Ibid., 42.

quality education was no longer available in the public schools. If that situation ever became reality, then neither blacks nor whites could receive equal educational opportunity.

The board's plan had not addressed the issue of educational quality, except through one largely undefined and unfunded magnet school. Judge Wiseman found the 1980 plan to be simply another pupil reassignment plan. If the schools were disrupted again without a strong effort to enhance their educational quality, more parents would flee to private schools.

Wiseman also indicated that the "osmosis effect," the use of white children as a principal learning resource for black children, had not had the desired result. "The gap between black and white achievement had narrowed slightly . . . but average black achievement in both math and reading is still well below national norms, and the gap between black and white achievement remains substantial."

The judge believed that white flight would surely undo the racial balance busing plan and would likely lead to a new dual school system. Black achievement scores under busing had not responded with the surge predicted by the "osmosis" model. Wiseman found that blacks would bear an onerous burden of busing under the proposed plan. Nor had the board's plan given attention to the need to enhance educational programs, since money was to be diverted to pupil transportation. In short, Wiseman held that the social, educational, and economic costs of busing were too high.

Wiseman examined the record of busing in Nashville and found that a remedy of the *Swann* type had not been effective. The rights of black people were violated in Nashville by vestiges of a dual school system. The court's job was to restore these victims to the position they would have occupied had the historic violations not occurred. The Supreme Court in *Swann* had assumed that, had it not been for state-imposed segregation, blacks would have lived geographically dispersed throughout the county—that is, blacks would have been assimilated into the mainstream culture. Assimilation was the restoration required by *Swann*, and busing was the tool to bring it about. But in the Nashville case, the plaintiffs did not want assimilation; they wanted cultural parity. Busing itself, according to the plaintiffs, was based on paternalistic and racist assumptions.

Wiseman's options were clear. If he accepted the board's plan, he would simultaneously crush black aspirations and engender another wave of white flight; white flight would ultimately lead to a new dual school system. If he acceded to the plaintiffs' requests and bused more whites into black area schools, he would acknowledge the black cultural arguments but stimulate greater white flight. White flight, as it led both to a new dual school system and to diminished financial support for the public schools, was the great nemesis, no matter which way he turned.

Wiseman could escape the nemesis only by rejecting busing and the assimilationist theory that underlay it. And that is just what he did. He would establish neighborhood elementary schools and require a minimum 15 percent of *either race* at the middle and high school levels. He would acknowledge the claims of the advocates of black culture and remedy the ill effects of historic segregation through enhanced *educational* services. And he would reject assimilation: "It was not the intent of *Brown* and its progeny to require blacks always to be in the minority; nor should these precedents have been read to require assimilation or amalgamation." To the judge, it was not undemocratic to have a system which recognized and respected racial differences in society. Dr. Leonard's arguments were compelling and were reflected in Wiseman's assessment of racial quotas: "A rigid adherence to racial ratios premised upon the social goal of assimilation, which in the process demeans, diminishes, or benignly neglects cultural and ethnic pride as well as differences, is not only constitutionally un-required but socially undesirable."[31]

Guidelines for the New Plan

The interpretive history of *Kelley* and the citations of constitutional law were but a preface and a justification for Wiseman's decision. The court rejected the school board's plan and ordered that a new plan be developed according to specific guidelines enumerated in the opinion. The court's guidelines eliminated busing in the early grades, minimized it in the upper grades, established either race as a minority, set the threshold of desegregation at 15 percent, and mandated special programs and services for underachieving youngsters. In short, Wiseman abandoned assimilation and accepted the claims of black cultural separatism. Wiseman ordered:

1. *Tier Structure.* A three-tier system (K4-4-4) was to be employed instead of a four-tier grade structure, since it was judged educationally better for students.
2. *Grades K-4 of a Neighborhood Character.* Neighborhood schools should be used in Grades K-4 with zone lines drawn to utilize facilities better and to maximize integration.
3. *Middle Schools with 15 percent Minimum of Either Race.* Middle

31. Ibid., 50.

schools (Grades 5–8) were to be based on clusters of elementary school zones, to bring about a minimum of 15 percent of either race in the minority. Noncontiguous zones could be used but should be held to a minimum, and wherever they were used, the nearest black or white children should be included to achieve the required 15 percent minority.

4. *Comprehensive High Schools with No Cross-Zone Busing.* Wiseman implicitly accepted the idea of *naturally desegregated* high schools in a ring around the city (Briley Parkway extended). He confirmed the closing of Bellevue and Joelton High Schools and in addition ordered outlying DuPont and Antioch High Schools closed. He permitted the construction of a new Madison-Goodlettsville Comprehensive High School and thus implicitly affirmed the board's plan to close traditional high schools in those two communities. He accepted the board's intention to build a new inner-city comprehensive high school (Pearl-Cohn), although he noted the redundancy of programs and facilities. He accepted the idea of an academic magnet high school with feeder academic magnets at the elementary school level.

5. *Educational Services As a Remedy for Historical Violations.* In place of busing Wiseman ordered design and implementation of various educational programs. They could be paid for, in part, by the savings from reduced busing. The judge specifically suggested:

- Regular intercultural experiences for children in predominantly white or predominantly black elementary schools (e.g., exchanges between schools).
- Reduced pupil-teacher ratios in schools where academic achievement is below the average for the system.
- Remediation efforts in schools or classes made up largely of socioeconomically deprived children who suffer from the continuing effects of prior discrimination.
- Any other ways the professional staff could develop to attack the problem of disparate achievement between black and white children.
- The design, implementation, and monitoring of black history and culture materials for inclusion in the regular curricula of all schools, and specific courses in black history and culture in the comprehensive high schools.

6. *Affirmative Action in Employment.* Wiseman had not yet held hearings on staff composition but was already persuaded that the old ratio of 80 percent–20 percent, white to black, had to be abandoned. He ordered the board to include in its new plan a

provision for affirmitive-action recruitment and hiring of black personnel as vacancies occurred by attrition.

7. *Sensitivity Training and Teacher Assignment.* Wiseman ordered further efforts to be made to see that all teachers went through training designed to increase their sensitivity to the special needs of black children. Moreover, the most sensitive teachers should be assigned to schools and classes where desegregation was problematic.

Conclusions

The implications of Wiseman's guidelines were striking. He had heard an enormous amount of testimony and had ordered a wholly new direction for desegregation in Nashville and, by example at least, for countless other communities across the country. In place of assimilation, he had accepted cultural dualism. In place of busing, he had mandated educational programs.

At first glance it seemed that Avon Williams and Dr. Hugh Scott had gotten all they had asked for. Neighborhood elementary schools meant that black youngsters could stay close to home. More financial resources, in the form of educational services, would be dedicated to their schools than to affluent suburban schools.

But Williams and the plaintiffs had not gotten something else they had wanted desperately—whites bused into the inner city. They had wanted neighborhood schools, *and* desegregation, but they had gotten only neighborhood schools. If 12 to 35 percent of the student body were not white (and the neighborhoods around most of the black community's schools would not generate those proportions), then their aims had been thwarted. They had wanted enough whites in the minority to give black children a "majority experience" and white children a "minority experience," and so to assure that the white community would remain attentive to black students' needs. In terms of status politics, the plaintiffs had not scored a victory. Whites would pay no homage to black culture at the elementary school level.

And at the high school level, Wiseman had not restored historic Pearl High School; he had merely agreed to the board's proposal to build a new inner-city comprehensive high school. Pearl had become the symbol of black heritage, and Wiseman had denied blacks this symbol. Wiseman was consistent, though; he also closed white Bellevue, Joelton, DuPont, and Antioch. The ring of comprehensive high schools would fulfill the needs of desegregation naturally.

The white communities had not really lost, even though the guidelines handed down were consistent with Dr. Scott's agenda. The whites, too, would have neighborhood elementary schools they so desired. Wiseman clearly had feared that more busing would alienate the white community still more, pushing Nashville ever closer to a new dual school system—public and private this time, and largely segregated by both race and class. Wiseman certainly must have hoped that a return to neighborhood schools would stop the flight from the public schools and perhaps even attract greater public enrollment and financial support.

Epilogue

When newspaper reporters gathered to pick up copies of the decision, one latecomer asked another, "Who won?" His colleague replied wryly, "The judge did." Judge Wiseman felt that the decision, once rendered, required explanation. The court testimony had convinced him that the future of public education in Nashville was tied to his decision. He wanted to restore pride in public education.

It came as no surprise, then, when Judge Wiseman accepted an invitation to address the Downtown Exchange Club. He began his speech with a question: "How many of you attended public schools?" A large majority raised their hands. Then the judge asked how many in the audience sent their children to public schools. The response was predictable. Among fathers and mothers who had moved through the public schools, few raised their hands. The problem was simply stated: there had been a steady erosion of support for public education, especially among the upper middle class.

Wiseman quoted the figures on white flight provided by Dr. Richard Pride in his court testimony. The judge explained that some of the flight might be attributed to the quest for moral values found in Christian academies, some to the perception of poor quality, and some to racism traveling under another guise. But if parents felt that the public schools were inferior educationally, Wiseman said, they should investigate more carefully. The public schools had a record to be proud of.

The schools needed help to become better still, though. Although Nashville achievement test scores were still a bit below the national average, the public schools, with all their diversity, had made rapid progress and only needed additional support to reach the average. Between 1974 and 1980 Nashville schools had produced twenty-five National Merit Scholars, and thirteen of them were from public high

schools. Harpeth Hall, an elite private academy for girls, had thirty-
five National Merit finalists, but Hillsboro and Hillwood, the adjacent public high schools, had thirty-four and eighteen respectively.
Moreover, of the Phi Beta Kappa members elected at Vanderbilt University that spring, six of the seven from Nashville were public high
school graduates.

Wiseman asked the business elite a simple question and suggested
his own answer.

> Why should we be concerned about erosion of support for the public
> schools? Why should it bother us if there appears to be a trend toward a
> sharp division of society, in which the children of the affluent attend
> private schools and the public school system exists for the poor and black?
> Why should it concern us that with such an erosion of public support there
> will inevitably be an erosion of the quality of education offered? The
> answer to these questions lies in the recognition—the realization—that
> public education has been the leavening agent by which our multi-ethnic,
> multi-racial society has been able to rise and become a whole loaf.
>
> It is *because* we had public schools, which most children attended, that
> we were able to assimilate so rapidly the great influx of immigrants from so
> many different cultures during the nineteenth century.
>
> It is *because* we had public schools, attended by rich and poor alike, that
> the American dream became a reality to so many of us. The concept of
> democracy, of a society in which hard work, perseverance, and talent would
> be rewarded regardless of the station from which one started, has been
> most notably evident in, and fostered by, the public schools.
>
> It is largely *because* we had public schools, in which children from the
> most diverse of backgrounds learned to live and work together at an early
> age, that we have been able to maintain social harmony in such a hetero-
> geneous conglomerate of people.[32]

32. Thomas Wiseman Jr., unpublished and undated speech, photocopy in Pride's
files.

CHAPTER TWELVE

The Triumph of Assimilation

Would Judge Wiseman's decision be appealed? "I don't know," said Avon Williams; "I may seek clarification from the court."[1] A national desegregation expert criticized the decision and predicted it would be overturned upon appeal. Busing opponents in the outlying areas mobilized to resist the plan, and one of their city Councilmembers went so far as to draft an educational voucher proposal. Others organized to change the Metro Charter to allow for an elected, instead of appointed, school board. But most parents applauded the Wiseman decision; it emphasized quality of education and public support for public schools.

The main actor in the drama remained Avon Williams. He was trying a case in Jackson, Tennessee, when the Wiseman order came down. Reporters pursued him there and found his reaction mixed. "I'm pleased with the court's philosophical position, the decision to do something about black studies and remediation, and the recognition that desegregation means more than just mixing children in schools," Williams said after reading the opinion. But he opposed the exclusion of grades K–4 from the busing plan. "Our position was simply that an effort be made to apply zoning to maintain some neighborhood characteristics, but that when integration could not be achieved in a (neighborhood) zone, busing be used with a more liberal ratio for minority presence."[2] Williams, always cautious with the press, gave no hint about a possible appeal of Wiseman's order. Instead he chose to wait until the school board prepared a plan based on the Wiseman guidelines.

Dr. Willis D. Hawley was not guarded in his reaction. Hawley, one of the nation's foremost experts in school desegregation, had recently accepted a position on the Vanderbilt University faculty. He stated that the Wiseman decision had national implications and would certainly be appealed and overturned. If Wiseman's order were to stand unchallenged, Hawley said, school systems around the country

1. *Tennessean*, May 22, 1980.
2. Ibid.

would return to court to try to eliminate busing in the early grades in their communities. For Hawley, exclusion of the early grades from busing was a crucial error in judgement. While he acknowledged that neighborhood schools in the early grades would probably arrest white flight and would certainly be popular with the community, he said that the Wiseman decision simply returned the schools to segregated status. Hawley repeated the research findings: the beneficial effects of desegregation on black achievement and race relations depended most on interracial contact in the early grades. "Most of the research says that if desegregation is going to be effective, it has to begin when children are young."[3] Hawley believed that the Sixth Circuit Court of Appeals would overturn the neighborhood elementary schools approach taken by Wiseman.

Meanwhile, other members of the community tried to make the school board more responsive to majority public opinion. Metro Councilman Charles "Bud" Hill said that he wanted an elected school board and the "elimination" of the public school system. Hill sponsored legislation that would distribute school tax money so parents could pay private school tuition.[4] The school board had voted to close Joelton and Bellevue High Schools, and Wiseman had ordered Antioch and DuPont High Schools closed as well. Each school served outlying white communities, and supporters of these schools vowed to keep them open. They sought a revision in the Metro Charter.

The charter adopted by referendum in 1962 had established a metropolitan government for Nashville and Davidson County. At that time, to remove it from political issues, the school board was established as a body appointed by the mayor. In the August 1980 general election, partisans of the schools scheduled for closure collected enough signatures to place the issue of an elected school board on the November 1980 ballot. The Committee for an Elected School Board (CESB) spent only sixty dollars on its campaign but won handily. County-wide, the referendum garnered 56 percent of the vote. It was the first revision of the Metro Charter by a political drive since Metro's inception in 1962. The first school board election would not take place until 1982, but the victory of parochial interests was evident in the voting patterns. The white outlying areas gave overwhelming support to the idea of an elected board. One of their leaders made clear why: "The people are sick and tired of having bureaucracy shoved down their throats whether they like it or not."[5] The symbolic aspects of the victory were not lost on the community, but the

3. *Banner,* June 16, 1980.
4. Ibid., May 22, 1980.
5. *Tennessean,* Nov. 5, 1980.

incumbent board was undeterred. Its members announced that they would proceed with the business of running the schools until their terms expired.

After Judge Wiseman's May 20, 1980, order, the Nashville *Banner* editorialized, "The Metro School Board has been sent back to the drawing board for a new desegregation plan, but not without some well-defined and precedent-setting blueprints from U.S. District Judge Thomas Wiseman."[6] The board studied Wiseman's ruling and decided that it would take several months to develop the plan fully. At a July hearing Judge Wiseman accepted the board's proposed timetable with minor revisions, and during the fall the planning process began in earnest. The board received reports from its staff and planning committees, just as it had the year before, but there was no urgency and little public interest. Wiseman's guidelines had laid out the plan's major features, and hence there was little room for partisan maneuvering.

The Wiseman Plan

The details of the "Wiseman Plan," as the latest desegregation draft was known, was first revealed in a meeting noticeably devoid of the emotional outbursts, packed crowds, or posters characteristic of earlier gatherings. On November 20, 1980, about 250 people gathered at East High School for the information session. No questions were permitted, but the crowd seemed receptive, if a little subdued, as zoning director Ray Osborne outlined school zones.

Osborne used a simple metaphor which captured the spirit of the new plan: in the past, the zoning plan has been the tail that wags the dog. For the first time in a decade we will let the dog wag the tail. . . . In this plan, the most important thing is not where the children will go to school, but what will happen when they get there."[7]

The language of Judge Wiseman's May 20 opinion had indicated firmly that he was concerned about white flight, the hardships placed on black children and the black community, and the continued erosion of public support for the schools. For these reasons, he had rejected the busing remedy dictated by *Swann*. After examining the board's 1980 plan, Wiseman had said, "The plan submitted by the board disparately onerates young black children with the burden of achieving desegregation." He had wondered if ratios could be

6. *Banner,* May 24, 1980.
7. *Tennessean,* Nov. 21, 1980.

achieved permanently or even initially. In one of the most revealing parts of his opinion, Wiseman had discussed the future of public education in Nashville. "The spectre that haunts all the parties in this case, this court, and the community is a public school system populated by the poor and black, and a private school system serving the affluent and white. . . . further disruption without massive efforts to make the public school system more attractive will further deteriorate public support and will engender more flight to private schools."[8]

In drawing up the Wiseman Plan, the planning team was faithful to Wiseman's tradeoff: reduce busing and enhance the educational program.

Pupil Assignment The pupil assignment section of the plan was simple, direct, and bound for controversy. The elementary years (Grades 1–4) would be spent in neighborhood schools. Middle schools (Grades 5–8) and high schools (Grades 9–12) would use limited busing to achieve a minimum of 15 percent either white or black minority in each school. Some school closings were necessary in order to maximize desegregation.

As Ray Osborne presented the specifics of the new plan to the community for the first time, the full implications of Wiseman's order became clear. Of seventy-six elementary schools, forty-nine would have student bodies 90 percent of one race! Fifty-seven of the schools would be majority white and nineteen majority black. Forty of the fifty-seven majority white schools would have enrollments more than 90 percent white; and nine of the nineteen black schools would have a similar extreme ratio. Of the nineteen majority black elementary schools, fourteen would be walk-in-schools. Of the fifty-seven majority white elementary schools, seventeen would be within walking distance for all their students.

The Wiseman Plan, then, sacrificed racial balance for neighborhood schools in the elementary grades. Clearly, Wiseman had hoped for a greater degree of desegregation under the provisions of his decisions than the planning staff produced. The intervenors in the case had used volunteers to draft their neighborhood school plan, and their plan's amateur character had not escaped Wiseman's watchful eye. "The expert staff of the (School) Board," he said, "can do a more refined job, drawing lines that achieve better utilization of space . . . and also maximizing the opportunities for integration." But as it turned out, the intervenors' plan had projected fewer one-race schools

8. Memorandum Opinion, May 20, 1980.

than the plan developed by the Metro staff. At the end of the first section of his presentation, Osborne said that the proposed plan closed thirteen schools, almost all in predominantly white areas.

As for the middle schools, there were to be twenty-four schools, seven of them majority black. Pearl was to become a middle school and was projected to be 77 percent black. Five middle schools were to include less than 15 percent black, but each of these was near that figure.

The plan included ten comprehensive high schools, two of them Pearl-Cohn and Madison-Goodlettsville—still on the drawing board. Pearl-Cohn, Whites Creek, and Maplewood were to be majority black schools, and the rest would enroll more than 15 percent black students.

The middle and high school plans stirred some comment, but greatest attention was paid to the elementary schools. There desegregation depended only on residential patterns, and most areas of the community were not residentially integrated.

Educational Programs   School officials did not try to justify their plan. Judge Wiseman's opinion gave justification enough. Wiseman had examined the performance of the 1971 plan and ordered a new approach stressing neighborhood elementary schools, school consolidation, and special educational programs. The staff printed and circulated crucial passages from Wiseman's opinion as part of their presentation of the educational component of the new plan:

"The gap between black and white achievement has narrowed slightly . . . [but it] remains substantial. . ."

"The 'osmosis' effect, or use of white children as a principal learning resource for black children, appears not to have had the desired result at least in isolation. These data strongly suggest the necessity for educational components both as an essential ingredient to the remedy and also as a reinforcement to parental perceptions of, and *support* for, this system."

"The remedial benefits of smaller pupil-teacher ratios in the early grades would far exceed any benefits from an 'osmosis' effect."

"The greatest concern [of parents] is with the quality of education received, or perceived to be received."[9]

Wiseman had gone on to order that the money saved through reduced busing should be reallocated to educational components providing intercultural experiences, reduced pupil-teacher ratios, remediation efforts, and other elements the professional staff felt were

9. Untitled brochure on file in Room 110 Metro Board of Education.

necessary for the improvement of educational services. Wiseman wrote in his opinion, "The plan of the Board will specifically address [the question of black history and culture] and propose methods of monitoring inclusion of such subject material into the regular curricula, as well as the offering of specific courses on black history and culture in the comprehensive high schools."

The various planning committees had responded to the language of the order. They had not reached final conclusions about appropriate curricula, but they were far along. The staff made clear that they were specifically addressing (1) Grade K–4 intervention and remediation, (2) black history, (3) multi-cultural education and intercultural exchange, and (4) desegregated academic magnets for gifted and talented students.

Comments on the Plan   The school board invited public comment on the proposed plan at its December 2 meeting. Reflecting the community's general satisfaction with the Wiseman Plan, very few activists turned out. Of the fifty people who attended, only nine spoke on the desegregation plan. What they said, however, revealed the continuing themes of desegregation politics.

Dr. Charles Kimbrough, local NAACP chapter president, attacked the Wiseman plan. He said, "The Nashville branch of the NAACP warns the Metro School Board that adoption of this plan for segregation of Metro public schools will be met with vigorous opposition and be fought in the Courts until it is held to be unconstitutional."[10]

Kimbrough hoped that Avon Williams and the *Kelley* plaintiffs would appeal Wiseman's order, but he served notice that the NAACP would intervene if Williams did not. The NAACP was not formally a party to the case, but the NAACP Legal Defense Fund, a separate organization, had handled appeals for the plaintiffs several times during the twenty-five-year history of the case.

Willis Hawley, newly appointed dean of George Peabody College for Teachers of Vanderbilt University, also addressed the board in opposition to the plan. Unlike Avon Williams, whose children attended a private school, Hawley had two children in Hillsboro High School; his commitment to desegregation was not merely academic. Hawley argued that the Wiseman Plan was flawed because desegregation's positive effects on minority achievement and racial attitudes were accomplished most clearly in Grades K–4. Multi-cultural progams, which the Wiseman Plan featured in lieu of busing for racial balance in the early grades, "do not significantly enhance interracial under-

10. *Tennessean*, Dec. 3, 1980.

standing in the absence of regular opportunities for interracial contact." Contradicting the arguments of black leaders like Hugh Scott, Hawley said there was no evidence that one-way busing "negatively affects the self-esteem or self-importance of minority children." Hawley went on to say that the Nashville case "will have national consequences," leaving no doubt that he thought the Wiseman trade-off was wrong.[11]

But the continuing split within the black ranks was dramatized when Leo Lillard addressed the board. Lillard, a black urban planner, had joined whites from Bellevue as intervenors in the court hearings. He predicted that students in the majority black inner-city elementary schools eventually would raise their achievement test scores to the level of those in white suburban schools. He said the proposed plan "has merit and will usher in a new day."[12]

Disruption and Appeal

On January 13, 1981, the Metro School Board, after discussing the desegregation plan for two meetings, approved it and forwarded the recommendations to Judge Wiseman. The board attached two conditions to its approval. First, the plan would require a $23 million dollar bond offering by Metro government to fund the two new comprehensive high schools (Pearl-Cohn and Goodlettsville-Madison). Second, the plan could not be fully operational until the new schools were constructed. The implementation date for the entire plan was set for August 1984.

The board was not unanimous in its approval of the plan. Barbara Mann, now one of three black dissenters, read a letter to the board explaining her opposition. Her main objection was the resegregation of the neighborhood elementary schools. "If we implement the plan," she said, "we will set in concrete a separatist mentality and nothing we can interject will be sufficiently strong to drown out our ambiguity or our lack of commitment to an open society." Although "far from perfect," Mann went on, busing was "far from being the perpetrator of all the evil as it has been portrayed."[13]

Avon Williams had until February 9 to respond to the school board's plan. On February 6 he filed his objections with the court. He cited five major flaws:

11. Ibid. *Banner,* Dec. 3, 1980.
12. *Banner,* Dec. 3, 1980.
13. Ibid., Jan. 28, 1981.

1. The plan would create massive resegregation in Grades K–4; forty-seven of the seventy-five elementary schools would be 90 percent one race.
2. The plan would place a disparate burden on black children in Grades 5–8; they would be bused to eleven schools in white neighborhoods, while whites would be bused to only one school in the inner city.
3. The plan called for the construction of a comprehensive high school in predominantly white Madison; Grades 7–9 could have been handled at Madison, and Grades 10–12 could have been handled at Maplewood, a predominantly black high school.
4. Pearl would be made a middle school; it could have been selected as an academic magnet high school.
5. The plan did not address the plaintiff's complaints about the board's practice of assigning majority white faculty to schools with black majorities; the plan also failed to address the plaintiffs' charges of discrimination in the assignment of black administrative personnel.[14]

Williams was consistent. He wanted more majority black schools in black neighborhoods with black teachers and administrators, and he felt that the plan did not deliver this. He would be satisfied only if more whites were bused into the inner city to fill the largely underutilized school buildings there. The board's 1980 busing plan secured desegregation but had burdened blacks unfairly, Williams argued; the present elementary grade pupil placement plan did not assure desegregation at all.

In the memorandum detailing his criticism, Williams went farther than he had ever gone before; he asked the court to give him time to prepare a desegregation plan for the plaintiffs, using expert help from elsewhere. Several times during court hearings Judge Wiseman had asked Williams if he would prepare a plan of his own, but Williams had always demurred. Now, however, he was ready to propose a plan himself, rather than simply criticizing the work of others. Wiseman agreed to delay hearings on the board's plan until Williams, too, had a plan ready.

During the lull, the Metro School Board voted to ask Judge Wiseman to make the State of Tennessee a co-defendant in the case, responsible for sharing with Metro the cost of the litigation. The board justified its request on grounds that Tennessee state law had mandated segregation and that therefore the state should share re-

14. Objections by Plaintiffs to Plan Submitted in Response to Court's Memorandum and Order of May 20, 1980 by the Plaintiff. Filed Feb. 6, 1981, District Court.

sponsibility for eliminating its vestiges.[15] Wiseman took the petition of the board under advisement.

On March 25 Williams filed his desegregation plan with the court. It had been prepared by HGH Associates, a group of academic desegregation experts. The plan utilized county-wide busing for racial balance, but other aspects of the plan were inconsistent with arguments Williams had made in court the previous year. Under the plaintiffs' plan, kindergarten children would not be bused, although Williams had repeatedly argued in favor of their inclusion. During the recently concluded hearings Williams had often criticized the Grade 1–4, 5–6 structure of the 1971 plan, calling it "educationally unsound in dividing kindergarten from first grade [and] in breaking up the educational continuity of Grades 1–3, Grades 4–6, and of the first six grades." The HGH plan, however did the same thing. It used "clustering" and "pairing" to desegregate elementary schools. Schools were grouped by twos, threes, or fours, and their grade structures were split. For example, one school would have Grades K–2, another would have K and 3–4, and still another 5–6. The plan called for students to attend three schools in the first six years, although Williams (as well as school staff) had argued in the 1980 hearings that this was educationally counterproductive.

These were not the only departures from Williams' earlier line of attack on the school board's plans. In 1980, the school board had proposed a goal of 32 percent black in each elementary school, with a 15 percent deviation acceptable. Williams had objected to this because "its basic premise that each school ought to be predominantly white [perpetuates] historic attitudes of black inferiority." Under the board's plan ten schools had been scheduled to be majority black; under the HGH plan, racial balance was again the goal. Only eight majority black schools were forecast.[16] The major feature of the HGH plan was its use of crosstown busing to achieve the racial ratios. The plan called for more long-distance busing than had ever been proposed by the school board. One cluster required students to be bused from the county line on one side to the county line on the other. The plan would increse busing for both whites and blacks.

When hearings began on March 30, 1981, Judge Wiseman signaled his impatience with both sides. He chided the school board for "slowwalking" the timetable for their plan. The board had said it could not implement the plan until 1984, when Pearl-Cohn and Madison-Goodlettsville High Schools were completed. Under questioning

15. *Tennessean*, Mar. 26, 1981.
16. *Banner*, Mar. 26, 1981.

from Wiseman, school officials indicated that the plan could be implemented in the southwestern part of the county, where there was excess capacity, in fall 1981, but the plan could not be moved ahead for the remainder of the county. Wiseman also told school officials that they had given too little attention to the development of academic magnet schools.

Wiseman had correspondingly little interest in Avon Williams' new plan. After only fifteen minutes of oral presentation, the judge indicated that he would strike the plaintiffs' elementary school proposal. Most of it, he said, was "totally antithetical to the order of the court." When Williams objected to the criteria presented in the court order, Wiseman cut him off, "If you object to the guidelines, I want you to appeal.[17]

There was no surprise when Wiseman issued his court order. He read it from the bench in Columbia, Tennessee, to interested observers and reporters. The order was brief, to the point, and in some ways savage.

The plaintiffs' plan for primary schools ignores the directives and guidelines of the May 20, 1980, order and is contradictory to the position taken last year by plaintiffs.

Specifically, it envisions substantial transportation of very young children out of their neighborhoods, denies parental involvement, and is subject to all the criticisms leveled by the plaintiffs and their expert witness (Hugh Scott) in the hearings of last year.

It ignores the Court's directive to establish a three-tiered system and establishes some K–1–2, some K–3–4 [schools] as well as other deviations from the Court's directive. For these reasons, as the Court observed earlier, it is impertinent to the issues framed and unresponsive to the Court's order. It is stricken.

The plaintiffs' middle school plan is hastily conceived and based on inadequate study and unfamiliarity with this system. It fails to consider transportation routes and natural barriers such as rivers, railroads, and interstates. It fails to consider building availabilities and building capacities and in general is a superficial offering. Based on these findings of fact, the plaintiffs' middle school plan is rejected.

The School Board's plan, as amended . . . in all of its components as well as pupil assignment, is approved.[18]

Two amendments were made to the school board's plan at Judge Wiseman's insistence: (1) the plan would include an academic magnet school, and (2) the plan would be implemented in the southwestern part of the county that fall. Wiseman was impatient: "The

17. *Tennessean,* Mar. 31, 1981.
18. *Banner,* Apr. 7, 1981.

Court is disappointed that the transition to a county-wide system of three tiers is not feasible immediately."[19]

The reaction to Wiseman's order was mixed. Informed partisans and officials speculated about the national impact of Wiseman's order. Would it signal a retreat from busing in the courts? Would Williams appeal the decision, and if so, what would be the outcome?

Avon Williams himself said nothing to the press about an appeal, but Willis Hawley did. "The singular character of this decision is that it is the first decision in a major city in which a federal judge has increased, by reason of his action, the amount of racial segregation in the schools . . . This is in some sense a historical decision. . . . you can believe a number of other communities that have resisted desegregation in the past will look to Nashville as the leader in the struggle to avoid busing."[20] Hawley was sure that Williams would appeal and that Wiseman would be reversed.

Plaintiffs had until May 18, a Monday, to file a notice of appeal with the court. Suspense and speculation built. Some said that Williams would not appeal; he had gotten what he wanted—reduction in the burden of busing, black majority schools, a new comprehensive high school for the inner city. Others said that he would appeal; he would not accept segregated schools in the early grades under any conditions. Listeners were reminded that "Williams wants white minorities in schools in the inner city."

Avon Williams waited until Friday, May 15, to file his notice of appeal, though the specifics would not be spelled out until a later memorandum. The appeal placed a cloud of indecision over plans for the ensuing school year.

The school system was under a court order to implement the Wiseman Plan and, over the summer, set about doing so. Teachers and principals were reassigned. Books, desks, and other equipment were shifted. Training sessions for teachers were offered. Parents affected by the order were noticeably cautious when explaining to their children where they would go to school that fall. Some took their children by the "new" school, and others sought information about which teachers would be there and how good they were. The parents' information networks buzzed.

Three weeks before schools were to open, Williams petitioned the sixth U.S. Circuit Court of Appeals in Cincinnati to stay the execution of Judge Wiseman's school desegregaion order. School officials responded that if a stay were ordered, the opening of school would

19. *Tennessean*, Apr. 1, 1981.
20. *Banner*, Apr. 7, 1981.

have to be delayed three weeks while pupils were reassigned, teachers reoriented, and bus routes redrawn. On August 19, 1981, two days before principals were scheduled to return to their schools for the new year, the sixth Circuit Court issued a stay of Judge Wiseman's order to implement the new school desegregation plan.

Although the appeals court would not hear the case until the late fall, the three-judge panel, in granting the injunction, said that Avon Williams was "likely to prevail on the merits of the appeal." The makeup of the panel itself signaled its members' sentiments, and their verbal jibes at Bill Willis suggested their lack of faith in Wiseman's Plan. George Edwards, chief judge of the Sixth Circuit, had written the court's rejection of the school board's appeal of the 1971 court order which originally had established busing. Judge Anthony Celebrezze had been a Kennedy liberal of cabinet rank; he too had approved the original 1971 plan. And Judge Nathaniel Jones had been the NAACP's chief counsel before appointment to the federal bench.

Willis hardly had a chance to present his arguments before the panel bore down on him. Edwards commented that the federal courts had had to drag the Metro board "kicking and screaming into the twentieth century." Celebrezze chimed in, "The Supreme Court has come down with so many decisions telling you what to do, there shouldn't be any difficulty." When Willis tried to argue the central point of Wiseman's opinion—that recent research, including some by black educators, had questioned the value of mere mixing of the races to achieve educational opportunity—Jones interjected, "You're quoting the wrong people to me." And Celebrezze added, "Experts are a dime a dozen."[21]

The judicial stay signaled impending defeat for the Wiseman Plan. Schools did not open on schedule, as administrators tried to reorganize according to the old plan. Twelve hundred teachers and other staff members had to be reassigned. Textbooks, desks, and libraries had to be removed and redeployed.

Anger, relief, and uncertainty reigned in the community. Many whites held Avon Williams responsible for the disruption, since he had waited until July 31 to ask the appeals court to stay implementation of the order.[22] Others faulted the school board. The reaction in the black community was mixed, but most believed the decision was appropriate. As the Reverend Kelly Miller Smith said, "Chaos is not desirable, but one should not blame the victim of segregation. . . . the chaos is the result of resistance to desegregation."[23]

21. Ibid., Aug. 20, 1981. *Tennessean*, Aug, 20, 1981.
22. *Banner*, Aug. 22, 1981.
23. Ibid., Sept. 4, 1981.

In the wake of school delays and court appeals, the citizens of Davidson County, by a five to one ratio overwhelmingly defeated a school tax increase referendum on September 3. The increase would have cost the average homeowner only about thirty dollars a year, but property owners were in no mood to provide more money for schools over which they had no control. One observer commented that the vote was a mandate "saying to elected officials and government, 'Don't raise my taxes until you prove you're managing well what you already have.'"[24]

The Sixth Circuit Court of Appeals

On October 19, 1981, the Metro Board of Education filed an unusual motion before judges of the Sixth Circuit Court. Attorneys Bill Willis and Marian Harrison had been stung by comments from the bench the previous August, so they asked two of the three judges on the panel to recuse themselves from hearing the appeal. Judge Nathaniel Jones was asked to disqualify himself because he had served as general counsel for the NAACP and had cooperated with the NAACP Legal Defense Fund. The petition suggested that Judge Jones might have a "preconceived notion about this case in which the NAACP Legal Defense Fund represents the plaintiff-appellants." Chief Judge George Edwards was asked to recuse himself because at the August hearing he had directed remarks at Willis which, "at a minimum attributed to [Willis] racist motives in challenging the only black judge on the panel."[25] Edwards' remarks at the time had left little doubt in the school board attorneys' minds that he was prejudiced against the board. Judge Wiseman had criticized the 1971 plan, approved by Edwards, for perpetuating the forbidden dual school system. Finally, the attorneys asked for the case to be heard *en banc*, that is, by all the appeals court judges (save those who recused themselves) instead of by the usual three-judge panel.

Reaction was swift and firm. In a tersely worded order, the two judges denied the request for recusal "on the ground that all actions taken and opinions formulated concerning this case have been taken and formulated in the regular course of judicial proceedings."[26] The appeals court also rejected the *en banc* request. In sum, the same three judges who had sided with Williams in August would again rule on busing in Nashville.

24. Ibid.
25. *Tennessean*, Oct. 20, 1981.
26. Ibid., Oct. 24, 1981.

The Plaintiffs' Argument   The plaintiffs filed their brief with the
Sixth Circuit Court on October 30, 1981. The brief identified the
major question for the court to consider: whether the district court
had erred in approving a "different remedy" which on its face resegregated Grades K–4, imposed a 15 percent either-race minimum presence as a desegregation standard, imposed a disproportionate
transportation burden on black schoool children, and failed to retain
and develop Pearl as a high school. The brief was interesting, to begin
with, in two ways. First, it was largely the product of Bill Lann Lee of
the NAACP Legal Defense Fund. Lawyers Avon Williams and Richard
Dinkins appeared to have been relegated to a consulting role. Second,
the brief largely ignored the arguments made by Williams in the
district court hearings. Specifically, it took special pains to mim-
imize Dr. Hugh Scott's testimony regarding the 15 percent racial
threshold of either race as a desegregation standard.

The plaintiffs' attorneys opened their arguments with a thirty-page
history of major events in the twenty-six-year-old lawsuit. The history section depicted a recalcitrant school board seeking delays in order
to obstruct desegregation. Even the 1971 busing plan had been undercut by board action, according to the brief. The proposed Wiseman
Plan was simply a new twist by a school board with a dismal record on
desegregation.

To prevail in the appeals court, the plaintiffs' attorneys had to show
that Wiseman had either misunderstood the facts of the case or
misapplied the relevant constitutional law. They played down the
factual record developed in Wiseman's court and emphasized his
faulty application of the law.

The NAACP Legal Defense Fund lawyers maintained that Nashville schools had never been fully desegregated. The last vestiges of
the dual school system had never been eradicated, so the district
court should have used a county-wide plan requiring racial balance in
each school. The plaintiffs argued that Judge Wiseman had erred
when he did not apply established constitutional remedies to a manifest case of southern school segregation.

To substantiate their argument, the plaintiffs' attorneys needed
evidence showing that Wiseman had affirmed some school board
action designed to maintain an unconstitutional dual school system.
They could find no such evidence. Wiseman had said that the school
board had executed the 1971 plan in good faith; the judge had believed
that the original 1971 court-ordered plan had been flawed. Ironically,
Chief Judge Edwards himself had approved the original busing order.
Wiseman's only criticism of the board concerned the optional transfer policy which had decimated Pearl. Even here, though, the facts did

not condemn the board. Wiseman's opinion gave the plaintiffs no help; there was no instance in the record of a clear violation of constitutional responsibility. So the plaintiffs argued the issue by citing a list of alleged wrongs perpetrated by the board. None of these wrongs had been acknowledged by Wiseman as violating the 1971 court order.

The plaintiffs' brief held that from 1973 to 1979 "the Board not only did not maximize desegregation, but engaged in a series of activities which ultimately led to a finding of 'de jure segregation' in implementation of the 1971 plan." Having made this finding, the argument continued, the court should have fashioned a remedy based on *Swann*. Instead, said the plaintiffs, the court had "gutted" *Swann*. Instead of applying the *Swann* racial balance remedy, the district court had changed the definition of a unitary school system "to remediation and quality education." This was a fundamental error, according to the plaintiffs, and it mistakenly had led to approval of the board's 1981 plan.[27]

All of the Wiseman innovations hung on this question: Was nine years' experience with busing sufficient experience to justify a new approach? Wiseman had thought so and on this premise had "broken new ground." The plainiffs thought not; for them, the schools never had been effectively desegregated and never would be if the Wiseman Plan was approved.

The NAACP lawyers appealed to precedent. Their argument was rooted in logic developed in five Supreme Court decisions: *Brown II* (1955), *Green* (1968), *Swann* (1971), *Penick* (1979) and *Brinkman* (1979).

Brown II imposed on school boards an "affirmative duty to disestablish the dual school system." *Green* said that school boards operating such systems were "clearly charged with the affirmative duty to take whatever steps might be necessary to convert to a unitary school system in which racial discrimination would be eliminated root and branch." *Swann* established busing for racial balance because school boards had to do more than abandon prior discriminatory purpose. *Penick* said that school boards had an affirmative responsibility to see that pupil assignment policies and school construction and abandonment practices "are not used and do not serve to perpetuate or reestablish the dual school system." *Brinkman* made judicial responsibility crystal clear:

The Dayton Board . . . had engaged in many post–*Brown I* actions that had

27. Plaintiff's Brief, *Kelley v. Metropolitan County Board of Education* (1980), file, District Court.

the *effect* of increasing or perpetuating segregation. The District Court ignored this compounding of the original constitutional breach on the ground that there was no direct evidence of continued discriminatory purpose. But the measure of the post–*Brown I* conduct of a school board under an unsatisfied duty to liquidate a dual system is the *effectiveness, not the purpose of the actions* in decreasing or increasing the segregation caused by the dual system. [emphasis added][28]

The effect of the board's actions in Nashville between 1971 and 1980 was, the plaintiffs argued, the resegregation of the schools. The school board had failed in its duty affirmatively to disestablish the dual school system, and Wiseman had totally ignored the Supreme Court's binding statements. These arguments led naturally to the conclusion that the 1981 school board plan, approved by Wiseman, was nothing more than massive resegregation, especially in Grades K–4.

Ultimately the plaintiffs argued for a county-wide busing plan with a racial balance formula of 32 percent black (plus or minus 10–15 percent) in all schools. Completely absent from the brief was Avon Williams' argument for "havens of black majority" and the need for whites to have a "minority experience." Amenities such as intercultural exchanges, intervention, and remediation programs for inner-city students were acceptable, but they could not take the place of busing. The plaintiffs' pleadings in the Sixth Circuit Court reiterated the "end racial isolation" theme so familiar in civil rights cases and totally ignored the two-cultures approach espoused by Dr. Scott and Avon Williams in the 1980 court proceedings. The NAACP Legal Defense Fund embraced busing for purposes of integration and implicitly accepted the assimilationist logic which had guided federal school desegregation policies since the 1960s.

The School Board's Argument   Marian Harrison and Bill Willis, attorneys for the defendant school board, filed their brief on November 23, 1981. They faced an immense challenge. They had unsuccessfully asked two justices to recuse themselves from the case and had unsuccessfully argued for an *en banc* hearing. Their present task was to justify Wiseman's departure from established legal precedent.

The attorneys argued that Judge Wiseman had not erred in directing the development of the 1981 desegregation plan. First they emphasized that the case was not about the imposition of a desegregation plan upon a segregated system trying to achieve desegregation for the first time. The board had faithfully implemented a

28. *Brinkman* quoted in plaintiff's brief.

Swann-style busing remedy for nine years. A new Wiseman remedy, based on accumulated experience, was warranted. The attorneys pointed out:

> The Plaintiffs have misstated the findings of the district court relating to the Board's implementation of the court's order of 1971. Rather than finding the Board had caused "*de jure* segregation," the Court found that the *Court order itself* had fostered resegregation. Furthermore, the Court found explicitly that the Board had implemented the 1971 order in good faith and had voluntarily expanded its scope. Based on this fundamental misconception, the Plaintiffs build their entire argument, never once citing a case where a court reviewed a comprehensive *Swann* remedy which has been in place for a decade.[29]

This, then, was the major issue in the school board case: the district court, sitting as a court of equity and guided by the Supreme Court rulings, had exercised legitimate power to bring forth a new remedy. If the district court had erred, it had done so only in not relinquishing jurisdiction back to the school board. Because the original court-ordered plan had been faulty, Judge Wiseman had decided that the district court had to fashion a new and better remedy.

The board's brief pointed out, with what could only have been bitter irony, that the plaintiffs, in their appellate brief, had disowned Hugh Scott and his argument. Only on appeal had the plaintiffs asserted that every school should meet a racial balance test; the testimony and pleadings before Judge Wiseman's bench had been quite different.

In short, the school board attorneys argued that Judge Wiseman had legal authority to order a new and more reasonable plan in the light of practical circumstances. This new plan, they believed, fell under the umbrella of constitutional precedent. *Swann*, they argued, established racial ratios as a "starting point in the process of shaping a remedy"—but, there was no "substantive constitutional right [to] any particular degree of racial mixing." Racial ratios had been used in 1971 as a starting point, but ten years had elapsed since then, and Judge Wiseman was no longer compelled to use them. Other strategies such as cultural enrichment programs were legitimate substitutes.

In legal circles there is an old maxim, "When you can't argue facts, argue law; when you can't argue law, argue facts." On appeal, the plaintiffs argued law, while the school board argued that facts changed the law. Without coining the phrase, the defendant's attorneys held that Nashville was a "second-round busing case." A decade

29. Defendant's brief, *Kelley* (1980), file, district court.

of experience had demonstrated that a new legal principle was needed.

The Circuit Court's Decision

Oral arguments before the now-familiar three-judge panel of judges began on December 10, 1981. It had been clear from the outset that the panel was predisposed against the Wiseman Plan, and especially against the return to one-race neighborhood schools. Judge Edwards said that the plan appeared to return the schools to "separate-but-equal."

The only chink in the pro-busing logic of the judges' questioning came from Judge Celebrezze, who asked Lee, "If the magnitude of white flight gets so great, how can you follow *Swann* [i.e., a racial balance approach]?[30]

After oral arguments, the judges took the case under advisement. They would, said a clerk, "give their opinion in a week or a year." In Nashville, school officials hoped for an early decision so that they could make whatever adjustments might be necessary before the next school year began. The decision and opinion of the court did not come until July 27, 1982.

Judge Wiseman had believed he was "plowing new ground" in approving Nashville's desegregation plan. Busing had been used for nine years, and Wiseman found it to have been a failure. So he had develped a strikingly different plan—one which rested on educational programs rather than racial ratios—to remedy the effects of longstanding state-imposed segregation. In the appeals court, the plaintiffs had argued law, the defendants facts; in the final decision, legal precedent prevailed.

Judge Edwards, speaking on behalf of the majority, declared that the case "offered no new legal issues and can and must be decided by this court on the basis of final decisions of the United States Supreme Court."[31] The judges approved the educational components of Wiseman's plan. But they rejected the 15 percent minority-of-either-race criterion for junior and senior high schools as well as the neighborhood K–4 schools. Instead, the court said, Nashville must use a racial balance approach; schools should be 32 percent black, plus or minus 15 percent, corresponding to the overall racial makeup of the

---

30. *Tennessean*, Dec. 11, 1981.
31. Opinion of the Sixth Circuit Court of Appeals, July 27, 1982, 1.

community. In his opinion, Edwards cited long passages from *Swann*, for him the definitive statement regarding southern school desegregation. *Swann* instituted busing for racial balance as the most appropriate (and, it appeared, the only) remedy for school segregation.

For the appeals court, educational achievement, the disparate hardships busing placed on blacks, community support for the schools, white flight, and cost, were secondary considerations. Only assimilation, in the form of the racial ratios, seemed important.

In sum, the judges decreed that, while neighborhood schools may be acceptable in a school system without a history of segregation, a plan must do more where such a history exists; it must make "every effort to achieve the greatest possible degree of actual desegregation." Some inconvenience and even awkward remedies may be necessary where neutral assignment plans fail to desegregate the schools.[32]

The courts' decision was not unanimous. The majority opinion represented the views of Judges Edwards and Jones. Judge Celebrezze wrote a sharp dissent. Observers speculated that the court's delay in issuing its ruling had been due to an effort by the majority to persuade Celebrezze to join them.

Celebrezze said that the district court had made no clearly erroneous findings of fact and had not abused its discretionary powers in forming a remedy. Indeed, in Celebrezze's view, the appeals court had overreached its own authority in overturning the Wiseman plan.

Celebrezze chided his colleagues for not studying the record of the case. If they had, he said, they would have come to his conclusion.

> After a careful reading of the record in this case, I believe that the Davidson County community, the Board of Education, and the district judge are making significant progress towards affording a constitutionally acceptable educational system and that this Court should allow the local community and federal court to proceed with their innovations and programs. In my view, the district court did not make clearly erroneous findings of fact and did not abuse its discretion in forming its remedy.[33]

Judge Celebrezze read *Swann* to mean that the court should use a racial ratio as a starting point, and Nashville had done so in 1971. But, he said,

> The Constitution does not require the district court to use a ratio which mirrors the makeup of the community. . . . The majority opinion seems to recognize that there is no constitutional right to any particular racial balance in schools. Yet the majority's requirement that the district court employ a ratio of 68 percent white and 32 percent black (plus or minus 15

32. Ibid., 19.
33. Ibid., 26.

percent) appears to be an attempt to establish such a balance. I fear that the precise racial mixture required by the majority on remand will, as a practical matter, create such a right.[34]

Those close to the case were not surprised by the decision. The Sixth Circuit Court's history portended this outcome. The Celebrezze dissent, however, was a surprise. It showed that opinions were changing; the debilitating effects of busing were now in the arena of judicial discussion. The Nashville *Banner* editorialized on the decision: "In medical terms, they [the Sixth Circuit majority] have performed a perfect operation, but the patient is in danger of dying."[35]

The appeals court remanded the case to Wiseman's court, where a new plan was to be drawn based on county-wide busing to achieve racial balance. The appeals court also required Wiseman to move expeditiously to hold hearings on the plaintiffs' remaining complaints: discrimination in faculty and staff assignments, attorneys' fees, and contempt motions against the school board. Now the largest question surrounding the case became whether or not to appeal to the Supreme Court.

The Supreme Court Appeal

The two-to-one ruling of the Sixth Circuit Court was handed down less than a month before school was scheduled to begin. The outgoing, appointed school board met for the last time on July 28, one day after the announcement. Bill Willis summarized the opinion, emphasizing the Celebrezze dissent. "The majority of the court did not analyze the detailed findings of fact made by Judge Wiseman to determine whether or not they justified the remedy. Therefore, it is our opinion that the basic questions presented in this appeal have not been ruled upon."[36]

In Willis' mind, the basic question was whether or not a federal district judge has the power and responsibility to tailor a new remedy in a desegregation case if the previous remedy did not achieve the desired result. After a few questions, the board, divided along racial lines, voted five to three to appeal the case to the Supreme Court.

The Celebrezze dissent had emboldened the departing board. "It is interesting to note that Judge Celebrezze sat on the court that approved the 1971 plan, and his latest pronouncements represent an

34. Ibid.
35. *Banner*, July 29, 1982.
36. *Tennessean*, July 29, 1983.

acceptance of the fact that the remedies set forth in the plan have not worked."[37]

The pending Appeals Court decision served as a background against which Metro voters elected their school board for the first time. Two blacks, Ike Northern and Dorothy Gupton, were chosen. Two Metro school-teachers, Tom Hightower and Charles Gann, retired the day before taking up their new posts. Three lawyers were elected: Dewey Branstetter, Dan Alexander, and Kent Weeks. Vern Denney, a minister and school activist, and Pat Bentrup, a nurse and mother, rounded out the board.

But the backgrounds of these board members were not as important as their views, and these became apparent quickly. A "conservative" coalition emerged in Alexander, Hightower, and Gann; their views paralleled those of the "outlying whites" on the former board. The "liberal" coalition was composed of the two blacks, Gupton and Northern. Denney, Branstetter, Bentrup, and Weeks held the center. Weeks was elected chair. His good cheer, intellect, and leadership would be tested early, for the first issue of the agenda asked whether Metro should continue the Supreme Court appeal.

National and local observers of the Supreme Court were convinced that the justices were looking for a busing case in which to make "new law." Justices Powell and Rehnquist had intimated as much in written opinions, and the Reagan administration was on record as being "against busing." The Nashville case seemed a likely candidate for judicial review. Judge Wiseman had, after nine years' experience, found busing ineffective and sought another solution. The appellate court decision had been compromised by the Celebrezze dissent, with its defense of Wiseman's approach and the community's effort to balance desegregation with educational quality.

While the Nashville case had much to recommend it as a likely candidate for Supreme Court action, it had liabilities as well. First and most important, Nashville was a southern school district. It had been guilty of *de jure* segregation and the district court had never declared it free of segregation. The Supreme Court had always taken a tough stance toward southern school districts, and perhaps a precedent limiting busing in a southern school desegregation case would give up too much, too soon. A second problem concerned Justice Thurgood Marshall, the only black on the Supreme Court. Marshall had represented the NAACP Legal Defense Fund in the Nashville case early in its history, and he would have to recuse himself if the Nashville case came to the Court. The Supreme Court almost surely

37. *Banner*, July 27, 1982.

would be reluctant to render a major decision on busing without Justice Marshall's participation.

It was something of surprise when, on November 12, 1982, the Solicitor General's Office in the U.S. Department of Justice filed a friend-of-the-court, or *amicus curiae*, brief in support of the school board. The brief petitioned the court for a review of the 1981 Wiseman desegregation plan. "There is no way to interpret our filing as a *per se* attack on busing," said U.S. Deputy Assistant Attorney General Charles Cooper. Nevertheless, the *amicus* brief improved the chances of Supreme Court review; normally the Justice Department waited for the Supreme Court to accept a case before it intervened.

The Reagan administration's position on busing was quite clear. A position paper written by Assistant Attorney General for Civil Rights William Bradford Reynolds stated, "We believe that effective and creative alternatives to busing do exist.[38] And the *amicus* brief argued that the appeals court "adopted too restrictive an interpretation of *Swann.*" The narrow interpretation rendered by the Sixth Circuit "severely restricts a district court's ability to assess the effect of earlier decrees in the light of experience."[39] Justice Department support for the Nashville appeal did not go unnoticed. On December 7, 1982, the six-member U.S. Commission of Civil Rights issued a statement saying it deplored the administration's effort to obtain a review of court-ordered busing. The administration's action was described as "yet another example of the administration's efforts to eliminate student transportation as a remedy for unconstitutional school segregation."[40]

Such protestations had been unnecessary; in January 1983, the Supreme Court, without comment, refused to take up the case. The Nashville case would not become a "landmark" in the nation's retreat from busing.

The Final Round

The scene was a familiar one. Metro school board attorneys and civil rights lawyers gathered again in the U.S. District Court to debate the merits of a desegregation plan. But this time the mood was different. Events of the previous two years had exhausted the protagonists, so by now, on January 27, 1983, an atmosphere of resigna-

38. Ibid., Nov. 13. 1982.
39. *Tennessean*, Nov. 13, 1982.
40. Ibid., Dec. 8, 1982.

tion reigned in the courtroom. Judge Wiseman ordered the parties to submit a new plan to him by April 1. In addition, he said, "I will not only encourage, I will direct counsel to have ongoing discussions about the possibility of a consent order in this case."[41] Such an order would mean that both parties would be directed to try for a negotiated settlement. Both the school board and Avon Williams expressed a desire to work harmoniously on the new plan; Williams had negotiated consent orders in several desegregation cases elsewhere.

Why the sudden spirit of cooperation? One reason was that by January 1983 collateral issues associated with the case had been resolved. A lingering matter involved back attorney fees for Williams and his co-counsel, Richard Dinkins. Williams contended that fees owed him were in excess of $1.4 million, but in early December, after hearings on the matter, Judge Wiseman had awarded only $139,214. Though bitterly disappointed, the plaintiffs' attorneys were pleased that the matter finally had been addressed by the court.

Another matter concerned the financial costs of desegregation. Two years earlier, the school board asked Judge Wiseman to make the State of Tennessee, the governor, the commissioner of education, and the State Board of Education defendants in the suit. School board officials contended that when the suit was filed in 1955 the state constitution, as well as numerous state statutes, mandated a segregated school system. The board felt that it should not bear the costs of desegregation alone. Judge Wiseman granted the board's motion, and though the matter was on appeal, it looked as if the state might yet bear some financial responsibility for integrating Nashville's public schools.

The complex issues of desegregation planning were well-known to the lawyers in the case, but members of the new elected school board were like fresh troops, eager to join the fray. The board had already had a two-day retreat in November to hear reports from school administration department heads, and another retreat had been scheduled for the weekend of January 27 to consider aspects of desegregation. When the Supreme Court announced its decision not to take up the Nashville case and Judge Wiseman speedily reacted, conservative members of the board said they would not participate in this closed-door session which was scheduled to be held at Vanderbilt. Hurriedly Kent Weeks consulted with other board members and with board attorneys. A meeting was called for Saturday night, January 28, in the conference room of Metro Schools Director Charles Frazier. There, the lawyers briefed the board, and frank discussions

41. Ibid., Jan. 27, 1983.

followed. All present agreed that these secret discussions were privileged attorney-client consultations and hence not subject to Tennessee's "sunshine" law.

The board, meeting in special session on February 1, began by considering whether to accept or reject the twelve criteria established by the previous board. As the board took up each criterion in turn, it became obvious that the issues, the discussions and the votes were very similar to those of the appointed board three years earlier.[42] The conservative coalition of Alexander, Hightower, and Gann sought to limit the plan's impact on white outlying areas.

The board was different, but its dynamics were the same. Similar, too, was the plan that began to take shape. The board met on February 7, 8, 10, and 22, to discuss the nature of the plan. It met on March 7, 10, and 15 to review specifics of a plan drawn up by its staff. Throughout, the public showed little interest in this abbreviated version of the now-classic drama.

On March 18, 1983, the board met to hear from parents and other interested parties. Almost all of the comments were directed at proposed school closings. At 6:30 P.M., after more than two hours of public testimony, the board adjourned until March 21. Mrs. Gupton said that this delay would give the board time to consider what had been said. The conservative coalition—Alexander, Gann, and Hightower—voted against the motion to adjourn. They apparently wanted to force a vote on the plan that night before the full house, but they also knew something else. Earlier Bill Willis had called from downtown to invite the board to meet in his law office later that evening. Something important had come up.

When the board assembled later that evening at Willis' office on Second Avenue North, those present were told that Avon Williams had sent a letter offering terms for a negotiated settlement.

Kent Weeks, as board chair, had begun to meet with Avon Williams not long after Judge Wiseman had indicated that he wanted the two parties to try to negotiate a settlement. Long before he had become board chair, Weeks had argued that the two sides should sit down and talk their way to a settlement. The Wiseman initiative was an opportunity he could not let pass. At an informal gathering before a board meeting in January, Weeks had told the board that he would like to try to talk to Avon Williams. There were mixed feelings but no outright "no"s. He had not reported to the board since that time, but Weeks and Williams had been talking privately, in the company of the

---

42. Minutes, Metropolitan Board of Public Education, Feb. 1, 7, 8, 10, 22; and Mar. 7, 10, 15, 18, 1983.

board's lawyers. The intensity of the negotiations had increased as
the board's plan took shape and Wiseman's April 1 deadline neared.
Williams took a group of informed black citizens, including participants in the 1979-80 planning process, into his confidence as ad-
visors.

In Willis's office the Williams letter was circulated.[43] The reaction
was surprise. Was this all he wanted? Williams had accepted the
major part of the board's pending plan, but he did want several
specific things. He wanted "inverse modification" of five clusters, by
which he meant that black children could stay in their own neighborhoods in the early grades, with whites being bused in, in contrast
to the prevailing pattern. He wanted certain schools in the black area
to remain open, especially Pearl, which was to be renamed the Martin
Luther King, Jr., Magnet School. If his terms were accepted, the
overall plan, supported by both parties, could be given to Judge
Wiseman and a consent decree issued. Over the weekend, the negotiations continued, letters were exchanged, and the basic bargain was
struck.

On March 21, 1983, Weeks announced that the parties were near
agreement. "For years people in this community have been asking
why we don't sit down and negotiate with the plaintiffs."[44] The press
was outraged that the negotiations had been going on in secret, but
most of the community was pleased to hear that the lawsuit would
finally end.

On the last day of March, the Metro School Board heeded pleas to
end the uncertainty brought on by protracted litigation and voted six
to three in favor of the negotiated desegregation plan. The conservative coalition voted against the agreement, but Vern Denney seemed
to speak for the majority when he said, "After twenty-seven years,
this community can no longer afford to debate, stall, and put children, parents, and staff—as well as taxpayers and taxpayers' money—
through the wringer of prolonged debate and argument in the
courts."[45]

The negotiated school plan institutionalized busing in the pairing
and cluster arrangements across the whole county. The basic pattern
bused children out of inner-city neighborhoods to suburban schools
in Grades 1–4 and reversed that configuration in Grades 5–6. Outly-

43. Only a sketchy account of these events can be given, since the state court has
enjoined participants from talking about this or other aspects of these events due to
pending litigation. The suit, *Head v. Hightower*, contends that the board violated the
states' sunshine legislation mandating open public meeting of government boards.
44. *Banner*, Mar. 21, 1984.
45. *Tennessean*, Mar. 30, 1983.

ing whites won some concessions. Antioch High School was left open for three years, and 309 children who lived on the eastern edge of Davidson County were exempted from busing. Some schools in the black community would be reopened, and some black children would be zoned to their neighborhood schools in the early grades. Pearl High School would be paired with Cohn High School as a single entity, which would use the current campuses until the new Pearl-Cohn Comprehensive School could be built on a new site. Then the historic Pearl building would become a magnet school, the Martin Luther King, Jr., Open-Zoned Magnet School for the Health Sciences.

These specifics were all contained in the consent order forwarded to Judge Wiseman on April 7, 1983. The board and the plaintiffs, traditional adversaries in *Kelley v. Board of Education,* agreed to combine forces if the plan were ever challenged by an intervening party. After many years of bitter struggle, the debate over busing died without a whimper in a near-empty federal courtroom.

CONCLUSION

The black struggle for racial equality has had a long and torturous history in the American South. After the heady days of Emancipation and Reconstruction, the traditional configuration of exploitation and paternalism returned in the form of Jim Crow separatism. Blacks remained at the bottom of the class and status hierarchies. The Second Reconstruction of the South began in the 1950s and grew to involve the whole nation. In an effort to shed light upon the whole configuration of racial politics in America, this book has recounted a small scene in the unfolding drama, the story of school desegregation in Nashville, Tennessee.

The Second Reconstruction began with the *Brown* decision and civil rights protests across the South. Its immediate goal was to guarantee that, without discrimination, black people would have access to the institutions of our society. But the ultimate goal was the fulfillment of a more compelling dream—equality with whites on both the class and status dimensions of American life. In the long term, it was hoped, equal access would make the fulfillment of that dream possible.

The civil rights movement's demands for access were in some ways remarkably successful. Status distinctions between blacks and whites almost disappeared in relatively impersonal societal institutions. In Nashville and across the South, blacks and whites were served at the same restaurants, buses, hotels, and water fountains. Equal access was guaranteed in more intimate communal institutions, too. Open housing laws were passed, and neighborhood schools were desegregated. Civic clubs and churches were compelled to abandon discriminatory postures. The racial complexion of communal institutions changed some, but despite the equal access proclamations, most remained predominantly one-race.

Equal access as a means of redistributing status—prestige, respect, and deference among people—had mixed results. The approach was more effective in desegregating societal institutions, where interactions are more temporary and less personal, than communal institutions, where relationships are more permanent and intimate. The redistribution of class benefits through an equal-access approach also met with mixed results. Job opportunities for blacks remained limited, although, under the constant pressure of civil rights organizations, the allocation of government-supplied services improved somewhat.

The equal-access focus of the early civil rights movement was displaced by affirmative action in the late 1960s. Many people argued, and the federal govenment was persuaded, that the equal-access approach was both too slow and inherently unfair. Slavery and its cousin Jim Crow, had immorally and illegally disadvantaged black people; as a result of that handicap, they could not compete effectively for the good things of life. A quicker-acting, more efficacious remedy was sought, one that moved the focus from opportunity to results. Affirmative action meant that a fair share of society's benefits—jobs, programs, services—had to go to blacks, unless there was a compelling reason why they should not. With affirmative action, the distribution of class and status benefits in our collective lives was to be altered substantially.

Busing for racial balance was an important part of the affirmative-action approach to the problem of racial inequality in society. Busing was designed to redistribute class and status benefits or, to put it another way, to reallocate educational services and social respect. The initial goal of busing, like that of all affirmative-action policies, was to assimilate black people into the body of American society and the soul of its culture. With busing, as at every step in the black surge toward equality, strong and persistent segments within white society resisted. But with busing, as all along the path, other whites supported the attempt to end racial discrimination in America.

An empirical assumption and a moral precept underlay the policy of busing for racial balance. The assumption and the precept, however, may vary greatly from group to group and over time. In its original formulation, busing policy was predicated on the assumption that there was one American society with one prevailing culture, from which blacks had been unfairly excluded, and on the moral conviction that blacks should be assimilated into that society and that culture. As the unanimous opinion in *Brown I* put it, "Opportunity . . . is a right which must be made available to all on equal terms."[1] From this perspective blacks had little to lose and everything to gain from the policy of busing. Since they had little heritage and brought little of value with them, it remained only for black

1. Derrick Bell, *Civil Rights*, 111.

children to be made into white children with dark skin. To use the metaphor in Kenneth Clark's original psychological study, desegregation would make the black doll "nice."

The arrogance of this position could not escape perceptive people, but another combination of assumptions could also lead to busing. Here the empirical assumption was that America consists of two unequal cultures, one black and the other white; and the moral assumption was that one overarching, consensual, color-blind culture should take the place of both. Children, like paint pigments, were to be mixed—a little black and a lot of white to make dove gray. Both cultures would contribute their best parts to create a new and better whole; children of both races would be assimilated into a third culture, and busing was the tool to achieve this.

A third pluralistic alternative is also possible. In this case the empirical assumption is that America is made up of many ethnic subcultures, and the moral precept is that each one must be encouraged and respected. Multi-cultural education is functional, even necessary, in a multi-cultural world. Bilingual educational programs are but one result of this type of thinking. Proponents of this view can be discovered in Nashville, but its real force is felt in New York, Miami, Houston, and Los Angeles, where ethnic diversity is greater and its contrasts more sharply drawn.

For the southern, white, Anglo-Saxon Protestants (WASPs) of Nashville, the first view is least wrenching, the third most so. For the first view takes for granted the superiority of white culture—its history, heroes, traditions, and values; in short, its way of looking at the world. School programs and policies should be directed toward keeping white culture in the ascendancy. But in the third view, the WASP culture is relegated to the position of one among many equally attractive ways of life. Busing would teach white children that theirs is not the only or necessarily the best lifestyle. If that is not what parents want their children to learn, they frequently look to the Christian academies for reinforcement.

Among blacks, the preference hierarchy is just the reverse. The multi-cultural approach puts black history and culture on par with white history and culture. Naturally, black parents want their children to know and appreciate themselves within a larger context of which they can be proud; feelings of personal self-worth spring in large part from pride in the culture of which one is a part. As much as whites, blacks want schools to contribute to the positive socialization of their children.

Busing is a redistributive policy.[2] It takes from those who have more and gives to those who have less. An equal distribution of educational services does not require busing; other mechanisms can insure that blacks get their fair share of modern facilities, textbooks, programs, and money.

Busing, however, was believed necessary for the reallocation of prestige, respect, and deference within the community. Busing for racial balance was intended to create situations in which blacks and whites shared equal status, and so to end racial prejudice based on skin color. But busing also creates conditions by which dissimilar subcultures with divergent lifestyles come into conflict. That happened in Nashville, and we suspect it has happened elsewhere as well. The conflict then is no longer about skin color *per se*; it is about values and atttudes toward work and play, good and evil, and "us" and "them." In Nashville the drive toward subcultural separatism could be found in both black and white communities after ten years' experience with busing.

Busing In Nashville

No aspect of the struggle for racial equality has been more protracted or traumatic than the desegregation of America's schools. Ironically, in the years since the 1954 *Brown* decision, the South has become the most desegregated section of the nation. In 1979, the U.S. Civil Rights Commission Survey of nationwide segregation found "the lowest average level [in] the Southeast."[3] Busing has been used more extensively in the South than in any other part of the country, and busing for racial balance has existed in Nashville longer than in almost any other city. Hence, the story of desegregation in Nashville can be used to inform the national debate.

What have we learned about school desegregation in Nashville? We know that there were two school systems—one for blacks and another for whites—until the late 1950s. These two systems both reflected and reinforced the inequality of services and status between the two races. We know that desegregation of schools by neighborhood under the grade-a-year plan did not alter the prevailing

2. Theodore Lowi, "American Business, Public Policy, Case-Studies, and Political Science," *World Politics* 16 (1964), 677–715. Ira Sharkansky, ed., *Policy Analysis in Political Science* (Chicago, 1970).

3. U.S. Commission on Civil Rights, *Desegregation of the Public Schools: A Status Report* (Feb. 1979). Southeastern states included: Tennessee, Virginia, North Carolina, South Carolina, Mississippi, Alabama, Georgia, and Florida.

patterns of inequality and separation very much. Schools remained identifiably black or white one-race institutions; the racial stigma remained. Modern facilities were built and modern programs implemented in Nashville's expanding, predominantly white suburbs. Blacks objected to both the status and service inequalities which persisted and renewed their struggle for equality in the courts.

Busing came to Nashville in 1971 not because of the strength of assimilationist sentiment in the community but because the federal courts had the authority and ultimately the power to force change. The courts wanted results, not just good intentions. Most whites complied with the busing plan, but they worked hard to make sure that their interests were protected within the newly desegregated schools. Hundreds of parents attended Citizens Advisory Committee meetings and questioned teachers and principals about school programs. Desegregation of schools was fine as long as their children were not "pulled down" in the process. Other whites, more fearful and financially able, placed their children beyond the reach of busing. The levels and patterns of this white flight persisted over the years and threatened to establish in Nashville a new dual school system, divided along class and racial lines.

Busing was not popular with white citizens, parents, or teachers. As our opinion surveys showed, after years of experience it was judged to have failed; whites believed that busing was harmful to children's educational development. Yet this belief does not square with the facts. Both our own research and the bulk of the research done elsewhere shows that educational achievement of white children was not adversely affected by busing.[4] On the other hand, the surveys showed that whites believed that busing did not improve race relations, and this sentiment seems accurate.

When aspects of the busing plan were being reconsidered by the Metro School Board in 1979 and by the district court in 1980, race relations seemed at low ebb, not among children but among adults. Conflict centered more often on subcultures and their symbols than on strictly educational services. School closures, especially the fate of Pearl High School, dominated the agenda, not because of the educational services the affected schools did or did not offer, but because of their symbolic importance to both the black and white communities. Both blacks and whites came increasingly to fight for racially homogeneous schools.

Blacks were brought to this position by their own experience with busing for racial balance. Their children were bused out of their

4. Hawley, *Effective School Desegregation.*

neighborhoods more often than whites were bused out of theirs. Many of the schools in black areas were closed, and white teachers and white parents dominated the schools in both communities. They found that their children were to be disadvantaged by being in the minority at schools. The gap between black and white academic achievement persisted, despite the promises of desegregation, after years of busing. All these effects, blacks felt, undermined the self-esteem of their children. The separatist impulse manifested by many leaders of the black community originated in these feelings. Only in majority black schools with black teachers, located in black neighborhoods, would black Americans be celebrated. Busing for racial balance denied blacks the right of subcultural equality and deprived black children of the emotional security necessary to achieve ultimate equality.

In 1982 a popular song with lyrics about racial harmony was recorded by Paul McCartney and Stevie Wonder. "Ebony and ivory," they sang, "live together in perfect harmony, side by side on my piano keyboard; Oh Lord, why don't we?" By the 1980s in Nashville, "Music City, USA," the piano metaphor was appropriate. Most whites and blacks preferred the company of their own kind, the distinctive values of their own separate cultures. After ten years of busing experience, neither blacks nor whites wanted subcultural assimilation, unless it was on their own terms. In 1983 the federal court re-established busing for racial balance in Nashville, but it could not end the politics of race.

Racial Politics and Public Policy

The essence of politics is conflict between groups for those things which are both valued and scarce. The politics of race will not end when blacks and whites, as self-conscious groups, are equal in class and status; leaders of the two races will be forever vigilant, alert to policies or trends which might upset the racial status quo. The politics of race can end only when one of two things occurs: (1) when people no longer think of themselves in racial terms above all else, but instead identify themselves first as parents or teachers, employers or employees, producers or consumers, and only secondarily as black or white; or (2) when present inequalities between the races are accepted as legitimate and temporary.

When individuals want to change public policies in an effort to improve their lives, they search for others with similar interests and perspectives. The problem with busing, and perhaps with other forms of affirmative action, is that it reinforces racial thinking. Racial ratios and school enrollment percentages dominated the courtroom debates on desegregation. People became so caught up in racial concerns that other common interests were submerged. In Nashville, busing divided and preoccupied parents. They worried about which race would be bused where rather than joining forces to convince growing numbers of non-parents that they should support public education. As a race-conscious policy, busing reinforces racial consciousness and stimulates racial conflict among adults. Hopefully, the benign multi-racial environment of integrated schools will immunize children against the virus of racial hostility, but if black and white children believe that their life chances are adversely affected by busing, the policy will have failed. What we have seen in Nashville is that prospect: adults of *both* races believe that busing is unfair and are surely telling their children this. Such feelings may be especially acute among blacks, the very group the policy was designed to help. If black leaders are convinced that busing for racial balance is restrictive and paternalistic, one more instance of whites telling blacks how to live their lives, then the prospect of failure has already become a reality. From slavery and Reconstruction to Jim Crow separatism, W.E.B. DuBois urged blacks to organize and fight every effort by individual whites and their socio-political system to subjugate the black race. Busing for racial balance in Nashville may be another form of subjugation in the eyes of Avon Williams, DeLois Wilkinson, Amos Jones, Leo Lillard, and others.

The second way in which the politics of race can recede is if the remaining inequalities between the two races are accepted by both races as legitimate and temporary. Thomas Sowell made this argument in *Race and Economics,* where he examined the patterns of success and failure of various ethnic groups in the U.S. Skin color, poverty, illiteracy, and prejudice could not explain the outcome. Instead, he found that those ethnic subcultures which emphasized an orientation toward the future, and in which members worked hard, saved, learned, developed skills, and disciplined themselves, were increasingly successful over the generations. Independence and self-reliance are key attributes, according to Sowell. In the past many black people have manifested these traits and been successful, but too often their successes have been obscured by the dependent, present-oriented culture among blacks which had its origins in slavery and Reconstruction and today is perpetuated by welfare-state liberalism. Many government policies, Sowell argued, reinforce unfortunate elements within the black subculture. Blacks, as individuals and as an ethnic subculture, can achieve class and status equality through their own efforts, if governmental policies are changed. But that achievement will take time, generations in fact, just as it took generations for other immigrant groups to make their way up the ladder of success. Sowell talked too about education and black achievement. He said that the relentless attack on segregation as a moral evil has obscured the practical issue of which things actually encourage black children's real achievement.[5] It is what *happens* in schools that is important. In Sowell, one hears the echoes of Booker T. Washington: patience, skills, hard work, and self-reliance. Nashville's own past resonates with these themes. At the turn of the century, James C. Napier and R.H. Boyd established banks, businesses, newspapers, and schools, and their legacy persists today.

Politics is a serious game played by serious people in search of advantages for themselves and others like them. As in any game, there are rules, and courts help to make those rules. Busing is one of the rules and not the final score.

The Future

Busing has meant many things to many people in Nashville since 1971. It has meant sending children far from home each day, closing schools, risking children's futures, and more. Parents, black or white, have been compelled both to acknowledge their own values and to respond to the court order. They could choose the safety of private schools or stay in the public schools and work there to see their values triumph. Teachers, black or white, could resign themselves to their fates or work to bring children to full potential in the public system.

In the course of our research we stumbled upon a planning document entitled "Schools for 1980." The report was prepared by the Metropolitan Planning Commission in summer 1964, to predict the configuration of the Metropolitan school system fifteen years in the future. "It is projected that there will be approximately 109,800 pupils enrolled in the Nashville-Davidson County Metropolitan Public School System in 1980." The actual figure in 1980 was close to 66,000. But who in 1964 could have foreseen the events that were destined to alter public education in Nashville? The planners who prepared the forecast can be pardoned their mistakes, given the tumultuous happenings of the ensuing decade and a half.[6]

5. Sowell, *Race and Economics.*
6. Metropolitan Planning Commission, Metropolitan Government of Nashville and Davidson County, Tenn., "Schools for 1980" (June 1964).

We allow ourselves the same leeway. But this much we are sure of: busing is a redistributive policy. It is an affirmative action by courts, designed to reallocate educational services and social respect between the races, using an institution which welds together society and community. It remains to be seen whether busing will achieve this aim; we will not know for a generation or more. In the meantime, the burden of busing must be borne.

BIBLIOGRAPHY

Books

Allport, Gordon. *The Nature of Prejudice*. Garden City, N.J.: Doubleday, 1958.

Altshuler, Alan A. *Community Control: The Black Demand for Participation in Large American Cities*. New York: Pegasus, 1970.

Bash, Harry H. *Sociology, Race and Ethnicity: A Critique of American Ideological Intrusions Upon Sociological Theory*. New York: Gordon and Beach, 1979.

Bell, Daniel, ed. *The New American Right*. New York: Citation Books, 1955.

Bell, Derrick A., ed. *Civil Rights: Leading Cases*. Boston: Little, Brown, 1980.

Bittker, Boris I. *The Case for Black Reparations*. New York: Random House, 1973.

Bullock, Henry A. *A History of Negro Education in the South From 1619 to the Present*. Cambridge, Mass.: Harvard Univ. Press, 1967.

Cahnman, Werner J., and Heberle, Rudolf, eds. *Ferdinand Tonnes on Sociology*. Chicago: Univ. of Chicago Press, 1971.

Cash, W. J. *The Mind of the South*. New York: Vintage Books, 1969.

Dillon, Wilton S., ed. *The Cultural Drama: Modern Identities and Social Ferment*. Washington, D.C.: Smithsonian Institution Press, 1974.

DuBois, W.E.B. *Black Reconstruction in America*. New York: Atheneum, 1977.

Edelman, Murray. *The Symbolic Uses of Politics*. Urbana: Univ. of Illinois Press, 1964.

_____. *Politics as Symbolic Action: Mass Arousal and Quiescence*. Chicago: Markham, 1971.

Egerton, John. *A Mind to Stay Here: Profiles From the South*. New York: Macmillan, 1970.

———. *Nashville: The Faces of Two Centuries, 1780–1980.* Nashville, Tenn.: Plus Media, 1980.

Folmsbee, Stanley J.; Corlew, Robert E.; and Mitchell, Enoch L. *Tennessee: A Short History.* Knoxville: Univ. of Tennessee Press, 1969.

Gallup, George H. *The Gallup Poll: Public Opinion, 1980.* Wilmington: Scholarly Resources, 1981.

Gordon, Milton M. *Assimilation in American Life.* New York: Oxford Univ. Press, 1964.

Graglia, Lino A. *Disaster By Decree.* Ithaca, N.Y.: Cornell Univ. Press, 1976.

Gusfield, Joseph R. *Symbolic Crusade.* Urbana: Univ. of Illinois Press, 1976.

Hamer, Phillip M., ed. *Tennessee: A History, 1673–1932.* New York: American Historical Society, 1933.

Harlan, Louis R. *Booker T. Washington: The Making of a Black Leader.* New York: Oxford Univ. Press, 1972.

Hawley, Willis D., ed. *Effective School Desegregation.* Beverly Hills: Sage, 1981.

Humphrey, Hubert, ed. *School Desegregation: Documents and Commentaries.* New York: Crowell, 1964.

Jencks, Christopher. *Inequality.* New York: Basic Books, 1972.

Johnson, Lyndon B. *The Vantage Point.* New York: Popular Library, 1971.

King, Martin Luther, Jr. *Why We Can't Wait.* New York: Signet Books, 1963.

———. *Where Do We Go From Here: Chaos or Community?* New York: Harper & Row, 1967.

Kluger, Richard. *Simple Justice: The History of Brown v. Board of Education and Black America's Struggle for Equality.* New York: Knopf, 1975.

Lamon, Lester C. *Black Tennesseans: 1908–1950.* Knoxville: Univ. of Tennessee Press, 1977.

Lasswell, Harold. *Politics: Who Gets What, When and How?* New York: McGraw-Hill, 1956.

Lester, Julius, ed. *The Seventh Son: The Thought and Writings of W.E.B. DuBois.* New York: Random House, 1971.

Marcus, Laurence R., and Stickney, Benjamin D. *Race and Education: The Unending Controversy.* Springfield, Ill.: Charles C. Thomas, 1981.

Matthews, Donald R., and Prothro, James W. *Negroes and the New Southern Politics.* New York: Harcourt, Brace and World, 1966.

Mauney, Connie Pat. *Evolving Equality: The Courts and Desegrega-

tion in Tennessee. Knoxville: Univ. of Tennessee, Bureau of Public Administration, 1979.

Meier, August. *Negro Thought in America.* Ann Arbor: Univ. of Michigan Press, 1969.

Moynihan, Daniel P. *Maximum Feasible Misunderstanding.* New York: Free Press, 1970.

Muse, Benjamin. *Virginia's Massive Resistance.* Bloomington: Indiana Univ. Press, 1961.

Myrdal, Gunnar. *An American Dilemma.* New York: Norton, 1944.

Orfield, Gary. *The Reconstruction of Southern Education.* New York: Wiley, 1969.

Phillips, Kevin. *The Emerging Republican Majority.* Garden City, N.J.: Anchor Books, 1970.

Rabinowitz, Howard N. *Race Relations in the Urban South, 1865–1980.* New York: Oxford Univ. Press, 1978.

Raines, Howell. *My Soul Is Rested.* New York: Bantam, 1977.

Richardson, Joe M. *A History of Fisk University.* University: Univ. of Alabama Press, 1980.

Saratt, Reed. *The Ordeal of Desegregation: The First Decade.* New York, Harper and Row, 1966.

Scott, Mingo, Jr. *The Negro in Tennessee Politics.* Knoxville: Univ. of Tennessee Press, 1966.

Sharkansky, Ira, ed. *Policy Analysis in Political Science.* Chicago: Markham, 1970.

Simpkins, Francis P., and Roland, Charles P. *A History of the South.* New York: Knopf, 1972.

Sowell, Thomas. *Race and Economics.* New York: David McKay, 1975.

Williamson, Joel. *The Crucible of Race: Black-White Relations in the American South Since Emancipation.* New York: Oxford Univ. Press, 1984.

Wolters, Raymond. *The Burden of Brown: Thirty Years of School Desegregation.* Knoxville: Univ. of Tennessee Press, 1984.

X, Malcolm. *The Autobiography of Malcolm X.* New York: Grove Press, 1964.

Zurcher, Louis R. *Citizens for Decency.* Austin: Univ. of Texas Press, 1976.

Articles, Periodicals, and Unpublished Works

"A Bad Day in Lamar." *Newsweek*, Mar. 16, 1970.

"A Bus in Their Future?" *Newsweek*, July 3, 1967.

"A Supreme Court 'Yes' to Busing." *Time,* May 3, 1971, 13–14.

"Ain't Nobody Gonna Touch King Claude." *Time,* Apr. 20, 1970.

Armor, David J. "A Response to 'The White Flight Controversy,' " *Public Interest* 51 (Oct. 1978), 113–15.

———. "On School Busing and the 14th Amendment." Hearings before the Constitution Subcommittee of the U.S. Senate Judiciary Committee, 1981 (mimeographed).

———. "The Evidence on Busing." *Public Interest* 28 (Summer 1972), 90–126.

———. *White Flight, Demographic Transition, and Future of School Segregation.* (Rand Corporation, Aug. 1978, p. 5931).

Becker, Henry J. "The Impact of Racial Composition and Public School Desegregation in Non-Public School Enrollment by White Pupils." Center for Social Organization of Schools, Johns Hopkins University, 1978 (mimeographed).

Bell, Daniel. "The New American Right." In Daniel Bell, ed., *The New American Right.* New York: Citation Books, 1955.

Berger, Monroe. "Desegregation, Law and Social Science." *Commentary* 23 (1957), 471–75.

Brideman, William W. "Racial Desegregation in Education." *School and Society* 97 (Oct. 1969), 345.

Cahn, Edmond. "Jurisprudence." *New York University Law Review* 30 (1955), 150.

Clark, Herbert L. "The Public Career of James Carroll Napier: Businessman, Politician and Crusader for Racial Justice, 1845–1940." D.A. diss., Middle Tennessee State Univ., 1980.

Clark, Kenneth, and Clark, Mamie. "Emotional Factors in Racial Identification and Preference in Negro Children." In Martin M. Grossack, ed., *Mental Health and Segregation.* New York: Springer, 1963.

———. "Racial Identification and Preference in Negro Children." In Theodore Newcomb and Eugene Hartley, eds., *Readings in Social Psychology.* New York: Holt, 1947.

Clotfelter, Charles T. "The Detroit Decision and 'White Flight'." *Journal of Legal Studies* 5 (Jan. 1976), 99–112.

Coleman, James S. "A Reply to Green and Pettigrew." *Phi Delta Kappan* 57 (Mar. 1976), 454–55.

———. "Racial Segregation in the Schools: New Research With New Policy Implications." *Phi Delta Kappan* 57 (Oct. 1975), 75–78.

———. "Response to Professors Pettigrew and Green." *Harvard Educational Review* 46 (May 1976), 217–24.

Coleman, James S.; Kelley, Sara D., and Moore, John. *Trends in School Segregation, 1968–1973.* Washington, D.C.: Urban Institute, 1975.

Cottle, T.J. "Speaking of Busing." *New Republic* 172 (Jan. 1975), 14–15.

Crain, Robert L., and Mahard, Rita E. "Desegregation and Black Achievement: A Review of the Research." *Law and Contemporary Problems* 42 (Summer 1978), 18.

"Decision Against De Facto." *Time,* June 30, 1967, 58.

Devins, Neal. "School Desegregation Law in the 1980s: The Courts' Abandonment of Brown v. Board of Education." *William and Mary Law Review* 26 (Fall 1984), 7–43.

"Dixie Takes the Bus." *Newsweek,* Sept. 13, 1971, 14.

England, J. Merton. "The Free Negro in Ante-Bellum Tennessee." *Journal of Southern History* 21 (1955), 54–56.

Estabrook, Leigh S. "The Effects of Desegregation on Parents' Selection of Schools." Ph.D. diss., Boston University, 1980.

Farley, Reynolds. "Racial Integration in the Public Schools, 1967–1972." *Sociological Forces* 8 (Jan. 1975), 3–26.

———. "Is Coleman Right?" 6 *Social Policy* (Jan.-Feb. 1976), 14–23.

"For Benign Neglect." *Current,* Mar. 14, 1970, 264.

Gallup, George H. "Gallup Poll of the Public's Attitudes Toward The Public Schools." *Phi Delta Kappan* 63 (Sept. 1981), 33–47.

Gallup Opinion Surveys, "Thirteenth Annual Survey of the Public's Attitudes Toward the Public Schools." Princeton, N.J., Spring 1981.

Garfinkel, Herbert. "Social Science Evidence and the School Desegregation Cases." *Journal of Politics* 21 (1959), 37.

Gatlin, Douglas S.; Giles, Michael W., and Cataldo, Everett F. "Policy Support Within a Target Group: The Case of School Desegregation." *American Political Science Review* 72 (1978), 985–95.

Giles, Michael W. "Racial Stability and Urban School Desegregation." *Urban Affairs Quarterly* 12 (1977), 499–510.

Giles, Michael W., and Gatlin, Douglas S. "Mass-Level Compliance with Public Policy: The Case of School Desegregation." *Journal of Politics* 42 (1980), 722–46.

Giles, Michael, Cataldo, Everett F., and Gatlin, Douglas S. "White Flight and Percent Black: The Tipping-Point Re-examined." *Social Science Quarterly* 56 (1977), 85–92.

Green, Robert L., and Pettigrew, Thomas F. "Conflicting Views of Research and Social Justice." *Phi Delta Kappan* 57 (Apr. 1976), 555–56.

———. "Urban Desegregation and White Flight: A Response to Coleman." *Phi Delta Kappan* (Feb. 1976), 399–402.

———. "Now Supreme Court Sets Rules for Busing Students." *U.S. News and World Report,* May 3, 1971, 12–14.

Hawley, Willis D. "Equity and Quality in Education: Characteristics of Effective Desegregated Schools." In Willis D. Hawley, ed., *Effective School Desegregation.* Beverly Hills: Sage, 1981, 297–308.

————. "The New Mythology of School Desegregation." *Law and Contemporary Problems* 42. Nos. 3–4 (Summer 1978).

Hofstadter, Richard. "The Pseudo-Conservative Revolt." in Daniel Bell, ed., *The New American Right.* New York: Citation Books, 1955.

"How Much Progress is Enough?" *Saturday Review,* July 17, 1971, 41.

Howe, Harold. "The Battle of the Buses." *The Economist* 221 (Oct. 1966), 60–64.

Jackson, Gregg. "Reanalysis of Coleman's Recent Trends in Social Integration." *Educational Researcher* 5 (Feb. 1976), 3–4.

Jennings, Robert H. Former city attorney, City of Nashville, Tenn. Interview, Feb. 12–15, 1982.

Kopanen, Nilo E. "The Myth of the 'Tipping Point.' " *Integrated Education* 4 (Aug.-Sept. 1966).

Konvitz, M.R. "Why One Prof Changed His Vote," *New York Times Magazine* (May 18, 1969), 60

Lamon, Lester C. "The Black Community in Nashville and the Fisk University Strike of 1924–1925." *Journal of Southern History* 40 (1974), 225–44.

Lipset, Seymour. "The Sources of the Radical Right." in Daniel Bell, ed., *The New American Right.* New York: Citation Books, 1955.

Lord, Dennis, and Catau, John. "School Desegregation Policy and Intra-School District Migration." *Social Science Quarterly* 57 (1977), 784–96.

Lowi, Theodore. "American Business, Public Policy, Case-Studies, and Political Science." *World Politics* 16 (July 1964), 677–715.

McConahay, John B. "Self-Interest versus Racial Attitudes as Correlates of Anti-Busing Attitudes in Louisville: Is It the Buses or the Blacks?" *Journal of Politics* 44 (1982), 692–720.

Mills, Nicholas. "Busing: Who's Being Taken for a Ride?" *Commonweal,* March 24, 1974, 51–60.

"Moynihan Memo on Civil Rights." *America,* May 1970, 28.

Nelms, Thomas S. Former attorney in the Legal Department, City of Nashville. Interview, Jan. 15–21, 1982.

Orfield, Gary. "Is Coleman Right?" *Social Policy* (Jan.-Feb. 1976), 24–29.

Pettigrew, Thomas F.; Useem, E.L.; Normand, C., and Smith, M.S. "Busing: A Review of the Evidence." *Public Interest* 80 (1973), 88–118.

Phillips, Paul D. "White Reaction to the Freedman's Bureau in Tennessee." *Tennessee Historical Quarterly* 25 (1966), 30–62.

Pride, Richard A. "Desegregation and Achievement Test Scores in Nashville, 1975–1979" (mimeographed).

───. "Patterns of White Flight: 1971–1979." Report submitted to the Board of Education, Metropolitan Nashville-Davidson County Public Schools, Apr. 2, 1980 (mimeographed).

Pride, Richard, and Woodard, J.D. "Busing Plans and White Flight: Nashville and Louisville." Paper presented at meeting of Southwestern Political Science Association, Houston, Tex., 1978 (mimeographed).

───. "Busing and White Flight: Implementation Plans in Three Southern Cities." Paper presented at meeting of Southern Political Science Association, Gatlinburg, Tenn., 1979 (mimeographed).

Raspberry, William. "Busing: Is It Worth the Ride?" *Washington Post*, Nov. 7, 1972.

Ravitch, Diane. "The 'White Flight' Controversy." *Public Interest* 51 (Spring 1978), 135–149.

Regens, James L., and Bullock, Charles S., III. "Congruity of Racial Attitudes Among Black and White Students." *Social Science Quarterly* 60 (Dec. 1979). 511–22.

Rigsby, Leo C., and Boston, John. "Patterns of School Desegregation in Nashville, 1960–1969." *The Urban Observatory* (Nashville: Vanderbilt Univ., Jan. 1971; mimeographed).

Robin, Stanley S., and Bosco, James J. "Coleman's Desegregation Research and Policy Recommendations." *School Review* 84 (May 1976), 352-63.

Rossell, Christine. "Assessing the Unintended Impacts of Public Policy: School Desegregation and Resegregation." Washington D.C.: National Institute of Education, 1978 (mimeographed).

───. "Busing and 'White Flight'." *Public Interest* 51 (Fall 1978), 109–11.

───. "Is It the Distance or the Blacks?" Boston: Boston Univ., 1979. Unpublished Paper.

───. "School Desegregation and White Flight." *Political Science Quarterly* 90 (Winter 1975–76), 675–95.

Rossell, Christine, and Ravitch, Diane. "A Response to 'The White Flight Controversy'." *Public Interest* 51 (Fall 1978), 109–13.

"School Desegregation: Lessons of the First Twenty-Five Years, Parts I and II." *Law and Contemporary Problems* 42, Nos. 3–4 (Summer 1978).

"Schools Make News." *Newsweek*, Feb. 17, 1969, 31.

Sheehan, Daniel S. "Black Achievement in a Desegregated School District." *Journal of Social Psychology* 107 (1979).

"Should Negro Children Be Bused to Suburban Schools?" *U.S. News and World Report*, Oct. 24, 1966, p. 28.

"Skelly Wright's Sweeping Decision." *New Republic*, July 8, 1967, 11.

Stinchcombe, Arthur L.; McDill, Mary; and Walker, Dollie. "Is There a Racial Tipping Point in Changing Schools?" *Journal of Social Issues* 25 (1969), 127–36.

Summerville, James. "The City and the Slums: Black Bottom in the Development of South Nashville." *Tennessee Historical Quarterly* 40 (1981), 182–92.

Survey Research Center, 1964, 1968, 1972 *National Election Studies*. Ann Arbor: Univ. of Michigan.

Taylor, Alrutheus A. "Fisk University and the Nashville Community, 1866–1900." *Journal of Negro History* 39 (1954), 111–26.

Taylor, William L. "Brown in Perspective." In Willis D. Hawley, ed., *Effective School Desegregation*. Beverly Hills: Sage, 1981, 297–308.

"Thank God for Governor Kirk." *Time*, Apr. 27, 1970.

"The Bus to Integration Bogs Down." *Life*, Mar. 16, 1970.

"Title VI: Southern Education Faces the Facts." *Saturday Review*, Mar. 20, 1965, 60.

Van den Haag, Ernest. "Social Science Testimony in the Desegregation Cases." *Villanova Law Review* 6 (1960), 69.

Weatherford, M. Stephen. "The Politics of School Busing: Contextual Effects and Community Polarization." *Journal of Politics* 42 (1980). 747–765.

Weinberg, Meyer. "A Critique of Coleman." *Integrated Education* 13–14 (Sept./Oct. 1975–76), 3–7.

Woodard, J. David. "Busing Plans, Media Agendas and Patterns of White Flight: Nashville, Tennessee and Louisville, Kentucky." Ph.D. diss., Vanderbilt Univ., 1978.

"What the Court Said." *New Republic*, Nov. 15, 1969.

"Yes, Virginia, There is a Constitution." *Newsweek*, Nov. 10, 1969, 35.

Public Documents

Alabama Acts: 1955. Vol. 1, No. 201, 492.

Armstrong v. Board of Education of the City of Birmingham. 333 F. 2d 47 (5th Circuit, 1964).

Audit. Metropolitan Government of Nashville and Davidson County, 1970, 1971 and 1980.

Brown v. Board of Education. 349 U.S. 294 (1955).

Calhoun v. Members of the Board of Education, City of Atlanta. Civil No. 6298, N.D. Ga. (Dec. 30, 1959).

Coleman, James S. *Equality of Educational Opportunity.* Washington, D.C.: Government Printing Office, 1966.

Cooper v. Aaron. 358 U.S. 1 (1958).

Dayton Board of Education v. Brinkman. 433 U.S. 406 (1977).

Evans v. Newton. 382 U.S. 296 (1966).

Kelley v. Board of Education of the City of Nashville. 20 F. 2d 209 (6th Circuit, 1959–1980).

Keyes v. School District No. One, Denver, Colorado. 413 U.S. 189 (1973).

Mayor and City Council v. Dawson. 350 U.S. 877 (1955).

Metropolitan Board of Education. "Ten Year Analysis of Enrollment Patterns." Nov. 1979, mimeographed.

Metropolitan Planning Commission, Metropolitan Government of Nashville and Davidson County, Tenn., "Schools for 1980." June 1964.

Metropolitan Public Schools. "Report on Standardized Testing." May 1980 (mimeographed).

Milliken v. Bradley. 418 U.S. 717 (1974).

National Advisory Commission on Civil Disorders. *Report.* Washington, D.C.: Government Printing Office, 1968.

Nashville *Banner.* 1954–1983.

Nashville *Tennessean.* 1954–1983.

Northcross v. Board of Education of the City of Memphis. 333 F. 2d 47 (5th Circuit, 1964).

Palmer v. Thompson. 403 U.S. 217 (1971).

Scott, Hugh. "A Black Perspective on Critical Social and Educational Factors Considered Pertinent to the Restructuring of Approaches to Desegregation in the Nashville-Davidson County Public Schools." Mimeographed. Exhibit A, *Kelley v. Board.*

Southern Regional Council. "School Desegregation, 1966: The Slow Undoing." Dec. 1966.

Swann v. Charlotte-Mecklenburg Board of Education. 402, U.S. 1 (1971).

U.S. Commission on Civil Rights. *Survey of School Desegregation in the Southern and Border States, 1965–1966.* Feb. 1966.

_____. "Survey of School Desegregation, 1966–1967." Washington, D.C.: Government Printing Office, 1967.

_____. *Reviewing a Decade of School Desegregation, 1966–1975: Report of a National Survey of School Superintendents.* 1977.

_____. *Desegregation of the Public Schools: A Status Report.* Feb. 1979.

U.S. Office of Education, Federal Security Agency. *Directory of Secondary Schools in the United States.* Washington, D.C.: Government Printing Office, 1949.

U.S. Office of Education. *Public Secondary Day Schools: 1958–1959,* Washington, D.C.: Government Printing Office, 1959.

U.S. Office of Health, Education and Welfare. *Digest of Educational Statistics, 1972, 1973, 1980.* Washington, D.C.: Government Printing Office.

University of Tennessee, Center for Business and Economic Research, *Tennessee Statistical Abstract, 1980.* Knoxville: Univ. of Tennessee, 1980.

1896   U.S. Supreme Court establishes the doctrine of "separate-but-equal" in *Plessy* v. *Ferguson.*

1954   U.S. Supreme Court overturns *Plessy* doctrine in *Brown* v. *Board of Education* saying that, "Separated educational facilities are inherently unequal."

1955   *Kelly et al.* v. *Board of Education of Nashville* filed; attorneys representing the plaintiffs are Z. Alexander Looby, and Avon Williams.

1955   Nashville Board of Education adopts plan to end "compulsory segregation" of Grade 1.

1957   On September 6, U.S. District Court declares Tennessee's School Preference Act unconstitutional. The act permitted parents to choose the public school their children would attend.

1957   On September 7, 13 black children register for Grade 1 in formerly all-white schools.

1957   On September 10, Hattie Cotton Elementary School dynamited, one wing destroyed.

1957   Parents' Preference Plan filed with District Court by Nashville Board of Education.

1958   U.S. Federal District Court throws out the Parents' Preference Plan and tells the Board to eliminate dual school system.

1958   Nashville Board of Education files plan to desegregate a grade-a-year over next 11 years. The plan is approved by the court and becomes known nationally as the "Nashville Plan."

1960   *Maxwell* v. *County Board of Education* filed against the Davidson County School Board to force desegregation of county as distinct from city schools.

1961   District Court orders the county board to desegregate grades 1-4 in order to match the city plan.

1964   Metropolitan Nashville-Davidson County government established. Metropolitan Board of Education to be appointed by mayor and confirmed Metro Council.

1970   *Kelly* plaintiffs return to court to seek additional desegregation. In July Judge Miller orders board to desegregate teaching staff on 80:20 white to black ratio in each school but permits more time to draw up pupil reassignment plan.

1971   Judge Morton rejects limited desegregation plans and calls for a team of outside experts to prepare a more comprehensive plan, which he subsequently orders implemented in fall 1971. The plan mandates busing.

1971   Busing-for-racial-balance (25% black ± 10%) begins in September; 100 schools are included but 33 outlying schools are excluded from the busing plan. Casey Jenkins leads protesting white parents.

1976-77 Board fails to adopt new desegregation plan to accompany the completion of comprehensive high schools it is constructing. The fate of Pearl High School becomes a public issue.

1979   Judge Thomas Wiseman re-opens *Kelley* case and, after hearings in July and August, orders the board to reconsider the entire plan.

1980   In March the board submits a county-wide, racial balance busing plan after extensive public input. During court proceedings, as in the planning process itself, blacks argue for majority black schools and a reduced burden of busing on their children and community.

1980   In May Judge Wiseman orders a new plan be developed with "neighborhood" elementary schools and a minimum 15% minority, *black* or *white*, in middle and high schools. He mandates enhanced educational programs in place of busing after nine years of experience with the policy.

1980   Voters approve revision of Metro charter to cause the election of the Metro Board of Public Education.

1981   In August, Avon Williams obtains a stay from the implementation of the Wisemen plan, which is scheduled for partial implementation that fall, pending a full hearing by the 6th Circuit Court of Appeals.

1982   The Court of Appeals reverses Judge Wiseman and orders the implementation of a county-wide racial balance busing plan. The school board decides to appeal the decision to the U.S. Supreme Court.

1983   In January the Supreme Court refuses to take up the *Kelley* case despite a petition by the Justice Department that it do so.

1983   The school board and the plaintiffs negotiate and agree to a consent order mandating a new county-wide racial balance desegregation plan modeled on the 1971 plan. The plan is implemented in the fall.

INDEX

The Burden of Busing has been composed into type on the Mergenthaler Linotron 202 digital phototypesetter in ten point Trump Medieval with two points of spacing between the lines. Trump Bold was selected for display. The book was designed by Jim Billingsley, typeset by Typecraft Co., printed offset by Thomson-Shore, Inc., and bound by John H. Dekker & Sons. The paper on which the book is printed bears acid-free characteristics for an effective life of at least three hundred years.

THE UNIVERSITY OF TENNESSEE PRESS : KNOXVILLE